FROMMER'S™

BED & BREAKFAST NORTH AMERICA

By Hal Gieseking

THIRD EDITION

Published by Prentice Hall Trade Division
A Division of Simon & Schuster, Inc.
Gulf + Western Building
One Gulf + Western Plaza
New York, NY 10023

ISBN 0-13-072414-9

Manufactured in the United States of America

CONTENTS _____

PART III

The 50 Best B&B Homes in North America

PREFACE

THE BEST OF THE B&B'S

I want to thank all the readers, owners of B&B homes, and reservation services for all of your suggestions and comments about the first two editions of *Frommer's Bed & Breakfast North America.*

In this third edition, we're taking advantage of what we've learned from you.

Many readers wanted to locate the *best* B&Bs in each area. They didn't want to wade through dozens of pages of listings and take pot-luck on their vacation home for a week or a weekend. They didn't want to drive miles down a country road only to find that the B&B they chose from a few words of description was a decaying wreck.

That's why we asked the top B&B reservation services in the U.S. and Canada to hand-pick their *best* B&Bs for this new edition—the kinds of places they'd recommend to their own best friends.

These are not necessarily the most expensive. We wanted B&Bs that offered real value for the money, along with luxurious amenities ranging from great breakfasts to unusually helpful hosts—and/or spectacular scenic locations.

It was not possible for us to visit each of the hundreds of the prime selections in this book. But each was inspected and picked by the people who know B&Bs best in their own area—the managers of local reservation services who may see dozens of B&B homes in the course of a year. I have relied heavily on their descriptions of their selections, particularly for the "insider's tips" throughout much of the text. The *real* "insiders" in the booming B&B industry are these managers. (Incidentally, no B&B home or reservation service has ever paid to get into this book. They are listed only because they *earned* the honor.)

If you are ever dissatisfied with any B&B home or reservation service included in this book, please write to me. If you find a B&B reservation service or spectacular home, please let me know. (Please see the "B&B Critics" response form at the back of this book.)

But now is the time to start planning your own vacation (or business trip) in the "best of the B&Bs." Just turn the page.

A DISCLAIMER: Although every effort was made to ensure the accuracy of the prices appearing in this book, it should be kept in mind that prices do fluctuate in the course of time, and that information does change under the impact of the varied and volatile factors that affect the B&B industry.

PART

I

Introducing
Bed & Breakfast

1

BED & BREAKFAST—

The *Friendly* Revolution in Travel

- Travel across the U.S. and Canada, and stay in a B&B home for as little as $25 to $50 a night—breakfast included. Or over $150 for a B&B suite with a spa and swimming pool.
- Get "inside" tips from your hosts on the area's best restaurants, shops, stores, sightseeing attractions.
- Make friends as you travel and become "part of the neighborhood," rather than paying guests at a hotel, welcomed only by an occasional bellman looking for a tip or a desk clerk who may not be able to find your reservation.
- Participate in activities with your host, which can range from shopping the local stores to sailing and lakeside picnics.
- Rather than staying in a cold, impersonal hotel with stain-resistant plastic furnishings, you may wake up in a colonial bedroom filled with antiques.

Many travelers in North America are waking up to the bed-and-breakfast way of travel.

There are now over 12,000 bed-and-breakfast homes operating in the U.S., and the number is climbing almost daily. Many of the states I surveyed reported that the B&B movement was growing so fast they had trouble keeping any list of homes current.

Small wonder. Travelers have discovered what incredible bargains B&B homes can be. The cost of a hotel room in the U.S. has climbed to an average of $70 a night, with many rooms in major cities topping $150 to $200 per night. The B&B homes offer comfortable, home-like lodgings for as little as $20 to $35 per night per single, $20 to

$50 per night double. It's true that you can also spend over $100 a night for some B&B rooms, but these are luxury exceptions in choice scenic locations, often with swimming pools, spas, and many other amenities.

But the real reason that the B&B way to travel has caught on is the sheer *friendliness* of many of the hosts. Vacationers and travelers are weary of the impersonality, coldness, and rudeness of many travel personnel. They are tired of passing through some of the most hospitable areas of North America, and meeting no local person other than a bellman or hotel cashier. People who have become B&B hosts are often outgoing and friendly, and they take real joy in welcoming others into their homes and communities.

This welcome shows up in many ways.

In some California B&Bs you may be greeted on arrival with good local wine and cheeses. In many homes the hosts serve far more than the typical continental breakfast (juice, roll, coffee/tea). They introduce their guests to the local specialties: not simply bacon and eggs but sourdough pancakes, English scones, fresh-fruit platters, smoked meats, blueberry coffee cake, New England clam cakes, creamed cod on toast, and many other luscious regional surprises you'd never find on a hotel breakfast menu!

Many of the hosts don't treat you like paying guests at all. Stay a few nights and you can practically become part of the family, gathering for cocktails around the fire in the evening with your hosts or even joining them for birthday parties and special local events. The stories I have gathered since I started researching this book indicate just how often hosts go out of their way to make their guests feel welcome.

Many hosts provide laundry facilities. Others will act as your sightseeing guides. Some with small boats or even yachts take guests out on lakes, rivers, and oceans. Many will pick up guests at airports, or bus and train stations. One host provides nightgowns and toothbrushes for guests whose luggage may have been lost by the airline. Many are happy to lend you bicycles for local touring, and give you maps, brochures, directions to interesting sightseeing. Still others give you membership cards to local country clubs, tennis clubs, swimming pools, etc. And when you want some company, they are often happy to oblige with breakfast or end-of-the-day conversations. As I said, this is a *friendly* revolution in travel.

Imagine the advantages of learning firsthand where the best restaurants are—from people who have lived in an area for years. You can learn what are the best times to visit Walt Disney World, which are the least crowded roads for New England leaf watching, which local stores are having sales. In these imperfect times, you also learn which local areas have high crime rates and should be avoided.

The hosts themselves are often fascinating people. Here is a random list of their occupations that I discovered in researching B&B organizations across North America: journalists, investment bankers, linguists, painters, musicians (many), tennis pros and buffs, a world-renowned expert on scotch whisky, doctors, lawyers, teachers (many), gardeners, and gracious widows, widowers, divorced people who love to cook and entertain.

B&B homes are full of surprises, very nice ones. When you check into some hotels, you know there's going to be a standard-size bed, a TV set, a scratch-proof, mar-proof dresser, and often the same graphics on the wall from hotel to hotel. But your room in a B&B home may have a cannonball bed from colonial times, a working fireplace, family antiques that span the centuries, and often original artwork on all of the walls. The homes themselves are often unique. A number of B&B homes are listed on the National Historic Register. Others are not really houses at all, but houseboats and yachts in which the hosts welcome you to a floating B&B. There are also working ranches, Boston town houses, New York luxury apartments, and remote Canadian farmhouses.

ABOUT THIS BOOK

B&B travel is not your typical run-of-the-mill travel. Of course you could get a bad B&B—a poorly maintained house, surly people, a stale roll for breakfast. But I've personally encountered all of these problems in modern, expensive hotels, and you probably have too.

B&B travel can be more fun and more personal and more relaxing than any kind of traveling you've ever done before. You can meet and make new friends all over the country and the world. You can also save a lot of money.

Talking about savings, think about this. Next time you and your spouse or friend have breakfast in a top hotel, add up the *total* cost, including the tip to the waiter and local sales tax. That cost alone may just about equal the cost of a typical bed-and-breakfast for two in many parts of the country.

This guidebook was written to help you make the most of your next trip. It contains one of the most comprehensive listings and descriptions of North American B&B reservation services ever published. Many of these services pre-inspect every single home on their list. I surveyed them *twice*—with a span of one year between each survey—to help ensure that I was including the most stable and long-lasting services of this fledgling cottage industry. Some asked if they had to pay to be included in this guidebook. I told them "of course not." My only criteria for their inclusion was how well they were serving the traveling public.

I found many of these reservation-service organizations to be extremely conscientious, personally *pre-inspecting* the B&B homes included in their lists.

This guidebook also contains a listing of some special B&B inns that have come to my attention, my selection of the "50 Best B&B Homes" in North America.

So come join the *friendly* revolution in travel—bed-and-breakfast. You're going to like it!

ANSWERS TO SOME COMMON QUESTIONS ABOUT B&B TRAVEL

Q. *Is B&B travel a new idea?*

A. Not at all. It's one of the oldest. In the 11th century, when monks and other pilgrims were walking to Rome or other holy sites, they frequently stopped overnight at private farms, monasteries, and homes. After breakfast in the morning, they were on their way—the first B&B guests.

In recent years the B&B movement has spread throughout much of Europe. Europeans frequently stop at homes with "Bed & Breakfast" or "Zimmer Frei" (room free) signs posted on the front lawn.

In the American depression years of the 1930s, "tourist homes" sprang up all over the countryside. For as little as $2 you could have a modest room and sometimes an equally modest breakfast.

However, the current B&B movement is much different. While there are still many modest homes offering a room and breakfast, the quality of most accommodations (and breakfasts) is light-years ahead of early tourist homes.

Q. *I get confused. I see B&B signs on hotels.*

A. It is confusing. Many small inns have taken to calling themselves bed-and-breakfast places. These can be very pleasant, and many of them are listed in this guidebook. But when I say "B&B" I'm talking about a room in a private home with at least a continental breakfast served to guests.

Q. *Why should I make a reservation through a B&B reservation-service organization? I see lists of individual B&B homes in books and brochures.*

A. You can, of course, make your own reservations directly with a B&B home. Some of these I've seen can be very good. However, because of zoning and other problems with neighbors, often the best B&B homes *never* appear in any public list. The only way you can book them is through a reservation-service organization.

The best of these organizations *pre-inspect* all prospective B&B homes before listing them.

Some of these organizations can occasionally be hard to reach. Many are small "mom and pop," or sometimes just "mom," operations. They have a list of B&Bs, a telephone, and an answering machine. Sometimes you may not be able to reach them until after 6 p.m. at night because the owners of the service work during the day. However, with a little persistence, you can usually get through. Almost all the organizations I have included in this guide have been in existence at least one year. I surveyed most of them *twice*, with a span of one year in between.

Q. *Can I use a B&B home for business travel?*

A. Of course—B&Bs are ideal for business travelers who want to reduce costs. The reservation-service organizations included in this directory have listed many of the major corporations that are located near their B&B homes.

B&B homes are also ideal for parents visiting children at college, single women relocating to a new community, skiers, vacationers visiting specific scenic attractions, national parks, and other recreation areas, and everyone who's tired of paying high hotel costs and sometimes getting second-class, impersonal treatment.

Q. *Can I travel with a pet?*

A. Some B&B homes, especially in rural areas, do allow well-behaved dogs and cats to stay with their owners. Always ask about this, however, when you make your reservation. I know of one cat owner who stayed in B&B homes all over the state of Colorado with Tabby joining him for breakfast every morning.

If you are allergic to dogs or cats, be sure to ask if any are in residence in the B&B home before you make your reservation.

Q. *Are there any disadvantages to B&B travel?*

A. Yes. There can be a lack of privacy. Sometimes you and your spouse or friend want to be alone together on vacation; the conversation of even a well-meaning hostess may be more than you want. You also may have to wait in line for a shared bathroom, just like at home if you have a large family. You also may feel guilty staying too long in the shower when you know that others are waiting.

You may find a few B&B homes that are disappointing. Barbara Notarius, president of Bed & Breakfast USA Ltd., reported on her visit to one: "I recently went out on an appointment to visit one prospective B&B for my network. I arrived at the appointed time. The place was beautiful from the outside, handmade by a custom cabinetmaker, very rustic and nestled in the woods by a running stream just outside a desirable country community. When I rang the bell, a woman came to the door and stared at me. I asked for the woman of the house from whom I had the first inquiry many weeks previously. The woman looked at me a bit bewildered and said 'No,' and just stood there. So I asked for the husband who had given me detailed directions only a few days before. Again this woman said 'No,' and continued to look at me. I finally said, 'Who are you? When will the family be back?' Her response was that she was a tenant and the family had had a spat the day before. The wife had left and [the woman] thought the husband had gone off flying shortly before I arrived. Since they obviously had forgotten about the appointment, I asked to have a look at the house anyway. She didn't mind, so in I went. Furniture was practically nonexistent, filth was everywhere, and even the room this woman was renting had only a sleeping bag over a piece of foam, no sheets."

Moral: It's a pretty good idea to have the B&B home inspected and approved by the reservation organization *before* you pull into the driveway.

2

HOW TO FIND BED & BREAKFASTS

- Many of the most fascinating B&B homes never advertise or post a B&B sign.
- New sources of B&B information are springing up almost every week.

This book is the key to hundreds of the better B&B homes throughout the U.S. and Canada.

Why "better"?

Because most of the most luxurious or interesting or historic B&B homes won't risk angry confrontations with their neighbors by posting a "Bed & Breakfast" sign on their lawn or advertising in a local publication. Even B&B homes that have received free publicity from a well-meaning reporter have encountered problems from zoning boards, health boards, and sometimes a whole block of people who have exaggerated fears about a "business" operating in the neighborhood.

Also, many B&B hosts feel much more secure if any prospective guests are screened by a reliable reservation-service organization. Otherwise they would be opening their homes to total strangers right off the street.

That's why so many of the really great B&B homes are *never* advertised or publicized. Some of these homes have swimming pools, country antiques and fireplaces in every room, and beautiful grounds. The way to find them is to call one of the reservation organizations listed in this book.

Use the unique "B&B Finder" cross index at the back of

this guide. For example, if you are parents of a son at Atlanta University, you could simply turn to the "Schools and Colleges" section and find which reservation agencies offer B&B accommodations near this school. If you want to attend a Shakespeare play at the Stratford Festival in Ontario, Canada, turn to the "Attractions" section for your B&B reservation service. If you are a business person tired of the plastic sameness and $100+ price tags of many hotels, check the reservation listings for a home in the city or area you plan to visit. This service can be particularly valuable for women travelers who enjoy the security and comfort of a home environment when they're out of town.

If you ever do get stuck and can't contact a reservations organization operating in the area you want to visit, there are several alternatives.

First, you can look in the local *Yellow Pages* phone directory. Reservation services and individual bed-and-breakfast homes will be listed under a new, separate "Bed & Breakfast" heading.

You can also write ahead to local chambers of commerce and state tourism offices (their addresses are listed in this guidebook). Many are now beginning to offer free lists of B&B homes or brochures about individual homes and farms.

Tourist information booths along state highways are also beginning to carry B&B brochures and information.

When you're visiting a resort area, stop in the local tourist office. Some can tell you about local availabilities, and may even be able to book you into a B&B on the spot.

In some rural areas (where neighbors are more tolerant or friendly), you will see "Bed & Breakfast" signs in front of some homes.

You also can now get information about B&B accommodations from the American Automobile Association. In a newsletter to other AAA clubs, the National Travel Department of AAA wrote, "Due to the rapid growth of interest in bed-and-breakfast facilities, we decided to review our method for presenting B&B data to AAA Clubs. In the future, in order to ensure that members receive current information pertaining to reputable B&B referral services, we will provide a listing of only those B&B referral services which screen their listings. In this way, the listing provided to clubs will reflect AAA's concern for property cleanliness, hospitable hosts, and ethical operations." (*Note:* AAA really meant "reservation"—not "referral" agencies.)

As the B&B movement keeps growing (and in some areas it's starting to roar along, picking up new momentum with each day), you'll find more and more sources of information.

When you're traveling in North America, take this guidebook along. It can introduce you to B&Bs all over the U.S. and Canada through a network of reservation-service organizations. It's among the friendliest, most inexpensive ways to travel today.

Want to stay in a B&B inn? You'll find a list of special ones that have come to my attention (listed by state following the B&B reservation-service information in Part II).

Want to stay in one of the finest B&B homes in North America? See Part III, "The 50 Best B&B Homes in North America." You can even become one of our judges in selecting the "50 Best" for the next edition of this book.

STATE TOURIST OFFICES

Many state tourist offices can supply you with names and addresses of some outstanding B&B homes and inns in their area, as well as good state maps and other travel information. Here is a complete list.

Alabama Bureau of
 Publicity and
 Information
532 S. Perry St.
Montgomery, AL 36104
 205/261-4169

Alaska State Division of
 Tourism
P.O. Box E
Juneau, AK 99811
 907/465-2010

Arizona State Office of
 Tourism
1480 E. Bethany Home Rd.,
 Suite 180
Phoenix, AZ 85014
 602/255-3618

Arkansas Department of
 Parks and Tourism
One Capitol Mall
Little Rock, AR 72201
 501/371-1087

California Office of Tourism
1121 L St., Suite 103
Sacramento, CA 95814
916/322-2881

Colorado Tourism Board
1625 Broadway, Suite 1700
Denver, CO 80202
303/592-5410

Connecticut Department of
Economic Development,
Tourism Division
210 Washington St.
Hartford, CT 06106
203/566-2496

Delaware Tourism Office
99 Kings Hwy. (P.O. Box
1401)
Dover, DE 19903
302/736-4271

Florida Division of Tourism
107 W. Gaines St., Rm. 505
Tallahassee, FL 32301
904/488-5606

Georgia Tourist Division
P.O. Box 1776
Atlanta, GA 30301
404/656-3590

Hawaii Visitors Bureau
2270 Kalakaua Ave., Suite
801
Honolulu, HI 96815
808/923-1811

Idaho Department of
Commerce
Division of Travel Promotion
State Capitol Building
Boise, ID 83720
208/334-2470

Illinois Office of Tourism
100 W. Randolf, Suite 3-400
Chicago, IL 60601
312/917-4732

Indiana Tourism
Development Division
1 N. Capitol Ave.,
Suite 700
Indianapolis, IN 46204
317/232-8870

Iowa Department of
Economic Development
200 E. Grand Ave.
Des Moines, IA 50309
515/281-3401

Kansas Travel and Tourism
Division
400 W. 8th St., 5th Floor
Topeka, KS 66603
913/296-2009

Kentucky Department of
Travel Development
Capitol Plaza Tower, 22nd
Floor
Frankfort, KY 40601
502/564-4930

Louisiana Office of Tourism
P.O. Box 94291
Baton Rouge, LA 70804
504/925-3850

Maine Department of
Economic and
Community
Development
Office of Tourism
189 State St.
State House Station 59
Augusta, ME 04333
207/289-5710

Maryland Office of Tourist
Development
217 E. Redwood St., 9th Fl.
Baltimore, MD 21202
301/333-6611

Massachusetts Office of Travel
and Tourism
100 Cambridge St.
Boston, MA 02202
617/727-3205

Michigan Travel Bureau
P.O. Box 30226
Lansing, MI 48909
517/373-0670

Minnesota Office
of Tourism
375 Jackson Walkway, 250
Skyway Level
St. Paul, MN 55101
612/296-2755

Mississippi Department of
Economic Development
Division of Tourism
P.O. Box 849
Jackson, MS 39205
601/359-3426

Missouri Division of Tourism
P.O. Box 1055
Jefferson City, MO 65102
314/751-3051

Montana Promotion
Division Department of
Commerce
1424 Ninth Ave.
Helena, MT 59620
406/444-2654

Nebraska Travel and Tourism
Division
P.O. Box 94666
Lincoln, NE 68509
402/471-3791

Nevada Commission on
Tourism
600 E. Williams
Carson City, NV 89710
702/885-4322

New Hampshire Office of
Vacation Travel
105 Loudon Rd.,
Box 856
Concord, NH 03301
603/271-2665

New Jersey Division of Travel
and Tourism
P.O. Box CN826
Trenton, NJ 08625
609/292-2470

New Mexico Tourism and
Travel Division
Economic Development and
Tourism Department
1100 St. Francis St.
Santa Fe, NM 87503
505/827-0295

New York Division of
Tourism
One Commerce Plaza
Albany, NY 12245
518/474-4116

North Carolina Travel and
Tourism Division
430 N. Salisbury St.
Raleigh, NC 27611
919/733-4171

North Dakota Tourism
Promotion Division
Memorial Building, Capitol
Grounds
Bismarck, ND 58505
701/224-2525

Ohio Office of Travel and
Tourism

P.O. Box 1001
Columbus, OH 43216
614/466-8844

Oklahoma Tourism and
Recreation Department
505 Will Rogers Building
Oklahoma City, OK 73105
405/521-2406

Oregon Tourism and
Recreation Department
595 Cottage St. NE
Salem, OR 97310
503/373-1230

Pennsylvania Bureau of
Travel Development
416 Forum Building
Harrisburg, PA 17120
717/787-5453

Rhode Island Department of
Economic Development
7 Jackson Walkway
Providence, RI 02903
401/277-2601

South Carolina Department
of Parks, Recreation, and
Tourism
1205 Pendleton St., Room
106, Edgar A. Brown
Building
Columbia, SC 29201
803/734-0136

South Dakota Division of
Tourism
P.O. Box 6000
Pierre, SD 57501
605/773-3301

Tennessee Department of
Tourist Development
320 Sixth Ave. North
Nashville, TN 37219
615/741-1904

Texas Tourist Development
Agency
P.O. Box 12008, Capitol
Station
Austin, TX 78711
512/462-9191

Utah Travel Council
300 N. State,
Capitol Hill
Salt Lake City, UT 84114
801/533-5681

Vermont Travel Division
134 State St.
Montpelier, VT 05602
802/828-3236

Virginia Division of Tourism
202 N. 9th St.,
Suite 500
Richmond, VA 23219
804/786-2051

Washington Department of
Trade and Economic
Development
Tourism Development
Division
101 General Administration
Building,
Bldg. AX-13
Olympia, WA 98504
206/753-5600

Washington Convention and
Visitors Association
1575 I St. NW,
Suite 250
Washington, DC 20006
202/789-7000

West Virginia Department of
Commerce
Tourism Division
2101 Washington St. East
Charleston, WV 25305
304/348-2200

Wisconsin Division of
  Tourism
123 W. Washington Ave.
(P.O. Box 7970)
Madison, WI 53707
  608/266-2147

Wyoming Travel Commission
Frank Norris, Jr., Travel
  Center
I-25 and College Drive
Cheyenne, WY 82002
  307/777-7777

TERRITORIES

American Samoa
  Government
Planning and Tourism
  Office
P.O. Box 1147
Pago Pago, AS 96799
  684/633-5187

Guam Visitors Bureau
P.O. Box 3520
Agana, Guam 96910
  671/646-5278

Marianas Visitors Bureau
P.O. Box 861
Saipan, CM Mariana Islands
  96950
  670/234-8327

Puerto Rico Tourism
  Company
P.O. Box 4435
San Juan, PR 00905
  809/721-2400

Virgin Islands Division of
  Tourism
P.O. Box 6400
Charlotte Amalie,
  St. Thomas, USVI 00801
  809/774-8784

3

HOW TO BE A B&B GUEST

- Use a reservation-service organization that pre-inspects the homes on its lists.
- Some B&B homes offer free pickup at airports and train and bus stations for travelers without cars.

While enjoying the hospitality and warmth of a typical B&B home may be as easy as saying "Pass the strawberry preserves," finding the right home for you and your family may require a little effort and advance planning.

First, I strongly recommend that you use a reservation service rather than taking pot-luck as you drive along the road or call a home that you've seen listed in a book. Any reservation service worth the fee that it usually receives from each rental (from the B&B host, not from you) will inspect the homes on its list. Or at a very minimum the service will quickly drop any homes that guests have complained about frequently.

It's true that you may occasionally find a gem on your own simply by stopping at a "Bed & Breakfast" sign. But the odds are against you because many of the best B&B homes aren't listed.

I've repeated this warning in other parts of this guide because I truly believe that booking your B&B home through an established reservation-service organization is the simplest, safest, and ultimately the most satisfying way.

However, before you call any reservation service, you should write down your basic needs. In many cases the reservation service will send you a free or low-cost brochure that describes the homes and locations available. You then phone or write the reservation service after you've made the selection. You will usually be required to confirm the reservation by a minimum payment of the first night's rental. Some services may require full payment in advance.

After you have a confirmed reservation from the reservation service, always call the host. This is a very important call because it will be your first contact with this very important person. You can begin to establish a friendship with that first call. Have a map handy so you can ask specific questions about the most direct route to the B&B home. (This is very important—I have been stranded at night in some remote rural areas looking for "the second road on the right.")

Many B&B hosts offer pickup services to carless travelers, free or at a small fee. If you arrive by plane, bus, or train, you may be able to have the host meet you at the airport or station.

It is always a good practice (and often required) that you pay the host any balance due for your entire B&B stay when you arrive. This also saves problems when you check out if the host is away.

Ask about the use of a house key, particularly if your host works and you want access to the house and your room during the day. You may be required to post a key fee.

Ask all about the use of the house and grounds. Some hosts give you kitchen privileges and allow you to fix your own breakfast whenever you're ready. One B&B guest surprised her host by making strawberry pancakes for her husband and the whole host family. "They were pleased," she said later. "But you could tell this wasn't their typical breakfast. They really thought I was serving them dessert."

There may be recreation facilities/equipment in the house and on the grounds—TV sets, stereos, barbecue pits, volleyball nets, swimming pools, sleds, etc. Find out if you're permitted to use them. Many hosts are happy to oblige.

In the house itself, is smoking permitted in your room? In certain areas? Or forbidden throughout the house. Do you have access to the family room, the living room, and the laundry facilities?

Never hesitate to ask if you need certain comfort items —an extra blanket for the bed, extra towels, etc. Some rooms have individual air conditioners or temperature controls. Ask for a demonstration of how to regulate them.

The host may give you a written set of "house rules." Follow them and treat the house as you would your own. Clear communication and common courtesy are the bases for a successful and happy B&B homestay.

Always sign the guestbook when you leave, with any personal comments about what you liked about the visit and your hosts. It's a great keepsake for the hosts. It also can lead to Christmas cards, social notes, and just possibly, a lifelong friendship.

4

HOW TO OPERATE A B&B HOME

- Some hosts make $10,000 and over a year. But the majority earn far less. However, they do make a lot of new friends from around the world.
- Take advantage of possible tax deductions when you use part of your home as a business.
- Expect the unexpected. B&B people have hosted everyone from motion picture and soap opera stars to casual visitors who ask to be married in their home!

A surprising number of people want to become B&B hosts and turn one or two spare rooms in their house into guest rooms. Some are widows, widowers, divorcees, and single people who are burdened by the rising costs and taxes of homeownership. The idea of earning anywhere from $15 to $80 per night for a room (depending on the quality and location of the home) can be very appealing.

Others are simply "empty nesters" whose children have gone off to college or careers and left them with extra rooms and an abnormally quiet house. They like the idea of meeting new people from around the U.S. and the world. Many of these hosts are college professors, doctors, lawyers, world travelers, company presidents, as well as automobile mechanics, shop foremen, secretaries, and bus drivers—a generous cross section of America.

Other people who become B&B hosts are frustrated innkeepers or restaurant owners. Many dream of one day owning their own inn on a mountain or designing their own restaurant serving "new American cuisine." Becoming a B&B host allows a person—at least partially—to satisfy some of these dreams.

However, before you go into this business (and it *must* be a business, not a hobby, if you hope to qualify for possible tax deductions on your house), you should look at the pros and cons with your eyes wide open. You may want to follow Ben Franklin's wise advice. Write down all the positives you can think of on one sheet, all the negative factors on another. Then look at both of them together. You may then quickly see what your decision should be.

Here are some things you should consider:

1. Don't expect to make much money. In fact, one B&B association estimated that only about 10% of the B&B homes make a profit at present. However, as every business person knows, "profit" is relative. You might make attractive and useful improvements in your home, such as new carpeting, drapes, furnishings. You might qualify for depreciation of your house (and furnishings) for tax purposes. And even if the IRS rules that you are pursuing B&B as a hobby, you may still be able to use expenses to offset any income from your B&B. That means you have to make *serious* efforts to rent the room regularly.

2. Look at your home objectively. Does (do) your spare room(s) have a good double or twin beds? Are the furnishings in good condition? Is there adequate closet space? Will your guests have access to a private bath, or will the bathroom be shared with the family and other guests? One knowledgeable hostess said, "Always sleep at least once in the room you plan to use for your B&B service. You may be surprised by street noises, or too bright a light in the early morning streaming in the windows—things you would be aware of only if you stayed in your own room." Often one of the key factors in how often the room is rented is the location of your home. If it's in or near a major interstate highway, a major city, scenic attraction, college, hospital, or major corporations, your chances of renting it regularly increase dramatically. Some reservation agencies have told me that a few B&B homes in really remote areas may only be rented about once a year!

3. Poll your whole family. How do they feel about having guests? Remind them that they may lose some privacy in their own home and that they may have to wait in line to use the bathroom. Everyone may have to cooperate to keep the whole house clean (particularly the bathroom) for the arrival of guests. This may be the time for a good family discussion before you make any decision. Do you have a pet? A dog that protects the home by nipping strangers could cost you a lawsuit.

4. Talk with a good lawyer or someone in local government who is familiar with regulations that may govern B&B operations. The real problem is that zoning laws across the country are often very vague about B&B homes. Some zoning laws seem to permit occasional boarders in a home. At other times riled neighbors, who fear that their property value or privacy may be threatened by strangers coming into the neighborhood, may contact the local zoning board for a ruling. Recently one woman in La Jolla, California, began to operate a B&B business in her home. She posted notices locally. Some incensed neighbors brought suit against her. Although she fought the legal action vigorously, her lawyers eventually advised her to close the business. These zoning laws are in flux all over the nation. However, some B&B homeowners are also winning their cases and getting favorable rulings from zoning boards. This is particularly true in states that are actively encouraging the growth of the B&B movement as a way of stimulating more tourism. Jean Brown, head of Bed & Breakfast International, writes, "Not one of the thousands of host homes I've had has ever been the subject of a complaint to a zoning commission."

Also ask your attorney to check local public health/safety laws/regulations that may apply to any commercial application of your home. For example, some areas may require smoke detectors throughout your home.

5. If you do decide to become a B&B host, you now must decide whether you want to operate independently or want to be connected with a local or national reservation service. *I strongly recommend that you register your home with a reservation service.* If you operate as an independent, you must advertise and promote your home in some ways to attract guests. That could mean putting small ads or generating publicity in local newspapers and magazines.

You might even put a small sign in front of your home. Unfortunately all of these activities could raise red flags for your neighbors or local officials. There is another problem. With your phone number on public display in an ad or in one of those books that describes independent B&B homes, you could be subject to unwelcome calls at any time of the day or night. You also would have little opportunity to screen the people who come into your home to spend the night. Instead you would be much better off using a reservation service that does not list your address or phone number in any of their literature. Let the reservation service screen prospective guests. (Before you sign up for any reservation service, ask about their screening activities.) You may want a service that handles all the financial details, even accepting credit-card payments, and forwards a check to you. A service typically charges you a small annual fee to cover administration/advertising costs plus a percentage of each rental (often 20% to 30%). When a service regularly brings you business and conscientiously screens prospective guests, they are more than worth their keep. If the service seems to be choosy about selecting homes for their network and wants to come out for a personal inspection of your home, be thankful! It means, that the service really cares about offering attractive accommodations to the public, and you are in very good hands. Some of the larger services even hold seminars and annual meetings for B&B hosts. This whole business is still in its infancy, and hosts are learning from each other. This guide contains one of the most complete listings of reservation services now operating. Turn to one operating in your area. If none, consider one that offers B&B listings across the U.S.

6. Check your home insurance coverage with your insurance agent. Tell him frankly what you plan to do. Ask what kind of coverage you have and how you would be protected if a paying guest were injured in your home. The standard homeowner's policy may only cover *two* boarders. As the B&B movement grows, the insurance industry is becoming aware of the problems and drafting special new policies. *Warning:* Insurance costs for B&B continue to increase—a major new problem.

I have deliberately listed the most negative factors, not to discourage you but to be sure that you understand that becoming a B&B host is not as simple as deciding you want to do it. That decision involves a commitment, and some careful attention to detail to avoid the pitfalls. However, there can be enormous personal rewards. Many of the stories I have heard from B&B hosts have been heartwarming. One hostess described the young lady who came to their bed-and-breakfast and liked their home so much that she asked to be married there. Other homeowners have met people from around the world who became fast friends. Barbara Notarius, president of Bed & Breakfast USA, Ltd., frequently offers her home as a B&B. She told of her first guest, a retired mining engineer from Australia. He had spent much of his life in remote areas of the world such as New Guinea and had hundreds of stories to tell. Soon Barbara's husband was skipping work so he could drive the guest around town. On another occasion, several of her house guests were musicians. Before they went to bed at night, they gave a chamber concert for Barbara and her family. "What a privilege!" she said.

But hosts also have to learn to be resilient and expect the unexpected. One hostess received a booking from a young woman for two people. When the two women arrived (one an actress who had recently appeared in a successful avant-garde film), they announced that they were gay and wanted to share a double bed. The hostess accommodated them, and had food for conversation at the next eight bridge parties with her friends. (If you operate a B&B home, you have to decide in advance if you will accept unmarried couples, singles, etc. This is another advantage of using a reservation service that knows your preferences.) Joan Brownhill, president of Pineapple Hospitality reservation service in New Bedford, Massachusetts, tells how she selects B&B homes and hosts: "We send out a 'Host Home' preliminary packet which tells of our philosophy as an agency. There is a form to be completed that gives a profile of the prospective host, and answers such basic questions as to whether the host will accept children and pets. Two interviewers then visit the home by appointment to check everything out. If it meets the standards we've set, we sign an agreement with the new B&B home. An annual fee to the agency is collected."

Even when you are listed with an agency and want additional guests, there are a number of ways you could discreetly attract a number of guests:

▪ If you are close to a local college, call or write the personnel office or office of student housing. Describe your home, its location, and room availability. Often visiting parents need an economical place to stay, especially with today's college costs being what they are. There also may be visiting professors or alumni who would welcome a home atmosphere. You might have some very stimulating guests.

▪ Contact the personnel office or corporate travel department of major corporations. Transferees and other visiting employees might make excellent prescreened guests. Women business travelers are particularly receptive to the relaxed B&B concept.

▪ Talk with local real estate agents. They may have out-of-town prospects who need a place to stay while looking for a new home. You'll not only earn extra income by providing hospitality, but you may also be making friends with new neighbors.

▪ Ask previous guests back. When you find particularly appealing and thoughtful guests, invite them back in the summer or winter. Always keep a guestbook and ask them to write their comments. You may be pleasantly surprised how many Christmas/holiday cards you receive from guests who enjoyed your hospitality. *Note:* If your guest originally came from a reservation-service organization, you should ask them to rebook through this organization rather than directly with you. The few dollars you would lose in commission are more than made up by keeping the goodwill of the reservation service that is advertising and generating business for you.

SOME TIPS FOR HOSTS—

"The Gift of Hospitality"

1. Show room and house and give guests an opportunity to unload their belongings.
2. Offer a drink/beverage and see if anything else is needed.

3. Take care of business, such as collecting money, signing the guestbook and contracts, giving a receipt (preferably within 20 minutes of the guests' arrival).
4. Answer questions and mention nearby attractions.
5. Supply guests with an information sheet containing questions and answers about your local area.
6. Collect brochures on sightseeing for your local area, as well as your state, and have them available for guests.
7. Offer a "Sue's Special": picnic basket breakfast in bed.
8. Collect menus from popular restaurants to leave in the guests' room.
9. Make coffee early. Find out when guests arrive what they prefer to drink in the morning. A Thermos of coffee outside the door, so the first cup of coffee can be drunk in bed, is a real treat for the real coffee drinker.
10. Put an umbrella stand with loan umbrellas near the door and tell guests about it.
11. Set up a game corner (garage sales are a wonderful source of these and other handy items).
12. Place extra toilet articles (small sample sizes) in drawers.
13. Use liquid soap in the bathroom so that no guest has to use anyone else's soap.
14. Offer a special guest tray including a fruit bowl, drinking glass, tissues, etc.
15. Have on hand books and magazines for your guests to read.
16. A hairdryer, makeup mirror, and curling iron from a garage sale may be lifesavers for your female guests.
17. Have newspapers on hand.
18. Have a good map on hand.
19. Copy the section of your local map showing your home and circle your house, restaurants, attractions, movies, etc., and run off enough copies so that each guest can take one with him/her.
20. Collect articles from your newspaper's attractions section and keep in a folder easily available to guests. Copies hold up better than newsprint originals.
21. Collect discount coupons from nearby attractions and restaurants for guests.
22. Save fast-food discount coupons too.

23. Leave a note on the guests' desk or bureau telling where they can order take-out pizza. Let them know if it's all right to eat on your deck or patio.
24. Deliver ice water to the guests' room in the evening.
25. Have iced tea available in the refrigerator or let guests know that they can always boil themselves hot water for tea or instant coffee.
26. Help your guests to feel comfortable in your home. Assure them that they should ask if there is something they need—extra towels, more pillows, etc.
27. Copy your special B&B recipes so guests can take them home.
28. Invite guests to watch you do your hobbies/special-interest activities (such as stained glass, pottery, etc.).
29. If you have a historic home, guests may be interested in its history and architecture. Take a course about tracing the history of your home and keep the results of your work accessible.
30. See if the historical society or other town group has a walking tour of the community published that your guests can take.
31. Be sensitive to your guests' need for privacy and space. Don't ever make a guest feel that he's there to amuse you. Be available for those who want to talk but in touch enough to recognize when a guest just wants to be left alone.
32. B&B attracts a lot of folks looking for romance. If your setting is conducive to this, encourage it. Offer guests some privacy in front of the fireplace, put out a decanter with a little after-dinner liqueur, etc. Flannel sheets are wonderful in cold climates.
33. Let your guests get to know you as an individual—your way of life, your part of the country.

(Suggestions from *Rocky Mountains—Bed & Breakfast* hosts, reprinted with the permission of Kate Peterson and Barbara Notarius)

COMMONLY ASKED QUESTIONS ABOUT HOSTING

Q. *How much should I charge for the room?*

A. The rate depends on several factors. The most impor-tant is location. Even a modestly furnished room in a modest house that is close to a popular ski slope can often command a premium rate. The condition of the room, its furnishings, and the general appearance of your home also should be considered. If the room has a private bath instead of a shared bath, you can also charge more. However, you want to be sure that the rate you charge is competitive and doesn't drive business away. Check the rates of other B&B homes in your area. Also, find out the rates of local hotels and motels. Your rate should generally be lower than hotel rates. Travelers expect B&B rates to be bargains.

Q. *What about income tax deductions?*

A. If your home is only used for B&B hosting 14 or fewer nights per year, you may not have to pay any income tax on what you make. However, if a room in your home is rented more than 14 nights a year, then you would have to declare all income. You would also be entitled to deductions that could range from depreciation on your furnishings, fees paid to reservation-service organizations, stamps, phone calls, etc. You also may be able to claim depreciation on your house and a percentage of certain housecleaning/ home maintenance costs. You should make (and report) a profit at least two out of every five years or the government may claim your B&B operation is a hobby—not a business —and disallow any business deductions. *Note:* You may be unable to deduct some smaller expenses as a result of the newly revised federal tax law. To avoid problems, work with a good accountant who can help you interpret the current IRS rules.

Q. *Should I tell my neighbors I operate a B&B home?*

A. No. Not unless you are a would-be Perry Mason anxious to plead your case before a local zoning board.

Q. *Should I charge sales tax?*

A. Check with local authorities about this. It may be necessary for you to get a tax number and collect sales tax on all B&B rentals. Don't follow the human tendency to just keep mum about any rentals or income. You could become liable for back taxes and penalties.

Q. *I have to leave for work early in the morning. How can I fix breakfast for guests or give them access to the house should they return while I'm away?*

A. You could leave breakfast ingredients in the refrigerator and give your guests kitchen privileges for a do-it-yourself meal. Some hosts also give their guests a key, charging a "key fee" of $5 or $10 (which is refunded when the guest returns the key). For your own security, you may give the guest a key only to the regular lock, not a deadbolt lock, if you have one. You then have the security of locking the deadbolt without worrying about any unreturned keys that might be floating around.

Q. *What about the possibility of theft? I am letting strangers into my home.*

A. Theft could happen. However, at least so far, B&B guests seem to be an unusually honest group of people. In talking with B&B hosts, I have yet to hear of an incident where a guest has taken as much as a teaspoon. (In contrast, talk with any major-city hotel, which regularly loses a large quantity of towels and room-service silverware and linen in the luggage of departing guests.) You would want to use some common sense in protecting your personal belongings. If your guests have active children, you might want to store away any obvious breakables. You also can get an extra measure of security by having all prospective guests screened by the reservation-service organization. Many of these organizations ask guests for personal references.

Q. *Should I print a "brochure" on my B&B home?*

A. It really isn't necessary. You might want to do a simple letter on your stationery which describes your home and the breakfast you serve, tells of any "house rule" restrictions (such as no smoking, no pets, etc.), and gives directions to your home. Offset print a quantity and send some to your reservation-service organization. Or mail one to the guest who calls and asks for directions or more information.

Q. *Will I make much money as a B&B host?*

A. As I've said before, you probably *won't* make a high income as a host. However, I have been told of hosts who make $10,000 or more a year. Others who are close to scenic attractions, major cities, resort areas, etc., reliably make several hundred extra dollars each month. One hostess recently used her B&B earnings to pay for an all-expense safari in Africa. But there are also some B&B homes in remote locations that are only rented as little as once a year. As the real estate people love to say about selling a house, the three most important factors are location, location, and location.

A LAST NOTE

Much of your reward of being a B&B host will come from meeting other people. Kate Peterson, coordinator of Bed & Breakfast Rocky Mountains, shared this letter she had received from one of her new hosts:

Dear Kate,

Clyde and I just wanted to let you know how delighted we are with our first experience hosting bed-and-breakfast travelers. The couple from Houston left just this morning. I know we have made new friends. They were so comfortable with us that they have already decided to return in June to stay. It's amazing to me that they have even referred some of their friends to us—all this in just the last few days. Yesterday was really special. It was my birthday. When I got home in the afternoon, they had a birthday card and a delicate dried-flower arrangement waiting for me. I was truly touched. Kate, we want to thank you for making this opportunity possible for us and for others. We are look-

ing forward to the next bed-and-breakfast travelers we can serve.

Sincerely,
Fairley

These are the *real* rewards of becoming a B&B host.

II

Directory of B&B Reservation Services and Selected B&B Inns in North America

SPECIAL NOTE TO READERS

Be sure to check the "Best B&Bs" section of each reservation-service listing. This is designed to give you an edge over other people calling the same reservation service. It describes the B&B homes that the services themselves consider their most appealing. Ask about them. Also you will learn about special services available from many B&B hosts just for the asking.

National and Regional B&B
Reservation Services

AMERICAN HISTORIC HOMES BED & BREAKFAST
P.O. BOX 336, DANA POINT, CA 92629

Offers B&B Homes In: 500 locations throughout the United States
Reservations Phone: 714/496-6953
Phone Hours: 9 a.m. to 5 p.m. Monday through Friday
Price Range of Homes: $25 to $65 single, $35 to $85 double
Breakfast Included in Price: Continental or full American; some specialties are cinnamon rolls, freshly ground coffee, smoked meats, fresh-baked breads, and "recipes from the Gold Rush days in Mother Lode Country"
Brochure Available: For $1 (includes listings)
Reservations Should Be Made: 2 weeks in advance (last-minute reservations accepted if possible)

Best B&Bs
■ Historic 22-room home in Boston, Massachusetts. Home is located just 15 minutes from the city. You can enjoy the antique collection and resident small poodle.

■ Victorian house in Arlington, Virginia. Close to metro and Washington, D.C. This home is also filled with antiques and is frequently included on house-and-garden tours.

■ Victorian house in San Diego, California. Has antique décor. Your hosts, George and Julian, serve a full breakfast.

BED & BREAKFAST HOSPITALITY
P.O. BOX 2407, OCEANSIDE, CA 92054

Offers B&B Homes In: Major cities and rural areas across the U.S. and Hawaii
Reservations Phone: 619/722-6694
Phone Hours: 9 a.m. to 6 p.m. Monday through Saturday; no holidays; answering machine
Price Range of Homes: $25 to $150 single, $36 to $170+ double
Breakfast Included in Price: Continental or full American; most hosts serve home-baked breads and muffins, fresh fruit in season, and farms serve their own eggs and produce.
Brochure Available: Free
Reservations Should Be Made: At least 2 weeks in advance; last-minute reservations accepted if possible

Best B&Bs

■ Large home on Lake Arrowhead, California. When you arrive, you will be treated to complimentary refreshments on the deck overlooking the lake. You will breakfast in the "Top of the Tower" with a view of the lake and cedar and spruce boughs. *Insider's Tip:* If you'd like a wood-burning fireplace for a romantic evening, choose the Lake View Suite. It also has a large deck and a full bar.

■ Greek Revival–style home in Cambria, California. This home was completed in 1873 and is registered with the Historic House Association of America. Completely refurbished in 1987, it has been decorated with antiques from the 1800s. *Insider's Tip:* This is a particularly convenient place to stay if you plan to visit Hearst Castle, just five miles away.

■ Queen Anne Victorian in San Diego, California. "It features an octagon window turret with a conical peak, has two double-story bays of windowed rooms, featuring stained glass, and you'll want to spend some time on the beautiful veranda with its spindle frieze and ballustrades." The home is high on a hillside above San Diego Bay (about two to three minutes from downtown San Diego). You'll find some nice touches here—fresh flowers in the room and complimentary wine and sherry.

BED & BREAKFAST INTERNATIONAL—SAN FRANCISCO

1181B SOLANO AVE., ALBANY, CA 94706

Offers B&B Homes In: San Francisco and all areas of tourist interest in California, including Los Angeles, Monterey Peninsula, San Diego, Wine Country, coastal and mountain regions; also, Las Vegas, New York City, and Hawaii
Reservations Phone: 415/525-4569
Phone Hours: 8:30 a.m. to 5 p.m. Monday through Friday, till noon on Saturday
Price Range of Homes: $40 to $100 double; a single is $6 discount on double rate
Breakfast Included in Price: Full American; the famous sourdough bread is served in many of the San Francisco host homes
Brochure Available: Free
Reservations Should Be Made: 2 weeks in advance preferred

Best B&Bs

■ Turn-of-the-century home in San Francisco, California. Just three miles from Union Square and Fisherman's Wharf. The bedroom/sitting room on the second floor is furnished with antiques and has a private bath. The double bed is extra-long, and there's a TV and telephone in the room. Weather permitting, guests may breakfast in the back garden.

■ Three-bedroom home in Las Vegas, Nevada. You can stay in a quiet residential section yet be within three miles of the "action" in the casinos along the Strip. You have a choice of two guest rooms. Guests may use the swimming pool, which is in a beautiful garden with patio furniture. Artwork and collectibles reflect the host's fondness for animals.

THE BED & BREAKFAST LEAGUE/SWEET DREAMS & TOAST

P.O. BOX 9490, WASHINGTON, DC 20016

Offers B&B Homes In: Washington, D.C., and adjacent suburbs
Reservations: 202/363-7767
Phone Hours: 9 a.m. to 5 p.m. Monday through Thursday, to 1 p.m. on Friday
Price Range of Homes: $30 to $55 single, $45 to $65 double

Breakfast Included in Price: Continental, although a few hosts do offer a full breakfast

Brochure Available: Free if you enclose a stamped, self-addressed no. 10 envelope

Reservations Should Be Made: As far in advance as possible (accepts last-minute reservations when possible); two-night minimum

Scenic Attractions Near the B&B Homes: All of the attractions of the nation's capital, including the White House, Smithsonian museums, National Gallery of Art, National Zoo, U.S. Capitol

Major Schools, Universities Near the B&B Homes: Georgetown, George Washington, American

Best B&Bs

■ See their "50 Best B&Bs" winner in Part III.

■ A 1915 home in Washington, D.C. In the residential section of the city which begins on the east side of the Supreme Court and the Library of Congress. This is an ideal location for visitors who want to stay close to the U.S. Capitol and the Mall. This comfortable B&B is owned by a hostess born in England who is a caterer. Her full English breakfasts demonstrate her culinary skills and are a very special treat. You have a choice of four guest rooms.

■ Federal-style brick town house in Washington, D.C. In the Woodley Park section just north of DuPont Circle. This area has numerous trees, restaurants, shops, and entertainment. You can walk to the Zoo, the Washington Cathedral, and the Adams-Morgan restaurant area. The Federal house retains much of its original charm, with decorative moldings, brass fixtures, and chandeliers. *Insider's Tip:* You are welcome to use the extensive library, which is filled with good reference sources on Washington.

■ Four-story Victorian in Washington, D.C. In the DuPont Circle section. This is an ideal location for business travelers as well as vacationers who have come to sightsee. This Victorian B&B has been loving restored by the hostess, who once owned an antique shop. It's filled with period furnishings and copies of old wallpapers. Guests have the use of a kitchen on the second floor and are invited to gather in the evening in the parlor with a TV/VCR. *Insider's Tip:* The hostess can arrange off-street parking at a fee of $6 per day.

BED & BREAKFAST REGISTRY LTD.
P.O. BOX 8174, ST. PAUL, MN 55108

Offers B&B Homes In: 47 states, Canada, Mexico, and the Caribbean
Reservations Phone: 612/646-4238
Phone Hours: 9 a.m. to 5 p.m. Monday through Friday (sometimes on Saturday, depending on need and season)
Price Range of Homes: $25 to $145 single, $30 to $200 double
Breakfast Included in Price: Most hosts serve a continental-plus breakfast: "The breakfast varies by region, and our hosts have their own family recipes which add something special to our guests' visits."
Brochure Available: Free with stamped, self-addressed envelope. Complete Host Directory available for $9.95 plus $1.50 for shipping.
Reservations Should Be Made: Advance reservations are encouraged.

Best B&Bs

- See their "50 Best B&Bs" winner in Part III.

- Victorian home in West Harwich, Massachusetts. This is the perfect location for enjoying Cape Cod. You can walk to the beach, or relax on the wrap-around porch and later take a dip in the pool. You will enjoy talking with your interesting hosts. One is a registered nurse, the other an oceanographer.

- Brownstone home in Chicago, Illinois. In the Lincoln Park neighborhood. Use this B&B as your base to explore nearby fine restaurants, playhouses, cinemas, and the famous Lincoln Park Zoo. Check that wonderful oak staircase and original stained glass.

BED & BREAKFAST SOCIETY INTERNATIONAL
307 W. MAIN ST., SUITE 2, FREDERICKSBURG, TX 78624

Offers B&B Homes In: All over the U.S., Canada, England, Ireland, Europe, and 18 other countries
Reservations Phone: 512/997-4712
Phone Hours: 24 hours daily
Price Range of Homes: $35 to $100, single or double
Breakfast Included in Price: Continental or full American; "Gourmet or unique breakfasts are increasing, as the hosts get away from purely simple continental breakfasts."

Brochure Available: "Bed & Breakfast World Directory & Guidebook" available for $6 plus $1.50 first-class postage

Reservations Should Be Made: As soon as possible (last-minute reservations are also welcome)

Scenic Attractions Near the B&B Homes: Information on area attractions available when the guest books

---

BED & BREAKFAST U.S.A. LTD.

P.O. BOX 606, CROTON-ON-HUDSON, NY 10520

Offers B&B Homes In: All over New York State, Florida, Western Massachusetts, Pennsylvania, and Washington, D.C.

Reservations Phone: 914/271-6228

Phone Hours: 9 a.m. to 3 p.m. Monday through Friday

Price Range of Homes: $20 to $75 single daily, $30 to $225 double daily

Breakfast Included in Price: Continental or full American (juice, eggs, bacon, toast, coffee)

Brochure Available: For $4

Reservations Should Be Made: 2 weeks in advance (last-minute reservations accepted if possible)

Scenic Attractions Near the B&B Homes: Sleepy Hollow Restorations, Lyndhurst Castle, Rye Playland, Caramoor Music Festival, Murcoot Park, Boscobel and Hyde Park mansions, Croton Clearwater Revival, Cold Spring antiquing, Baseball Hall of Fame, Howe Caverns, Corning Glass, Saratoga, Vanderbilt Mansion, ice caves, plus the attractions of New York City

Major Schools, Universities Near the B&B Homes: Sarah Lawrence, Iona, Manhattanville, Pace, Vassar, Westchester Community College, SUNY New Paltz, Ithaca College, Cornell, Hamilton & Kirkland, Colgate, Skidmore, Russell Sage, Rensselaer Polytechnic Institute, Elmira College, Columbia.

Best B&Bs

■ See their "50 Best B&Bs" winner in Part III.

■ Federal Colonial mansion in Churchtown, Pennsylvania. This B&B puts you right in the heart of Pennsylvania Dutch Country. You will have plenty of diversions here: a piano, TV, VCR. The breakfast room is filled with antiques. *Insider's Tip:* The host can arrange for you to have dinner with a nearby Amish family, a warm and unusual experience.

■ Brownstone triplex in New York City, N.Y. Close to the Museum of Natural History. *Tip to Business Travelers:* Hosts are involved with a catering business and will arrange for a complete gourmet dinner for you and your guests at a cost of $25 per person, plus the cost of the food. This could be a home-entertaining touch to a business meeting.

■ Island waterfront home in Miami Beach, Florida. In addition to the great water views, the big attraction is the unusual pool—a home for tropical fish and plants as well as people. Also a hot tub nearby. If you come by private boat, you can tie up at their dock.

CHRISTIAN BED & BREAKFAST OF AMERICA
P.O. BOX 338, SAN JUAN CAPISTRANO, CA 92693

Offers B&B Homes In: 350 cities all over the U.S.
Reservations Phone: 714/496-7050
Phone Hours: 9 a.m. to 5 p.m. Monday through Friday, plus
  weekend evenings from 6 to 9 p.m.
Price Range of Homes: $20 to $40 single, $30 to $55 double
Breakfast Included in Price: Continental or full American; spe-
  cialties offered in some areas, such as high English tea served
  on 100-year-old china in prize-winning table setting
Brochure Available: For $1
Reservations Should Be Made: 2 weeks in advance (last-minute
  reservations accepted if possible)

Best B&Bs _____
■ Home in Napa Valley, California. You can doze off in front of a romantic fireplace in your own suite. Located near the wineries.

■ Home near Disneyland, California. So close you can watch Disneyland fireworks from the balcony. This B&B is great for families: only $45 buys a suite with two sleeping areas, plus full breakfasts.

COHOST, AMERICA'S BED & BREAKFAST
P.O. BOX 9302, WHITTIER, CA 90608

Offers B&B Homes In: Northern and Southern California and in
  many other states
Reservations Phone: 213/699-8427

Phone Hours: 8 a.m. to 9 p.m. daily, or anytime on answering machine

Price Range of Homes: $30 to $35 single, $25 to $75 double

Breakfast Included in Price: Full breakfast; co-hosts specialize in regional foods, such as a typical Mexican breakfast with huevos rancheros and tortillas, or country biscuits and gravy with ham and eggs, or eggs Benedict and fruit compotes

Brochure Available: $1 if you send a stamped, self-addressed no. 10 envelope

Reservations Should Be Made: 2 weeks in advance (last-minute reservations accepted if possible)

Best B&Bs

■ See their "50 Best B&Bs" in Part III.

■ Ranch-style home in suburban Los Angeles, California. Has an unobstructed view of the ocean. The hosts will share membership privileges with you in the private beach club right across the road. Breakfast specialties include honey-baked ham, French toast, or quiche.

■ Home in Newport Beach, California. When you stay here, you'll be near the tip of the Balboa Peninsula. Special decorative touches: used brick and natural wood, stained-glass windows, and a raised-hearth fireplace. Located about 40 minutes from Disneyland. Daily ferry service to Catalina Island (May to October).

The Northeastern States

B&B Reservation Services

NUTMEG BED & BREAKFAST
222 GIRARD AVE., HARTFORD, CT 06105

Offers B&B Homes In: Connecticut (125 homes)
Reservations Phone: 203/236-6698
Phone Hours: 9:30 a.m. to 5 p.m. Monday through Friday
Price Range of Homes: $35 to $70 single, $40 to $95 double
Breakfast Included in Price: Continental or full American; many homes serve full breakfast, often featuring nut breads and croissants
Brochure Available: $3 for a complete directory
Reservations Should Be Made: 2 weeks in advance (last-minute reservations accepted if possible)

Scenic Attractions Near the B&B Homes: Mystic Seaport, Sturbridge Village, etc. (guests are advised of attractions in the area before arrival)
Major Schools, Universities Near the B&B Homes: Yale, Wesleyan, Trinity, Coast Guard Academy, Hotchkiss, Kent, Pomfret, Lakeville, Choate, Rosemary Hall, Wallingford and Miss Porter's Farmington prep schools

Best B&Bs

■ An 1837 farmhouse in Mystic, Connecticut. Only five minutes from the Seaport. *Insider's Tip:* Ask for the room on the first floor. It's large and has a working fireplace. This home is called "Brigadoon" and may take you back to a more romantic era.

■ Victorian home in North Stonington, Connecticut. You can go to sleep in a double canopy bed. Two of the rooms have a private bath. One single room has a shared bath.

BED & BREAKFAST LTD.
P.O. BOX 216, NEW HAVEN, CT 06513

Offers B&B Homes In: Connecticut; Providence and Newport,
Rhode Island; and selected Massachusetts areas
Reservations Phone: 203/469-3260
Phone Hours: 5 to 9:30 p.m. weekdays and 24 hours weekends
during the academic year; in summer, 24 hours daily
Price Range of Homes: $35 to $50 single, $45 to $75 double
Breakfast Included in Price: Continental or full American; varies
with individual home
Brochure Available: Free if you send a stamped, self-addressed
no. 10 envelope; call to assure availability
Reservations Should Be Made: Prefer 1 week in advance (last-
minute reservations accepted if possible)

Scenic Attractions Near the B&B Homes: New Haven Coliseum,
Long Wharf Theater, Powder Ridge ski area, Shubert Theater,
Connecticut shore, Mystic Seaport, Peabody and British Art
Museums, antique shops, historic country villages
Major Schools, Universities Near the B&B Homes: Yale,
Wesleyan, Southern Connecticut State, Albertus Magnus, Hop-
kins, Choate, Milford Academy, Hamden Hall, Coast Guard
Academy, Taft

Best B&Bs

▪ Vintage home in New Haven, Connecticut. This house can accommodate a small army, with 12 rooms and 4½ baths. Close to
Yale and downtown New Haven. In summer, take a dip in the
pool.

▪ Colonial home in Greenwich, Connecticut. If you've been to
Greenwich, you know what a lovely (rich!) town this is. You can
stay in a carefully restored home near the water which has three
fireplaces and a formal garden.

COVERED BRIDGE BED & BREAKFAST
P.O. BOX 447, NORFOLK, CT 06058

Offers B&B Homes In: Cornwall, Kent, Sharon, Norfolk,
Litchfield, Lakeville, and other towns in the northwest corner of
Connecticut; the Berkshires—Lenox, Great Barrington, Shef-
field, Stockbridge, Williamstown—in Massachusetts; Shaftsbury
in Vermont; East Haddam, Old Mystic, North Stonington, West-
port, and Killingsworth in southern Connecticut

Reservations Phone: 203/542-5944
Phone Hours: 9 a.m. to 8 p.m. daily
Price Range of Homes: $40 to $100 single, $45 to $120 double
Breakfast Included in Price: Most offer full breakfast or continental plus (cereals, homemade breads and muffins, juices, fruit, coffee, tea)
Brochure Available: Free
Reservations Should Be Made: 2 weeks in advance (last-minute reservations accepted if possible)

Scenic Attractions Near the B&B Homes: Tanglewood Music Festival, Williamstown Theater, Jacob's Pillow, Sharon Playhouse, Norfolk Chamber Music Festival, Music Mountain, Appalachian Trail, white-water canoeing, skiing, antiques, Lime Rock car racing, state parks, White Flower Farm
Major Schools, Universities Near the B&B Homes: Williams, Bennington, Simon's Rock at Bard, Hotchkiss, Kent, Salisbury, Berkshire, Indian Mountain Gunnery, Taft

Best B&Bs

- See their "50 Best B&Bs" winner in Part III.

- Colonial home in Bethlehem, Connecticut. This home was built two years before the start of the American Revolution! It's located on 70 acres of hills. The huge fireplace in the living room has a baking oven, crane, and pot hooks for use over an open fire. You have a choice of seven bedrooms (four with fireplaces). *Insider's Tip:* Are you a tennis buff? There's a tennis court on the premises, available to guests.

- Colonial farmhouse near New Hartford, Connecticut. "The grounds include a spring-fed pond for swimming and fishing, a barn for horses, chickens, and pigs, and beautiful flower gardens. There are several old brick fireplaces for guests to enjoy." All four guest rooms are decorated with antiques.

B&B Inns

THE INN AT CHESTER
318 W. MAIN ST., CHESTER, CT 06412

Reservations Phone: 203/526-4961
Description: The inn was built during the war years of

1776–1778. There are 48 bedrooms and baths filled with antiques, period pieces, and Oriental rugs. Now completely restored, it's a beautiful inn.

Nearby Attractions: Parks, summer theaters, river activities
Special Services: Tennis, exercise room, fireplaces, sauna, large and small conference rooms
Rates: $80 double

COPPER BEECH INN
MAIN STREET, IVORYTON, CT 06442

Reservations Phone: 203/767-0330
Description: This is a gracious home in a woodland setting. There are four guest rooms in the main house and nine additional rooms in the old carriage house.
Amenities: Complimentary breakfast of fresh fruit, cold cereals, muffins, juice, coffee or tea

Nearby Attractions: The seaport town of Essex with charming old sea captains' homes, an old railroad, antique shops, Gillette Castle, the Goodspeed Opera House, Ivoryton Playhouse, local beaches
Special Services: The inn's limo will pick up guests at local marinas, airports, and the Amtrak stations.
Rates: $75 to $135 double in high season (May through October)

HOMESTEAD INN AND MOTEL
5 ELM ST., NEW MILFORD, CT 06776

Reservations Phone: 203/354-4080
Description: All the rooms in this 140-year-old Victorian inn have been recently renovated. The front porch overlooks the town green. Rooms in the motel are also available to guests.
Amenities: Expanded continental breakfast

Nearby Attractions: Lake Waremug, Indian Archeological Institute, two wineries, art galleries, museums
Special Services: Innkeeper in residence 24 hours a day for your convenience
Rates: $50 to $60 single, $60 to $70 double

---------- B & B Reservation Services ----------

BED & BREAKFAST OF MAINE
32 COLONIAL VILLAGE, FALMOUTH, ME 04105

Offers B&B Homes In: Maine
Reservations Phone: 207/781-4528
Phone Hours: 6 to 11 p.m., plus 24 hours daily via an answering
machine
Price Range of Homes: $35 to $50 single, $40 to $95 double
Breakfast Included in Price: Full American; "We encourage
hosts to serve hearty breakfasts. At least fresh breads and real
butter; blueberry pancakes are popular and fresh fruit cups and
jams."
Brochure Available: $1
Reservations Should Be Made: 2 months in advance for July
through mid-October

Scenic Attractions Near the B&B Homes: Daily cruise to Nova
Scotia, clam bakes, lobster festivals, craft shows, foliage tours,
art festivals, island cruises, coastal resort activities
Major Schools, Universities Near the B&B Homes: U. of
Maine, Bates, Maine Maritime, Northeastern, Westbrook, Bow-
doin

Best B&Bs _____

- See their "50 Best B&Bs" winner in Part III.

- Federal-style house in Buxton/Bar Mills, Maine. This 1805 home
is located about 17 miles west of Portland. Guests are invited to
enjoy the fireplaces in the living room and the den. Breakfast is
served on the sunporch overlooking the lawns and gardens. Sorry,
no smoking in the living room.

- Old house on Deer Isle in Stonington, Maine. The house overlooks Penobscot Bay (wonderful place for viewing the windjammers
that ply these coastal waters). You reach Deer Isle by a two-lane

bridge. *Insider's Tip:* Ask for the largest guest room. It has a water view. Home no. 27.

▪ Refurbished home in Bass Harbor, Maine. Would you like to stay in a sea captain's home right on a knoll overlooking the ocean? You just found it. This B&B is close to the Oceanarium and the Gilley Bird Museum. Interested in woodcarving? The host is a woodcarver. Home no. 56.

▪ Contemporary home on Mount Desert Island, Southwest Harbor, Maine. The reservation organization describes this as "one of the prettiest spots on Mount Desert Island." From the glassed-in family room and the several decks, you can enjoy a fabulous view. The property borders Acadia National Park. You can begin your hike, or jog through the woods right from the back door. *Insider's Tip:* You can rent bicycles and canoes in the village. Home no. 57.

BED & BREAKFAST DOWN EAST, LTD.
BOX 547, MACOMBER MILL ROAD, EASTBROOK, ME 04634

Offers B&B Homes In: Maine, statewide; including Acadia National Park, Mount Desert Island area, coastal, inland, rural, western lakes and mountains
Reservations Phone: 207/565-3517
Phone Hours: 8 a.m. to 7 p.m. Monday through Friday, to 11 a.m. on Saturday
Price Range of Homes: $35 to $50 singles, $40 to $80 double
Breakfast Included in Price: Most hosts give guests a choice between continental and full American; some specialties served are blueberry scones, popovers, and "toad-in-a-hole"
Brochure Available: $3 for 45-page directory
Reservations Should Be Made: At least 2 weeks in advance (last-minute reservations accepted if possible)

Scenic Attractions Near the B&B Homes: Acadia National Park, Jackson Laboratory, Bar Harbor, scenic coastal areas, historic sites, museums, hiking trails; ski areas
Major Schools, Universities Near the B&B Homes: U. of Southern Maine, Portland, Gorham, Colby, Waterville, Bates, Lewiston, Bowdoin

Best B&Bs

▪ Federal home in Kennebunkport, Maine. Close to beaches, town, and restaurants. You have a choice of five guest rooms, three with private bath. You can spend some time in the large yard and talk with your hosts, a friendly couple who moved here from New Jersey in 1984.

■ A 1772 home in Freeport, Maine. This home was built by O. Israel Bagley right before the start of the American Revolution. You can choose from five bedrooms that have handmade quilts and rugs. One room has a working fireplace. Be sure to see the kitchen—it has a huge fireplace and a beehive oven. Six acres of woods surround this B&B.

B&B Inns

TOWN MOTEL AND GUEST HOUSE
12 ATLANTIC AVE., BAR HARBOR, ME 04609

Reservations Phone: 207/288-5548
Description: Combining old-fashioned comfort with modern convenience, the guest rooms have pull-chain "johns," marble sinks, and period furniture. Some rooms feature working fireplaces and porches.

Nearby Attractions: Acadia National Park, fishing, swimming, golf, tennis, restaurants
Special Services: Color TV
Rates: $35 single, $66 to $95 double

NORSEMAN INN
HCR-61, BOX 50, BETHEL, ME 04217

Reservations Phone: 207/824-2002
Description: This 200-year-old building complex sits on four acres of land in the western foothills of Maine.
Amenities: Full breakfast with fruit of the season, as available

Nearby Attractions: Excellent hiking and camping facilities, downhill and cross-country skiing
Special Services: Activity room, living room with large fireplace, lounge with bar service
Rates: $50 single, $60 double, in winter; $35 single, $45 double, in summer

BLUEHILL FARM COUNTRY INN
P.O. BOX 437, BLUE HILL, ME 04614

Reservations Phone: 207/374-5126
Description: An old turn-of-the-century farm situated at the foot of Blue Hill Mountain, all its rooms overlooking 48 acres of field, pond, and woods. A barn was recently added to provide seven new guest rooms.
Amenities: Squeezed orange juice, fruit of the season, local Camembert cheese on fruit plate, their own granola, cereals, fresh-baked muffins, breads, or popovers—all served with fresh-ground coffee

Nearby Attractions: Acadia National Park, Kneisel Music Camp, Blue Hill Fair
Special Services: Snowshoeing and skiing
Rates: $55 single, $65 double, in summer; $45 single, $55 double, in winter

TOPSIDE
MCKOWN HILL, BOOTHBAY HARBOR, ME 04538

Reservations Phone: 207/633-5404
Description: A historic sea captain's house furnished with antiques —all rooms have a private bath and a refrigerator.

Nearby Attractions: Reid State Park, Carousel Music Theater, Boothbay Dinner Theater, golf, boat rides
Rates: $80 single, $90 double, in summer; $50 single, $75 double, in spring and fall

WHITEHALL INN
52 HIGH ST. (P.O. BOX 558), CAMDEN, ME 04843

Reservations Phone: 207/236-3391
Description: This 1834 building has operated as an inn since 1901. Edna St. Vincent Millay stayed here. The inn is furnished

with antiques and Oriental rugs. The porches have rocking chairs for the guests.
Amenities: Full country breakfast and dinner included

Nearby Attractions: Camden State Parks, many accessible islands
Special Services: Tennis court
Rates: $80 single, $130 double, in summer

LINCOLN HOUSE COUNTRY INN
LINCOLN HOUSE, DENNYSVILLE, ME 04628

Reservations Phone: 207/726-3953
Description: Built in 1787, this four-square colonial sits on 95 acres overlooking the Dennys River. The building has been carefully restored and has earned a place on the National Register of Historic Places.
Amenities: Full country breakfast; dinner is included.

Nearby Attractions: Campobello Island, Roosevelt International Park, Moosehorn National Wildlife Refuge, Cobscook State Park, Reversing Falls
Special Services: Salmon fishing, whale watching, swimming, tennis
Rates: $65 single, $125 double

CRAB APPLE ACRES INN
RTE. 201, THE FORKS, ME 04985

Reservations Phone: 207/663-2218
Description: This 1835 farmhouse on the Kennebec River has seven guest rooms and two shared baths. The new log lodge has six additional guest rooms with private baths. There are quilts on all beds and a wood-burning stove in the kitchen.
Amenities: Complimentary continental breakfast is served.

Nearby Attractions: White-water rafting on the Kennebec River, Fall Foliage Festival (package trips available), canoeing, hunting, fishing, cross-country skiing
Special Services: They will make full arrangements for your rafting trips.
Rates: $44 to $50 double with shared baths, $56 to $61 double with private baths.

THE GREEN HERON INN
OCEAN AVENUE (P.O. BOX 2578), KENNEBUNKPORT, ME
04046

Reservations Phone: 207/967-3315
Description: Built in 1908 on an inlet of the Kennebunk River,
  300 yards from the ocean, this inn has no two rooms alike.
Amenities: A hearty breakfast included in the room rate

Nearby Attractions: Colonial village with historic houses. Trolley
  Museum, beaches, shops, art galleries
Rates: $35 to $50 single, $48 to $75 double; special rates by the
  week or by month

THE WINTER'S INN
P.O. BOX 44, KINGFIELD, ME 04947

Reservations Phone: 207/265-5421
Description: This gracious old mansion sits above the town cemetery where the old monuments look down on three graceful
  curves of the Carrabassett River. The architect/owner restored
  this old Victorian with care and furnished it in the proper style,
  right down to the stuffed armadillo over the fireplace in the
  parlor, mid-18th-century portraits, and Egyptian knickknacks.
Amenities: Breakfast features stuffed French toast, quiche, omelets, homemade preserves.

Nearby Attractions: Sugarloaf, Robert Trent Jones golf course,
  white-water rafting, tennis court
Special Services: Swimming pool
Rates: $70 to $90 double in fall, $50 to $70 double in winter
  and summer

PUFFIN INN BED & BREAKFAST
97 MAIN ST. (P.O. BOX 2232), OGUNQUIT, ME 03907

Reservations Phone: 207/646-5496
Description: This 150-year-old sea captain's home, tastefully decorated with period furniture, is set on landscaped grounds
  abounding with flowers.
Amenities: Continental breakfast

Nearby Attractions: Perkins Cove, Ogunquit Playhouse, Rachel Carson Wildlife Preserve, Marginal Way (a footpath along the rocky coast)
Special Services: Guidance in planning your day and a local map
Rates: $55 to $75 double

CRAIGNAIR INN
CLARK ISLAND ROAD, SPRUCEHEAD, ME 04859

Reservations Phone: 207/594-7644
Description: The inn is set in a tiny town of 100, formerly a granite quarry, overlooking the ocean and Clark Cove.
Amenities: Full breakfast with fruit from the garden, eggs, bacon, sausage, muffins, cereal, coffee and tea; full-service restaurant featuring local seafood

Nearby Attractions: Lighthouse, ferry to offshore islands, Montpelier (Gen. H. Knox's home), Monhegan Island
Special Services: Pickup service, swimming in an old quarry
Rates: $40 single, $60 double, in summer; $36 single, $54 double, in winter; rates include breakfast

EAST WIND INN AND MEETING HOUSE
MECHANIC STREET (P.O. BOX 149), TENANTS HARBOR, ME 04860

Reservations Phone: 207/372-6366
Description: An authentic coastal inn, the three-story frame building, with a wrap-around porch, is located at the water's edge. It's furnished with period antiques, and singles, doubles, and suites are available.

Nearby Attractions: Farnsworth Art Museum, Owls Head Transportation, ferry to Monhegan Island, Vinalhaven and Islesboro, antique shops, lighthouses, and movie theaters
Special Services: A passenger sailing vessel leaves from the wharf daily
Rates: $65 to $150 double in summer, $52 to $115 double in winter

KAWANHEEINN LAKESIDE LODGE
LAKE WEBB, WELD, ME 04285

Reservations Phone: 207/585-2243 (207/778-4306 in winter)
Description: The main lodge has a large stone fireplace capable of taking four-foot logs; on the second floor are ten comfortable bedrooms. Eleven cabins face the lake, and can accommodate from two to seven guests; each cabin has a living room with a stone fireplace, one or two bedrooms, a private bath, and a screened porch.

Nearby Attractions: Mount Blue, and Tumbledown and Bald Mountains, hiking trail
Special Services: Lake for swimming or boating, sandy beach
Rates: $45 double in summer

DOCKSIDE GUEST QUARTERS
HARRIS ISLAND ROAD (P.O. BOX 205), YORK, ME 03909

Reservations Phone: 207/363-2868
Description: On a peninsula jutting out into the harbor at York, the main lodge was an early seacoast homestead. Four contemporary multi-unit cottages and a dining room building complete the complex. The furnishings of the public rooms include antiques, ship models, and choice marine paintings. Most bedrooms have their own bath and direct access to the porch or lawn.
Amenities: Buffet-style continental breakfast served on the ocean-side porch

Nearby Attractions: The center of York Village is a National Historic District and the buildings are open to the public.
Special Services: Marina, boat rentals, special yachting excursions, spacious grounds, lawn games
Rates: $41 to $74 double

MASSACHUSETTS

———————— B&B Reservation Services ————————

BED & BREAKFAST AGENCY
44 COMMERCIAL WHARF, BOSTON, MA 02110

Offers B&B Homes In: The heart of historic downtown Boston
Reservation Phone: 617/720-3540
Phone Hours: 9 a.m. to 10 p.m. daily
Price Range of Homes: $55 to $70 single, $65 to $95 double
Breakfast Included in Price: Continental or full American
Brochure Available: Free
Reservations Should Be Made: As soon as possible ("Rooms go
  quickly")

Scenic Attractions Near the B&B Homes: Historic Boston Har-
  bor and Faneuil Hall, Paul Revere's House, Old North Church,
  Haymarket, the New England Aquarium
Major Schools, Universities Near the B&B Homes: Boston
  University, Harvard, MIT, Northeastern, Emerson

Best B&Bs
■ An 1840 granite building in Boston, Massachusetts. This building
was once a warehouse and features many antique touches—
exposed brick and heavy wooden beams. From your guest room
you will have a view of the sailboats in Boston Harbor.

■ An 1881 Victorian town house in Boston, Massachusetts. Close
to Copley Place and the Hynes Convention Center. You have a
choice of three guest rooms. *Insider's Tip:* One is a garden
apartment. The host serves a full gourmet breakfast.

■ Five-story home in Beacon Hill, Boston, Massachusetts. This B&B
has a tree-lined roofdeck on a charming cobblestone private
street. A continental breakfast is served.

FOLKSTONE BED & BREAKFAST
P.O. BOX 931, BOYLSTON, MA 01505

Offers B&B Homes In: Worcester County
Reservations Phone: 508/869-2687
Phone Hours: 9 a.m. to 1 p.m. Monday through Friday, and also on many weekends
Price Range of Homes: $45 to $90 single, $45 to $90 double
Breakfast Included in Price: Continental (juice, roll or toast, coffee) or full American with such specialties as beef or chicken hash, homemade English muffins, omelets to order, pancakes with seasonal fruits and berries
Brochure Available: For $1
Reservations Should Be Made: 2 weeks in advance (last-minute reservations accepted when possible); MasterCard and VISA accepted

Scenic Attractions Near the B&B Homes: Sturbridge Village, Worcester Science Center, Higgins Armor Museum, Horticultural Society
Major Schools, Universities Near the B&B Homes: U. Mass. Medical Center, Clark U., Worcester Polytech, Anna Maria College, Atlantic Union College, Holy Cross

Best B&Bs

■ Georgian farmhouse in Auburn, Massachusetts. This B&B is only minutes away from the interchange of Interstates 90, 290, and 395 and Mass. Rtes. 12 and 20. Breakfast is served in the great room, often cooked at the huge hearth. A two-room suite is available.

■ An 1864 mansion in Brookfield, Massachusetts. This unusual home was built by the town's shoe baron, and it's elegant. Says the reservation service, "This location is the first choice for antique lovers." Your choice of three guest rooms, two with private dressing rooms and marble fireplaces.

BED & BREAKFAST, BROOKLINE/BOSTON
P.O. BOX 732, BROOKLINE, MA 02146

Offers B&B Homes In: Boston proper (including Beacon Hill, Back Bay, Brookline, Cambridge), Cape Cod, Nantucket Island, Gloucester, Swampscott, Nahant, and other Massachusetts areas

Reservations Phone: 617/277-2292
Phone Hours: 10 a.m. to 4 p.m. Monday through Friday
Price Range of Homes: $40 to $50 single, $50 to $65 double
Breakfast Included in Price: Continental breakfast can include homemade jams such as "Beach Plum" on Cape Cod, cranberry muffins, croissants, cereal, "Anadama bread"; several hosts serve full breakfasts.
Brochure Available: Free. For accommodations lists, send $1 and a stamped, self-addressed no. 10 envelope.
Reservations Should Be Made: Anytime—"first come, first served"

Scenic Attractions Near the B&B Homes: All of Boston's attractions are minutes away by subway; the Museum of Fine Arts, Gardner Museum, and Fenway Park are especially convenient to several of the host homes.
Major Schools, Universities Near the B&B Homes: Harvard, Boston U., Tufts, Simmons, Wheelock, plus centers for international visitors and studies

Best B&Bs

■ English brick home in Brookline, Massachusetts. This home, actually three attached town houses joined by a balcony across the front, is listed in the National Registry of Historic Places. Many of the furnishings were collected by the hostess during her world travels (she speaks fluent Spanish). You're close to downtown Boston.

■ Ranch in Newton, Massachusetts. Beautifully decorated home that was designed and built by the owner's architect husband. The landscaping is very attractive as seen through the numerous picture windows. The hostess is a retired librarian.

■ Victorian apartment in Greater Boston, Massachusetts. This home is located on a tiny, two-mile circle of land—Nahant. It's connected to the mainland by a causeway. Queen-size bed, a block from the beach—what more could you ask for?

GREATER BOSTON HOSPITALITY
P.O. BOX 1142, BROOKLINE, MA 02146

Offers B&B Homes In: Boston, Cambridge, Newton, Needham, Wellesley, Winchester, Marblehead, Salem, Swampscott, Charlestown, Belmont, Brighton, Massachusetts
Reservations Phone: 617/277-5430

Phone Hours: 24 hours daily

Price Range of Homes: $40 to $60 single, $40 to $90 double

Breakfast Included in Price: Full American, which may include homemade peach preserves and scones, hot chocolate, buttermilk pancakes, bagels with smoked salmon and cream cheese, croissants . . . and a vegetarian/macrobiotic home serves fresh carrot juice, rice muffins with tofu cream cheese, hot oatmeal, apple-pear crunch, brown rice, tea or coffee.

Brochure Available: Free

Reservations Should Be Made: 2 weeks in advance (last-minute reservations accepted if possible)

Scenic Attractions Near the B&B Homes: Boston Symphony, Boston Pops, Boston Ballet, Christian Science Church, Kennedy Library, Museum of Fine Arts, Isabella Stewart Gardner Museum, Faneuil Hall, Quincy Market, Freedom Trail, Chinatown, Beacon Hill, N.E. Aquarium

Major Schools, Universities Near the B&B Homes: Harvard, M.I.T., Boston U., Boston College, Emmanuel, Lesley, Pine Manor, Northeastern, Simmons, Wellesley, Massachusetts College of Art, New England Conservatory, Tufts, Babson, Brandeis

Best B&Bs

▪ Two renovated town houses in Boston, Massachusetts. These town houses were modeled after a small European inn. They are located in the heart of Boston's Back Bay area, minutes from the Prudential Center, Copley Square, and the Christian Science Center. Continental breakfast and later in the day—refreshments and hors d'oeuvres are served on the outdoor deck (weather permitting). B&B no. 26.

▪ Elegant home in Boston, Massachusetts. Located in the Victorian section. The host has created some "fantasy rooms" for a very different kind of B&B. There is the "British Officers Room" with a private library. "The French Dining Room" has a king-size bed, French antiques, and a Waterford chandelier. A "London Drawing Room" has a canopy bed. All rooms are air-conditioned and have private telephones. *Insider's Tip:* A full breakfast is served right in your room. B&B no. 7.

BED & BREAKFAST—CAMBRIDGE AND GREATER BOSTON

73 KIRKLAND ST., CAMBRIDGE, MA 02138

Offers B&B Homes In: Cambridge, Boston, Cape Cod
Reservations Phone: 617/576-1492
Phone Hours: 9 a.m. to 6 p.m. Monday through Friday; on Saturday from 2 to 6 p.m.
Price Range of Homes: $39 to $66 single, $55 to $80 double (prospective guests must join this B&B's organization for a $6 fee)
Breakfast Included in Price: Full American (juice, eggs, toast, coffee)
Brochure Available: Free
Reservations Should Be Made: 3 weeks in advance (last-minute reservations accepted when possible)

Scenic Attractions Near the B&B Homes: Boston's Freedom Trail, Museum of Fine Arts, John F. Kennedy Library, Museum of Science, Fogg Museum, Gardner Museum, Longfellow Home, Boston Harbor, Boston Symphony, and Boston Pops
Major Schools, Universities Near the B&B Homes: Harvard, M.I.T., Boston U., Tufts, Simmons

CHRISTIAN HOSPITALITY

636 UNION ST., BLACK FRIAR BROOK FARM, DUXBURY, MA 02332

Offers B&B Homes In: The New England States, also in New York, New Jersey, Virginia, Maryland, Tennessee, and Florida
Reservations Phone: 617/834-8528
Phone Hours: 9 a.m. to 9 p.m. Monday through Saturday
Price Range of Homes: $35 to $50 single, $35 to $65 double
Breakfast Included in Price: Continental or full American
Brochure Available: Free if you send a stamped, self-addressed no. 10 envelope
Reservations Should Be Made: 2 weeks in advance (can accept some last-minute reservations)

Scenic Attractions Near the B&B Homes: Historic homes of Boston, the Plymouth and Cape Cod areas, White Mountains and Green Mountains
Major Schools, Universities Near the B&B Homes: Boston College, Gordan College, Stonehill

Best B&Bs

■ White farmhouse near Augusta, Maine. This home overlooks 72 acres of private pond (swimming and boating). It was built in 1830 and has a tree-lined, stone-walled driveway. *Insider's Tip:* Good place for a family. Kids can watch the lambs frolic in the nearby fields.

■ New England Colonial near Conway, New Hampshire. Staying in this B&B will put you close to Lake Winnepesaukee and the White Mountains. Fireplaces in the bedrooms! You will enjoy the hostess, who is an author and quilt maker.

HOST HOMES OF BOSTON
P.O. BOX 117, WABAN BRANCH, BOSTON, MA 02168

Offers B&B Homes In: Boston, Brookline, Cambridge, Quincy, Concord, Framingham, Needham, Wellesley, Westwood, Weymouth, and other areas

Reservations Phone: 617/244-1308

Phone Hours: 9 a.m. to noon and 1:30 to 4:30 p.m. Monday through Friday; closed weekends and holidays (or an answering machine with same-day callback in winter)

Price Range of Homes: $40 to $80 single, $45 to $93 double

Breakfast Included in Price: "Hearty" continental (may include home-baked muffins, scones or croissants, bran and yogurt, fresh fruit) or full American (depending on the host or day of the week)

Brochure Available: Free; free directory

Reservations Should Be Made: 2 weeks in advance (late reservations accepted if possible)

Scenic Attractions Near the B&B Homes: "All of the cultural, recreational and educational offerings of Boston." This includes the Fine Arts Museum, Museum of Science, Freedom Trail, Faneuil Hall and Quincy Market, Boston Symphony, Hynes Convention Center, Bayside Exposition Center, Lexington and Concord, and Old Sturbridge Village.

Major Schools, Universities Near the B&B Homes: Boston College, Boston U., Harvard, Simmons, Brandeis, Tufts, M.I.T., Wellesley College, Pine Manor, Babson, Northeastern, New England Conservatory

Best B&Bs

■ Beacon Hill town house in Boston, Massachusetts. Huge house in the heart of historic Boston. The guest room is spacious and on the third floor. TV is located in the second floor parlor. Full breakfast served in the dining room.

■ Lakeside home in Newton, Massachusetts. This is a handsome, elegant home with high ceilings and wood detail. Two large guest rooms are available. Boston is eight miles away; the subway, three blocks.

NEW ENGLAND BED & BREAKFAST, INC.
1045 CENTRE ST., NEWTON CENTRE, MA 02159

Offers B&B Homes In: Boston and other special places in New England
Reservations Phone: 617/498-9819 or 617/244-2112
Phone Hours: 9 a.m. to 2 p.m. daily (498-9819 is a 24-hour service)
Price Range of Homes: $30 to $45 single, $40 to $57 double
Breakfast Included in Price: Continental (juice, roll or toast, coffee)
Brochure Available: Free
Reservations Should Be Made: 2 weeks in advance (last-minute reservations accepted if possible)

Scenic Attractions Near the B&B Homes: All Boston attractions, sand and dunes of Cape Cod, mountains and streams of New Hampshire and Maine, rolling hills of Vermont, Freedom Trail, historic Concord and Lexington, theaters and museums
Major Schools, Universities Near the B&B Homes: Harvard, Boston College, Boston U., Berkeley School of Music, Lesley, Northeastern, La Salle, Bentley, Brandeis

PINEAPPLE HOSPITALITY, INC.
47 N. 2ND ST., SUITE 3A, NEW BEDFORD, MA 02740

Offers B&B Homes In: Massachusetts, Rhode Island, Connecticut, Maine, New Hampshire, Vermont
Reservations Phone: 617/990-1696
Phone Hours: 9 a.m. to 7 p.m. Monday through Friday, April to November; 11 a.m. to 7 p.m., November to April

Price Range of Homes: $33 to $65 single, $55 to $130 double
Breakfast Included in Price: Continental or full American
Brochure Available: "Directory of host homes and small inns for all New England" for sale at $5.95
Reservations Should Be Made: 2 weeks in advance (24-hour last-minute surcharge)

Scenic Attractions Near the B&B Homes: Attractions throughout New England

Best B&Bs

■ See their "50 Best B&Bs" winner in Part III.

■ Country house in Manchester, Vermont. This B&B dates back to 1880 (with many additions since then). You will find a fireplace in the living room and a woodstove in the dining room. *Insider's Tip:* Ask for bedroom 1 upstairs; it has a view of Mount Equinox. Breakfast specialty of the house is homemade scones (blueberry, raspberry, cranberry, and orange).

■ Victorian house in New Bedford, Massachusetts. Want to see the famous New Bedford Whaling Museum? It's only six blocks away. This home, built in the 1870s, is bright and cheerful. If you'd like some tips about downhill and cross-country skiing, ask your hosts. They're both avid skiers.

ORLEANS BED & BREAKFAST ASSOCIATES
P.O. BOX 1312, ORLEANS, MA 02653

Offers B&B Homes In: Cape Cod, from the Harwiches to Truro
Reservations Phone: 508/255-3824
Phone Hours: 8 a.m. to 8 p.m. Monday through Friday (also accepts calls on weekends and holidays)
Price Range of Homes: $50 to $90 per room per night
Breakfast Included in Price: Expanded continental (juice and fruit in season, home-baked breads); some hosts are gourmet cooks and do large omelets, French toast, etc.
Brochure Available: For $1
Reservations Should Be Made: 3 weeks in advance (last-minute reservations accepted when possible)

Scenic Attractions Near the B&B Homes: Cape Cod National Seashore, whale watch, beaches, bike trails, museums, art galleries, antique and crafts fairs

Best B&Bs

■ "The Red Geranium" home in Orleans, Massachusetts. Located right on the main street, this country-style home offers easy access to village shopping and fine dining. The ocean and bay beaches are nearby. The home is completely furnished with antiques. Mary Chapman, executive director of Orleans Bed & Breakfast Associates, describes this B&B as "a little gem. It is most like a small pension (that you might find in Europe). Guests meet at breakfast to share delicious foods at tables set with beautiful antique china and unusual seasonal décor."

■ "Winterwell" home in Orleans, Massachusetts. This is a restored 18th-century Cape Cod farmhouse almost right on top of Skater Beach. It is also close to town and a bird feeder. Guests are invited to share the living room for TV and reading.

BE OUR GUEST, BED & BREAKFAST
P.O. BOX 1333, PLYMOUTH, MA 02360

Offers B&B Homes In: Plymouth and the neighboring towns of Hingham, Scituate, Kingston, Duxbury, Marshfield, and Quincy
Reservations Phone: 617/837-9867
Phone Hours: 9 a.m. to 9 p.m. daily
Price Range of Homes: $36 to $45 single, $40 to $65 double
Breakfast Included in Price: "Continental breakfast is required, but most hosts serve a good hearty, full breakfast . . . pancakes and blueberries, zucchini bread (homemade vegetables from garden), and croissants are the favorites."
Brochure Available: Free
Reservations Should Be Made: 2 weeks in advance preferred, but will try to make reservations the same day as your arrival in town

Scenic Attractions Near the B&B Homes: Plimoth Plantation, the *Mayflower* ship, Plymouth Rock, Cranberry World, Commonwealth Winery, Edaville Railroad, Plymouth Wax Museum, historic homes, beaches, state parks, whale watching, deep-sea fishing, sailing
Major Schools, Universities Near the B&B Homes: Bridgewater State College, and all major Boston schools, colleges, and universities within 30 to 60 miles

Best B&Bs

■ Antique Federal Colonial in Kingston, Massachusetts. Located only five miles from historic Plymouth Center. Beautifully decorated adjoining guest rooms are available. Full breakfast is served in the dining room. B&B no. 400.

■ Ranch-style home in Scituate, Massachusetts. In the Scituate Harbor area. Three guest rooms, each decorated with a mix of modern and antique furnishings. Decks allow guests to sit and relax in the cool ocean breeze. Within walking distance of Scituate Harbor, the marina, and all shops and restaurants. B&B no. 605.

BED & BREAKFAST CAPE COD
P.O. BOX 341, WEST HYANNISPORT, MA 02672

Offers B&B Homes In: Cape Cod, Nantucket, Martha's Vineyard, Gloucester, Cape Ann, and the Greater Boston area
Reservations Phone: 508/775-2772
Phone Hours: 8:30 a.m. to 6 p.m. (answering machine off-hours)
Price Range of Homes: $38 to $50 single, $48 to $175 double
Breakfast Included in Price: Continental or full country; home-baked specialties such as native berry pancakes and preserves and home-made bread and muffins are often served.
Brochure Available: Free
Reservations Should Be Made: 2 or 3 weeks in advance (last-minute reservations possible but choices are often limited)

Scenic Attractions Near the B&B Homes: Ferries to Martha's Vineyard and Nantucket, Heritage Plantation, Sandwich Glass Museum, Cape Cod National Seashore and Park, Audubon Sanctuary, Cape Playhouse, Melody Tent, Falmouth Playhouse, golf courses, deep-sea fishing, lake trout fishing, sandy beaches, bike paths
Major Schools, Universities Near the B&B Homes: Woods Hole Oceanographic Institute, Cape Cod Community College, Cape Cod Conservatory of Music and Art, Boston universities and colleges (1½-hour drive).

Best B&Bs

■ See their "50 Best B&Bs" winner in Part III.

■ An 1898 cottage in Gloucester, Cape Ann, Massachusetts. This is the place to sit back on the 100-foot wrap-around porch and watch the ships sail by. This home has been completely restored and sits majestically on a hillside overlooking the Annisquam River. All guest rooms have a water view. B&B no. 30.

■ Renovated Victorian in Barnstable, Massachusetts. Located just a few steps off the Old Kings Highway. Each bedroom is complete with decorative wall coverings, period furnishings, and fresh flowers. All have private baths. *Insider's Tip:* Room 4 on the third floor is extremely private—perfect for honeymooners. Right outside this room a porch provides a place for relaxation. This B&B is in a very quiet rural setting.

BED & BREAKFAST FOLKS
48 SPRINGS RD., BEDFORD, MA 01730

Offers B&B Homes In: Concord, Lexington, Westford, Groton, Chelmsford, Dunstable, Pepperell, Roxborough, Lowell, Tynesboro, Reading, and Bedford
Reservations Phone: 617/275-9025
Phone Hours: 8 a.m. to 10 p.m. Monday through Friday; also on weekends and holidays
Price Range of Homes: $40 to $60 single, $45 to $65 double
Breakfast Included in Price: Continental plus
Brochure Available: Free
Reservations Should Be Made: 2 weeks in advance (also attempts to accept last-minute reservations)

Scenic Attractions Near the B&B Homes: Concord, Lexington, Walden Pond, ski areas, Boston, Cambridge

Best B&Bs _____
■ See their "50 Best B&Bs" winner in Part III.

BERKSHIRE BED & BREAKFAST HOMES
P.O. BOX 211, WILLIAMSBURG, MA 01096

Offers B&B Homes In: Sturbridge area; Pioneer Valley (Springfield, Northampton, Amherst); also in Berkshire Country and eastern New York
Reservations Phone: 413/268-7244
Phone Hours: 9 a.m. to 7 p.m. Monday through Friday, on Saturday to 1 p.m.

Price Range of Homes: $30 to $55 single, $35 to $95 double
Breakfast Included in Price: Continental or full American; some
hosts will also prepare gourmet dinners
Brochure Available: Free; directory of hosts also available for
$3
Reservations Should Be Made: 2 weeks in advance; at least one
month in advance for choice housing during the Tanglewood
concert season

Scenic Attractions Near the B&B Homes: Basketball Hall of
Fame, Sturbridge Village, Deerfield Village, Tanglewood,
Jacob's Pillow, Mohawk Trail, downhill and cross-country ski
trails
Major Schools, Universities Near the B&B Homes: Williams
College, U. of Massachusetts, Amherst, Smith, Mount Holyoke,
Hampshire, Western New England, North Adams State

Best B&Bs

■ See their "50 Best B&Bs" winner in Part III.

■ Oversize Cape in Sturbridge, Massachusetts. Good place to
stay if you plan to visit Sturbridge Village (five minutes away).
Breakfast is served on a large screened-in porch in warmer
months.

■ Federal-style home in Cherry Plain, New York. This home was
built in the 1790s and is surrounded by forests, brooks, and
ponds. After a day of hiking, fishing, or skiing, you can return
home to cheese and crackers. A full breakfast is served in the
morning and a gourmet dinner in the evening.

HAMPSHIRE HILLS BED & BREAKFAST ASSOCIATION

P.O. BOX 307, WILLIAMSBURG, MA 01096

Offers B&B Homes In: The hills of western Massachusetts
Reservations Phone: 413/634-5529
Phone Hours: After 6 p.m.; each home must be phoned directly;
obtain numbers from the brochure or call the above number.
Price Range of Homes: $35 to $45 single, $45 to $70 double
Breakfast Included in Price: Continental or full American, which
can include such regional specialties as maple syrup, farm-fresh
eggs, and homemade blueberry muffins

Brochure Available: Free if you send a stamped, self-addressed no. 10 envelope

Reservations Should Be Made: 2 weeks in advance (last-minute reservations accepted if possible)

Scenic Attractions Near the B&B Homes: William Cullen Bryant Homestead, Historic Deerfield, DAR State Park, Chesterfield Gorge, Jacob's Pillow Dance Festival, Tanglewood Music Center, Williamstown Theater, Sterling Clark Museum, cross-country and downhill skiing, hiking trails, cycling, canoeing, tennis, golf

Major Schools, Universities Near the B&B Homes: Smith, Amherst, Hampshire, Mount Holyoke, U. Massachusetts, Deerfield Academy, Eaglebrook Prep

Best B&Bs

■ Cumworth Farm in Cummington, Massachusetts. Good family place. You can watch the activities of a working farm—gathering maple syrup, vegetables, and berries in season. This 200-year-old farmhouse offers six bedrooms and a choice of continental or American breakfast. You're close to cross-country and downhill skiing. For reservations, call 413/634-5529.

■ The Hill Gallery home in Worthington, Massachusetts. The "gallery" in the name of the home is not an artifice; this spacious four-bedroom contemporary really *does* have an art gallery. You can relax on a spacious sundeck or patio. *Insider's Tip:* If you really want privacy, a separate cottage is available. For reservations, call 413/238-5914.

B&B Inns

BAY BREEZE GUEST HOUSE

P.O. BOX 307, BEDFORD, MA 02553

Reservations Phone: 617/275-7551

Description: Located on Cape Cod Bay at Monument Beach, Bay Breeze has several comfortable rooms that overlook the beach.

Nearby Attractions: Shawmet National Park, Sandwich Glass Museum, Heritage Plantation

Special Service: Boat rides on the Cape Cod Canal, deep-sea fishing

Rates: $25 single, $30 to $35 double, in summer

DEERFIELD INN

THE STREET, DEERFIELD, MA 01342

Reservations Phone: 413/774-5587
Description: Located in the center of Historic Deerfield on The
    Street with 12 beautifully restored museum homes; the inn has
    23 guest rooms with period furnishing, private baths, and air
    conditioning.

Nearby Attractions: Historic Deerfield with extensive collections
    of paintings, prints, furniture, silver, ceramics, textiles, and
    other decorative arts
Special Services: Private function rooms; full-service restaurant
    on the premises
Rates: $133 B&B, $205 MAP

SHIPS KNEES INN

BEACH ROAD (P.O. BOX 756), EAST ORLEANS, MA 02643

Reservations Phone: 508/255-1312
Description: Built over 150 years ago, the inn is a restored sea
    captain's house that gives you old-style New England lodging
    surrounded by the charm of yesterday while offering the conve-
    nience of today. Many of the guest rooms have beamed ceil-
    ings, quilts, and four-poster beds. Several rooms have an ocean
    view and the master suite has a working fireplace.
Amenities: Continental breakfast

Nearby Attractions: Nauset Beach, Cape Cod National Seashore
Special Services: Swimming pool, tennis
Rates: $40 to $95 double; open all year

SEA BREEZE INN

397 SEA ST., HYANNIS, MA 02601

Reservations Phone: 508/771-7213
Description: A group of Cape Cod—style buildings with weath-

ered shingles, Sea Breeze has some rooms with an ocean view. All rooms have private bath and color TV.
Amenities: Juice, cereal, fruit, bagels, muffins, toast, coffee.

Nearby Attractions: John F. Kennedy Memorial, boats for Martha's Vineyard or Nantucket, sightseeing boat around the harbor and the Kennedy Compound, three minutes' walk to the beach
Rates: $60 to $75 double in summer, $45 to $55 double in winter

CANDLELIGHT INN
53 WALKER ST., LENOX, MA 01240

Reservations Phone: 413/637-1555
Description: In the heart of historic Lenox Village, the inn has a turn-of-the-century elegance and is lit by candles and fireplaces.

Nearby Attractions: Tanglewood, Norman Rockwell Museum, Jacob's Pillow, Berkshire Playhouse, skiing, tennis, golf, swimming, boating
Special Services: Weekend entertainment in the piano bar
Rates: $120 to $150 double in summer and fall, $60 to $100 in winter and spring

WHISTLER'S INN
5 GREENWOOD ST., LENOX, MA 01240

Reservations Phone: 413/637-0975
Description: This is a French/English Tudor mansion built in 1820 in the heart of the Berkshires overlooking seven acres of gardens and woodlands. Central to the inn is its cozy library and elegant music room.
Amenities: A continental-plus breakfast featuring home-baked blueberry muffins and breads, eggs or cheeses, coffee, tea, and juice served on the sun porch and terrace

Nearby Attractions: Miles of riding, hiking, and cross-country ski trails; Tanglewood, Norman Rockwell Museum, Chesterwood, many historical houses, Jacob's Pillow Dance Festival, a variety of sporting activities
Special Services: Complimentary sherry and afternoon tea
Rates: $60 to $170 double in summer, $50 to $150 double in winter

UNDERLEDGE INN
76 CLIFFORD ST., LENOX, MA 01240

Reservations Phone: 413/637-0236
Description: This Victorian mansion has been completely restored and now has nine rooms, many with fireplaces, and all with private baths.
Amenities: Continental breakfast

Nearby Attractions: Tanglewood, Jacob's Pillow, Norman Rockwell Museum, Berkshire Theater
Special Services: Solarium
Rates: $75 to $130 double in summer, $60 to $95 double in winter

THE QUAKER HOUSE INN AND RESTAURANT
5 CHESTNUT ST., NANTUCKET, MA 02554

Reservations Phone: 508/228-0400
Description: This 1847 Quaker-style inn is located in the heart of Nantucket Island's historic district. Each of its nine guest rooms is appointed with antiques, queen-size beds, and private baths.

Nearby Attractions: Nantucket Whaling Museum, dozens of historic homes open for tours, art galleries, sandy beaches, sailing, golf, tennis
Rates: $95 double in summer, $75 double in spring and fall

NEW HAMPSHIRE

─────── B&B Reservation Services ───────

NEW HAMPSHIRE BED & BREAKFAST
R.F.D. 3, BOX 53, LACONIA, NH 03246

Offers B&B Homes In: 40 communities throughout New Hampshire
Reservations Phone: 603/279-8348
Phone Hours: 10 a.m. to 5 p.m. Monday through Friday
Price Range of Homes: $35 to $85 single, $40 to $85 double
Breakfast Included in Price: Most homes serve full American breakfasts, including organically grown foods, real maple sugar, homemade cheese, and even pies and ice cream! Others serve a hearty continental breakfast.
Brochure Available: For $1
Reservations Should Be Made: 2 weeks in advance (last-minute reservations accepted if possible)

Scenic Attractions Near the B&B Homes: Lake Winnipesaukee, Lake Sunapee, White Mountains, Merrimack Valley, ski areas, arts and crafts shows, historic sites, and museums
Major Schools, Universities Near the B&B Homes: Dartmouth, Plymouth State, Colby-Sawyer, Keene State, Tilton Academy, New Hampton School; Holderness, Brewster Academy, St. Paul's, and Concord Schools

Best B&Bs ─────────────────────────────

■ Contemporary home on Lake Winnisquam, Laconia, New Hampshire. This home offers great mountain views and a beach area. *Insider's Tip:* Stay upstairs if you want some lake views through your window. Stay downstairs if you want to use the Jacuzzi.

■ Hilltop home near North Conway, New Hampshire. You'll see why this whole area is called "the Switzerland of America" with its high mountains and rushing brooks. This B&B offers a view of Mount Chocorua. A tennis court and other outdoor yard games are near the large porch.

B&B Inns

THE BRADFORD INN
MAIN STREET, BRADFORD, NH 03221

Reservations Phone: 603/938-5309
Description: This Federal-style building was opened in 1898 as a hotel. It contains individually decorated rooms, a spacious parlor, a grand staircase, and wide halls.
Amenities: Full breakfast, gourmet dinners

Nearby Attractions: Lake Sunapee; Sunapee, Winslow, and Rollins State Parks; Franklin Pierce's home; boat cruises
Special Services: Bus pickup in town, sailing and skating nearby
Rates: $59 to $79 double; multinight discount

MOUNTAIN LAKE INN
RTE. 114, BRADFORD, NH 03221

Reservations Phone: 603/938-2136, or toll free 800/662-6005
Description: Built by Bradford's first settler about 15 years before the American Revolution, the inn has country-casual furnishings with true period antiques. It's located on 167 acres with trout streams, waterfalls, and a quarter mile of beachfront on Lake Massasecum.
Amenities: Full country breakfast

Nearby Attractions: Boat and dinner cruises; three national parks; golf, tennis, racquetball, horseback riding, hiking, fishing
Special Services: Private beach, cookout areas, swimming, bicycles for guests, snowshoeing and cross-country skiing
Rates: $80 double with private bath

THE PASQUANEY INN
STAR RTE. 1, BOX 1066, BRIDGEWATER, NH 03222

Reservations Phone: 603/744-9111
Description: This turn-of-the-century inn on the edge of Newfound Lake has a long front porch facing the lake. Single and double rooms with shared or private bath are available.
Amenities: Features French/Belgian cuisine

Nearby Attractions: In the center of the state within range of most outdoor attractions
Special Services: Recreational barn, boats, bikes, sandy beach
Rates: From $84 double

FRANCONIA INN
RTE. 116, EASTON ROAD, FRANCONIA, NH 03580

Reservations Phone: 603/823-5542
Description: This resort offers quiet country life with mountain views from the Easton Valley. The 35 rooms have recently been redecorated and renovated.

Nearby Attractions: Mount Washington, Cannon Mountain Tramway, Tite Flume, the Old Man of the Mountains, White Mountain National Forest, ski areas
Special Services: Pool, hot tub, gliding, skiing, sleigh rides, ice skating, biking all on premises
Rates: $65 to $125 double in summer and fall, $60 to $90 double in spring

SUNNY SIDE INN
SEAVEY STREET, NORTH CONWAY, NH 03860

Reservations Phone: 603/356-6239
Description: This converted and expanded 1850s New England farmhouse has casual and comfortable rooms with private or shared bath, plus a living room with fireplace and TV
Amenities: Full breakfast

Nearby Attractions: White Mountains, four major downhill ski areas, three golf courses, museums
Special Services: Bus depot pickups
Rates: $22 to $50 single, $32 to $55 double

LAKE SHORE FARM
31 JENNESS POND RD., NORTHWOOD, NH 03261

Reservations Phone: 603/942-5521
Description: A family farmhouse expanded to accommodate guests, it has been under the same family management for 63 years.
Amenities: Full breakfast

Nearby Attractions: Shaker Village, Strawberry Banke Capitol Complex, a variety of outdoor sports
Special Services: Games room, tennis, volleyball, Ping-Pong, badminton, horseshoes
Rates: $41 double in summer, $36 double the rest of the year

THE CAMPTON INN
RTE. 175N (P.O. BOX 282), CAMPTON, NH 03223

Reservations Phone: 603/726-4449
Description: An 1835 New England farmhouse, the inn is at the foot of the White Mountains. All rooms are individually decorated with antiques. Private and shared baths available.
Amenities: Full breakfast includes the house specialty: baked apple pancake puff.

Nearby Attractions: White Mountain National Forest, Polar Caves, The Flume, Old Man of the Mountains, Lost River, Squam Lake (filming site of *On Golden Pond*)
Special Services: Guest refrigerator, bus pickup, laundry service
Rates: $34 to $40 single, $48 to $60 double

─────────── B&B Reservation Services ───────────

HAMPTON BED & BREAKFAST
P.O. BOX 378, EAST MORICHES, NY 11940

Offers B&B Homes In: Eastern part and rural areas of Long Island
Reservations Phone: 516/878-8197
Phone Hours: 10 a.m. to 10 p.m. Monday through Friday (accepts weekend calls)
Price Range of Homes: $45 to $65 single, $70 to $125 double
Breakfast Included in Price: Continental breakfast (juice, roll or toast, coffee); also such regional specialties as homemade blueberry and raspberry muffins
Brochure Available: Free with stamped, self-addressed envelope
Reservations Should Be Made: 2 weeks in advance (last-minute reservations accepted if possible)

Scenic Attractions Near the B&B Homes: Historic area with famous Hamptons nightlife, beaches, and golf
Major Schools, Universities Near the B&B Homes: Southampton College

Best B&Bs
■ Old Victorian in Bellport, New York. This B&B is within walking distance of the bay and ocean ferry, and serves a full country breakfast.

■ Tudor villa in Montauk, New York. Offers three double guest rooms, all with private bath and color TV with HBO films. You can walk to the ocean, tennis courts, and the village.

BED & BREAKFAST ROCHESTER
P.O. BOX 444, FAIRPORT, NY 14450

Offers B&B Homes In: Around the Rochester area, and down into the Finger Lakes of New York State
Reservations Phone: 716/223-8877
Phone Hours: 9 a.m. to 9 p.m. or "any time within reason"
Price Range of Homes: $40 to $50 single, $45 to $65 double
Breakfast Included in Price: Full breakfast, which may include apple muffins, apple oatmeal, German coffee cake, Dutch oven pancakes, crêpes, cheese strata, fruit salad, and other specialties
Brochure Available: Free if you send a stamped, self-addressed no. 10 envelope
Reservations Should Be Made: 2 or 3 weeks in advance (last-minute reservations accepted if possible); $3 booking fee

Scenic Attractions Near the B&B Homes: Eastman House of Photography, Strong Toy Museum, Genesee Country Museum, Letchworth Park, Sonnenberg Gardens, Lake Ontario, wineries, fishing derbies, scenic Finger Lakes region
Major Schools, Universities Near the B&B Homes: U. of Rochester, Brockport, Geneseo, St. John Fisher, Rochester Institute of Technology, Nazareth

Best B&Bs

■ "Woods Cabin" in Fairport, New York. Here is your chance to steal away into a small hideaway in the forest. You can build your own fire in the large fireplace in the living room. The house has antique furnishings and natural-wood walls. You feel as if you're in a distant rustic world, yet you're actually only 20 minutes from downtown Rochester. Or you can stay in the B&B home right next door, "Woods Edge." This home is furnished with antique country pine. Your hosts are interesting: she creates stone mosaic pictures; he is a college professor (mechanical engineering).

■ Tudor home in Rochester, New York. Known as the "Dartmouth House," this B&B is close to restaurants, antique shops, and the interesting Park Avenue area. You are also close to museums, concerts, the major business section, and parks.

■ Contemporary home on Lake Ontario, Ontario, New York. This home is right on the edge of a cove. The water almost surrounds, so it's almost like living on an island. The hosts are retired but still very active in sailing, skiing, gardening, and woodworking—and ready to talk about any of those subjects with you.

BED & BREAKFAST LEATHERSTOCKING RESERVATIONS

389 BROADWAY RD., FRANKFORT, NY 13340

Offers B&B Homes In: Eleven-county area of central New York, including Utica, Cooperstown, Clinton, and along the Mohawk River Valley
Reservations Phone: 315/733-0040
Phone Hours: 7 a.m. to 10 p.m. daily
Price Range of Homes: $20 to $50 single, $30 to $70 double
Breakfast Included in Price: Full American, with such special treats as blueberry pancakes, French toast with New York State maple syrup, zucchini bread
Brochure Available: Free; directory also available for $2
Reservations Should Be Made: 2 weeks in advance (last-minute reservations accepted when possible)

Scenic Attractions Near the B&B Homes: Adirondack Park area, Fort Stanwick, Howe Cavern, Farmers Museum, Baseball Hall of Fame, Utica Brewery
Major Schools, Universities Near the B&B Homes: Colgate, Hamilton & Kirkland, Utica College, Herkimer, Fulton, Cobbleskill, St. Elizabeth School of Nursing, SUNY at Marcy, Utica School of Commerce

Best B&Bs

▪ See their "50 Best B&Bs" winner in Part III.

▪ Victorian home in Waterville, New York. Every room of this B&B reflects the hostess's talents with quilts and needlework. Guest rooms include a twin-bedded room with private bath. Other rooms are furnished with antiques and collectibles. Full breakfasts with homemade breads and muffins, juices, and eggs.

AAAH! BED & BREAKFAST #1 LTD.

P.O. BOX 200, NEW YORK, NY 10108

Offers B&B Homes In: New York City (also in London and Paris)
Reservations Phone: 212/246-4000, or toll free 800/776-4001; FAX (212)686-2578
Phone Hours: 9 a.m. to 5 p.m. Monday through Friday and 10 a.m. to 2 p.m. on Saturday (answering machine after hours and Sunday)

Price Range of Homes: $40 to $75 single, $50 to $100 double, and $250 luxury suites ($100 credit at first-class restaurant inclusive)
Breakfast Included in Price: Yes
Brochure Available: Free
Reservations Should Be Made: As soon as possible—early reservations ensure the best selection

Scenic Attractions Near the B&B Homes: All New York City attractions
Major Schools, Universities Near the B&B Homes: Columbia, Hunter, NYU, Adelphi

ABODE BED & BREAKFAST LTD.
P.O. BOX 20022, NEW YORK, NY 10028

Offers B&B Homes In: Manhattan, Brooklyn Heights
Reservations Phone: 212/472-2000
Phone Hours: 9 a.m. to 5 p.m. Monday through Friday and 10 a.m. to 2 p.m. on Saturday; answering machine other hours
Price Range of Homes: $50 to $75 single, $60 to $95 double; plus $80 to $250 for unhosted studio to three-bedroom apartments
Breakfast Included in Price: Most are continental, consisting of juice, assorted rolls, muffins, condiments, and coffee or tea; some hosts serve a full breakfast.
Brochure Available: Free
Reservations Should Be Made: As soon as possible (last-minute reservations accepted if possible)

Scenic Attractions Near the B&B Homes: New York City's theaters, museums, parks, art galleries, architecture, etc.
Major Schools, Universities Near the B&B Homes: NYU, Columbia, Hunter, Baruch, Fordham, Marymount

Best B&Bs _____
■ Gramercy Park apartment in New York City. You will stay in a beautifully decorated two-bedroom apartment. One guest room has an antique oak double bed, 25-inch TV, telephone, stereo, and air conditioning. The whole apartment is filled with antique and traditional furniture. *Insider's Tip:* The host will lend you a key to Gramercy Park, New York City's only private park.

BED & BREAKFAST NETWORK OF NEW YORK

134 WEST 32ND ST., SUITE 602, NEW YORK, NY 10001

Offers B&B Homes In: New York City
Reservations Phone: 212/645-8134
Phone Hours: 8 a.m. to 6 p.m. Monday through Friday
Price Range of Homes: $50 to $60 single, $70 to $90 double, hosted; $80 to $200 unhosted
Breakfast Included in Price: Yes, except for several unhosted homes
Brochure Available: Free
Reservations Should Be Made: Several weeks in advance

Scenic Attractions Near the B&B Homes: All New York City attractions
Major Schools, Universities Near the B&B Homes: NYU, Columbia

Best B&Bs

■ This reservation service organization has classified their best homes by the first names of the hosts and hostesses. You can request these homes with that name.

■ "Dawn"—a duplex penthouse apartment on the West Side of Manhattan. This is a penthouse B&B that overlooks the Museum of Natural History and Central Park. The terrace has a greenhouse. Both guest rooms have private baths. *Insider's Tip:* While both rooms have cable TV, one also has a VCR. Ask for that if you'd like to watch a late-night film rental. Or maybe show a videotape you've just shot of Manhattan.

■ "Bevy"—a duplex loft in the heart of Soho, Manhattan. This is the place to stay if you would like to be close to all of the Soho art galleries, shops, and restaurants. The exposed brick and original artwork add to the charm of this unusual getaway.

■ "Barbara"—a luxury doorman building on the Upper East Side of Manhattan. This home "has it all" (as they like to say in New York): a working fireplace, stereo, and wrap-around terrace with garden, and great views (from the 19th floor). On a practical note, if you've been traveling for a while, you can use the laundry facilities in the basement.

■ "Peter"—a luxury doorman building on the West Side of Manhattan. Located steps from Carnegie Hall, Lincoln Center, and the Broadway theaters. The apartment has good views, a balcony, and cable TV. Guest room has a queen-size bed, private bath, and powder room.

■ "Ester"—a duplex brownstone on the West Side of Manhattan. Located about half a block from Central Park, it offers a backyard (pretty rare in Manhattan), exposed-brick rooms, and air conditioning.

BED & BREAKFAST IN THE BIG APPLE (URBAN VENTURES, INC.)
P.O. BOX 426, NEW YORK, NY 10024

Offers B&B Homes In: New York City (over 500 accommodations)
Reservations Phone: 212/594-5650
Phone Hours: 9 a.m. to 5 p.m. Monday through Friday, on Saturday to 3 p.m.
Price Range of Homes: $35 to $60 single, $45 to $85 double
Breakfast Included in Price: Continental (juice, roll or toast, coffee)
Brochure Available: Free
Reservations Should Be Made: 2 weeks in advance (last-minute reservations accepted if possible)

Scenic Attractions Near the B&B Homes: Broadway theaters, Central Park, skyscrapers, famous restaurants, and all the many other "Big Apple" attractions
Major Schools, Universities Near the B&B Homes: Columbia, NYU, Pace

Best B&Bs _____

■ See their "50 Best B&Bs" winner in Part III.

■ Apartment in new building on E. 76th Street, Manhattan. Spacious apartment with a double bed and private bath. B&B no. 2015.

■ Home on Gramercy Park, Manhattan. A former mayor of New York used to call this place home. Now you can too. One slight disadvantage—you have to climb three flights of stairs. One advantage—it's a grand sweeping staircase. Once you get to your room, you have a good view of the park. B&B no. 3019.

■ Town house on E. 62nd Street, Manhattan. Host offers breakfast in bed or join the group around a large kitchen table. One room has a working fireplace. The living room that is used by the guests also has a working fireplace. *Insider's Tip:* If you're traveling with your family, you could take over a special two-bedroom two-bath suite.

RAINBOW HOSPITALITY
9348 HENNEPEN AVE., NIAGARA FALLS, NY 14304

Offers B&B Homes In: Niagara Falls, Chautauqua, Lewistown, Youngstown, east to Rochester and Buffalo, and south to Pennsylvania

Reservations Phone: 716/283-4794 or 716/881-9977

Phone Hours: 9 a.m. to 3 p.m. weekdays, on Saturday to noon

Price Range of Homes: Modest, $35 to $45; moderate, $45 to $55; luxury, $60 to $85

Breakfast Included in Price: Continental or full American, according to the individual home

Brochure Available: $1 if you send a stamped, self-addressed no. 10 envelope

Reservations Should Be Made: 2 weeks in advance (last-minute reservations accepted if possible)

Scenic Attractions Near the B&B Homes: Niagara Falls, Canada, Lewistown Art Park, Fatima Shrine, Fort Niagara, Kleinhans Music Hall and Buffalo's theater district, Chautauqua Institute, four large amusement complexes, lakes, rivers, convention centers, antique and outlet shopping, museums and art galleries, winter sports

Major Schools, Universities Near the B&B Homes: Niagara U., SUNY at Buffalo, Buffalo State, Canisius

Best B&Bs
■ Dutch Colonial on Chautauqua Lake, New York. Located on an 11-acre wooded estate. A private beach and dock are available. Other nearby attractions include local winery tours, Midway Amusement Park, and a sail on the Sea Lion. Winter sports include skiing, snowmobiling, and ice fishing.

BED & BREAKFAST OF LONG ISLAND
P.O. BOX 392, OLD WESTBURY, NY 11568

Offers B&B Homes In: Eastern Long Island Hamptons beach area, Amagansett, Southampton, Garden City, Glen Cove, Syosset, Peconic, Southold, Mattituck, Rockville Center, Port Jefferson, Sayville, Westbury, Manhasset, East Islip, Roslyn, East Northport, Baldwin

Reservations Phone: 516/334-6231

Phone Hours: 9 a.m. to 12:30 p.m. Monday through Friday; answering machine to 10 p.m. weekdays, 10 a.m. to 9 p.m. weekends

Price Range of Homes: $48 to $68 single, $58 to $125 double

Breakfast Included in Price: Continental or full American, plus regional specialties like homemade beach plum jam, sautéed mushrooms and eggs, blueberry muffins, waffles, buttery croissants, carrot cake, quiche

Brochure Available: Free if you send a stamped, self-addressed no. 10 envelope

Reservations Should Be Made: 2 weeks in advance (last-minute reservations accepted if possible)

Scenic Attractions Near the B&B Homes: Sag Harbor Customs House, Whaling Museum, John Drew Theater, Guild Hall Art Exhibits, Home Sweet Home Museum, Parrish Museum, Shinnecock Indian Reservation, Halsey Homestead, Montauk Hither Hills State Park, sport fishing, Watermill Old Mill Museum & Windmill

Major Schools, Universities Near the B&B Homes: Hofstra, Adelphi, SUNY at Stony Brook, Southampton College, Dowling College, C. W. Post, Kings Point Marine Academy, Webb Institute, LaSalle Academy

Best B&Bs

■ See their "50 Best B&Bs" winner in Part III.

■ Second-oldest house in Manhasset, Long Island, New York. Built in 1840, to be exact and completely restored. From the huge dining room with its three chandeliers and the original carved fireplace to the doors with original brass hinges, this home is a gem. There are several guest rooms, with sitting rooms nearby on separate landings with TV. You can walk to the Long Island Railroad for the trip to New York City, or drive to the beach.

■ An 1800 home in Amagansett, Long Island, New York. This old home has just about everything—a swimming pool and Jacuzzi, a huge country kitchen, and a windowed dining room with hanging plants. Shaker-style furnishings in some of the rooms. You can walk to the beach, less than a mile away. Your hosts include a part-time actress and a writer.

A REASONABLE ALTERNATIVE, INC.–BED AND BREAKFAST ON LONG ISLAND

117 SPRING ST., ROOM 6, PORT JEFFERSON, NY 11777

Offers B&B Homes In: Nassau and Suffolk Counties, from Great Neck to Orient, from Hempstead to the Hamptons, from Garden City to Montauk
Reservations Phone: 516/928-4034
Price Range of Homes: $32 single; rates are adjusted seasonally and subject to change.
Breakfast Included in Price: Continental (juice, roll or toast, coffee); occasional extras and regional specialties provided in some homes; New York sales tax for breakfast is extra.
Brochure Available: Free if you send a stamped, self-addressed no. 10 envelope
Reservations Should Be Made: 2 weeks in advance (last-minute reservations accepted if possible)

Scenic Attractions Near the B&B Homes: Bethpage Recreation Village, Hargreaves Vineyards, Sag Harbor Whaling Museum, Sag Harbor Museum and Custom House, game farm and zoo, Fire Island National Seashore, Montauk Lighthouse, Jones Beach, Westbury Music Fair, Stony Brook museum complex, Sagamore Hill, Vanderbilt Planetarium, Sunken Meadow State Park
Major Schools, Universities Near the B&B Homes: Hofstra, Adelphi, C. W. Post, SUNY at Stony Brook

AMERICAN COUNTRY COLLECTION OF BED & BREAKFAST HOMES AND COUNTRY INNS

984 GLOUCESTER PL., SCHENECTADY, NY 12309

Offers B&B Homes In: Northeastern New York, Vermont, and western Massachusetts
Reservations Phone: 518/370-4948

Phone Hours: 10 a.m. to noon and 1 to 5 p.m. Monday through Friday (answering machine always on)

Price Range of Homes: $30 to $80 single, $40 to $125 double (rates in and around Saratoga, N.Y., increase approximately 50% in August, the racing season)

Breakfast Included in Price: Breakfasts range from homemade continental to traditional American. There are also elegant four-course gourmet breakfasts. Many Vermont and New York country breakfasts include maple syrup tapped right on the farm. Special treats include waffled French toast, hot fruit soufflé, and blueberry walnut pancakes.

Brochure Available: Free if you send a stamped, self-addressed no. 10 envelope; directory for $3

Reservations Should Be Made: 3 weeks in advance (over a month in advance during the peak travel seasons)

Scenic Attractions Near the B&B Homes: Several in the Saratoga area, near the Saratoga Race Course, Empire State Plaza in Albany, Baseball Hall of Fame in Cooperstown, Bennington Museum and Battlefield, Hyde Park and the Roosevelt Estate, Shaker Museum, Catskill Game Farm, Tanglewood and Lenox, Massachusetts

Major Schools, Universities Near the B&B Homes: Skidmore, SUNY at Albany and SUNY at Cobleskill, Williams, Smith, Bennington, Middlebury, U. of Vermont, Union College

Best B&Bs

▪ Greek Revival home in Fair Haven, Vermont. The reservation service describes this as a "textbook Greek Revival." It is nicely situated on 3½ acres of mostly gardens and lawns. The five guest rooms are individually decorated in soft hues. Each has a window view of mountains and farms. The formal parlor, TV room, and breakfast room are open to guests. B&B no. 077.

▪ Old farm house in Manchester, Vermont. In 1890 this building was home to a tenant farmer. Now it has been restored and furnished with eclectic old furnishings and antiques. The setting is perfect, at the foot of the Green mountains, bordered by a brook. B&B no. 080.

ELAINE'S BED & BREAKFAST AND INN RESERVATION SERVICE
143 DIDAMA ST., SYRACUSE, NY 13224

Offers B&B Homes In: Cazenovia, Fayetteville, Clay, Jamesville, Syracuse, Skaneateles, Liverpool, Seneca Lake, Baldwinsville, Lafayette, Watertown, Vernon, Hamilton, Red Creek, Lenox
Reservations Phone: 315/446-4199
Phone Hours: 10 a.m. to 8 p.m., daily
Price Range of Homes: Starts at $32 single, $42 double, with shared bath, to $75 for suites and studio apartments
Breakfast Included in Price: Each is different—some continental, some more elaborate. Advance requests for special diets are honored. Includes such items as homemade muffins, cantaloupe, cereal, orange juice.
Brochure Available: $1.25 with stamped, self-addressed envelope
Reservations Should Be Made: By phone at least two weeks in advance, and a deposit sent immediately

Scenic Attractions Near the B&B Homes: Erie Canal Museum; Erie Canal Boat Cruises; Beaver Lake Nature Center
Major Schools, Universities Near the B&B Homes: Syracuse University, LeMoyne College

Best B&Bs

■ A Queen Anne Revival home in Syracuse, New York. This comfortable home offers two large corner guest rooms with fireplaces. The wrap-around porch is filled with wicker chairs.

■ Hill home near Syracuse, New York. From this hilltop perch you can see 35 miles and three lakes. Yet you are only 15 minutes from downtown Syracuse. *Insider's Tip:* Be sure to see the unique solarium full of plants.

B&B Inns

THE HEDGES
BLUE MOUNTAIN LAKE, NY 12812

Reservations Phone: 518/352-7325
Description: In a historic Adirondack camp with unique architecture, the inn's rooms are furnished with antiques. There are 15 separate cottages set on secluded Blue Mountain Lake.

Amenities: Full breakfast cooked to order; complimentary bed-time snack

Nearby Attractions: The Adirondack Museum, Adirondack State Park with miles of hiking trails
Special Services: Clay tennis court, canoes and rowboats, swimming
Rates: $108 to $132 double July to September; in June and October deduct 10%.

THOUSAND ISLANDS INN
335 RIVERSIDE DR., CLAYTON, NY 13634

Reservations Phone: 315/686-3030
Description: Serving the public since 1897, the inn's 17 sleeping rooms were remodeled in 1980 with private bath and cable color TV. Most rooms have a view of the St. Lawrence River, and central fire and smoke-detector systems have been installed.
Amenities: Full breakfast with flapjacks, sourdough bread French toast, broccoli-and-cheese omelet, among the specialties

Nearby Attractions: Shipyard Museum, Town Hall Museum, Thousand Island Craft School & Textile Museum, fishing and water sports
Special Services: Scenic boat and airplane tours of the Thousand Islands, fishing charters
Rates: $37 single, $47 double, in summer

CECCE BED & BREAKFAST INN
166 CHEMUNG ST., CORNING, NY 14830

Reservations Phone: 607/962-5682
Description: In a Mediterranean setting with rooms designed in period style ("Eastlake," Victorian, Louis XIV master bedroom), the guesthouse is within walking distance of historic Corning.
Amenities: Continental breakfast

Nearby Attractions: Corning Glass Museum, Rockwell Museum of Western Art, 1796 Patterson Museum, Hammondsport Wineries, Watkins Glen, the Finger Lakes

Special Services: Kitchen and living room available for guests
staying three days or longer
Rates: $35 single, $40 double; VISA and MasterCard accepted

BIG MOOSE INN
BIG MOOSE LAKE, EAGLE BAY, NY 13331

Reservations Phone: 315/357-2042
Description: Single and double rooms are available in this rustic
lakeside lodge; up to 40 people may be accommodated.
Amenities: Continental breakfast

Nearby Attractions: Blue Mountain Museum, Old Forge,
Enchanted Forest
Special Services: Cocktail lounge, a variety of summer and
winter sports available
Rates: $32 single, $39 double, with shared bath; $55 single, $60
double, with private bath

SOUTH MEADOW FARM LODGE
CASCADE ROAD, LAKE PLACID, NY 12946

Reservations Phone: 518/523-9369
Description: There are beds for ten in these rooms, built around
a living room with fireplace and a piano. The "Honeymoon
Cottage" is a converted maple sugar house with a woodstove,
where candles provide the only light.
Amenities: Large farm breakfast

Nearby Attractions: Winter Olympic site
Special Services: Cross-country skiing, farm chores to share in,
camp rates available.
Rates: $32 single, $64 double; for a three-day midweek package,
$29 single, $57 double

PINE HILL ARMS
MAIN STREET, PINE HILL, NY 12465

Reservations Phone: 914/254-9811 or 914/254-9812
Description: Established in 1882, the hotel lies between two ski

centers. The 25 rooms have been completely remodeled and have private baths. The lounge has a large stone fireplace.

Nearby Attractions: Skiing, bicycling, golf, tennis, horseback riding, tubing, fly fishing
Special Services: Hot tub spa and sauna, exercise equipment, swimming pool
Rates: $45 single, $90 double, in winter; $25 single, $40 double, in summer

TIBBITTS HOUSE INN

100 COLUMBIA TURNPIKE, CLINTON HEIGHTS, RENSSELAER, NY 12144

Reservations Phone: 518/472-1348
Description: This 130-year-old farmhouse with an 84-foot enclosed porch has comfortably furnished rooms with shared bath, plus an apartment with an old keeping room with beamed ceiling and a corner, raised-hearth fireplace.

Nearby Attractions: The State Capitol and the Empire State Mall (two miles away), a 45-mile hiking and biking path along the Hudson and Mohawk Rivers
Special Services: Patio, picnic tables, spacious glass-enclosed porch, ample parking
Rates: $38 single, $40 double

RHODE ISLAND

B&B Reservation Services

ANNA'S VICTORIAN CONNECTION

5 FOWLER AVE., NEWPORT, RI 02840

Offers B&B Homes In: Newport, Middletown, Jamestown, Portsmouth, Tiverton, Bristol
Reservations Phone: 401/849-2489

Phone Hours: The number above gives you an answering machine 24 hours. Your call will be returned from 8 a.m. to 11 p.m. in summer, 10 a.m. to 2 p.m. and evenings in winter, every day of the week.

Price Range of Homes: $35 to $150, per room, with surcharge for third person.

Breakfast Included in Price: Juice, fresh fruit, home-baked goods, coffee or tea.

Brochure Available: Free

Reservations Should Be Made: In advance, with full first night's deposit; VISA, MasterCard, American Express, En Route accepted

Scenic Attractions Near the B&B Homes: Newport Beaches, mansions, boat shows, jazz, folk festival, international jumping derby, music festival, Virginia Slims and Volvo Tournaments, sailing, navy base, Newport Yachting Center

Major Schools, Universities Near the B&B Homes: Portsmouth Abbey, St. Georges, Salve Regina, U. of Rhode Island, Brown U., Bryant College, Roger Williams College, Providence College

Best B&Bs

■ Turn-of-the-century home in Newport, Rhode Island. Susan, the hostess, is an RN, with an empty nest. She has used some creative ideas in preparing special rooms—"Wicker," "Brass Bed," and "Lace." Each name denotes the main feature of the antique décor of that room. Susan serves a hearty continental breakfast in the Eastlake sitting room.

■ Commodore Perry Victorian cottage in Newport, Rhode Island. Ten years ago the hosts, Sondra and Jim, celebrated their marriage with the purchase of a large cottage two blocks from the center of town. In the last decade they have carefully restored their home and offices (they practice psychology together). The entire third floor is devoted to B&B guests. Breakfast may consist of waffles, muffins, and fruit. Two children in the family, Kate and Dan, have made the painful but generous decision to share their toys with the children of visiting B&B guests.

BED & BREAKFAST OF RHODE ISLAND, INC.
P.O. BOX 3291, NEWPORT, RI 02840

Offers B&B Homes In: Rhode Island and Massachusetts
Reservations Phone: 401/849-1298
Phone Hours: 9 a.m. to 5 p.m. Monday through Friday (9 a.m. to 8 p.m. Monday through Friday and 10 a.m. to 2 p.m. on Saturday during summer)
Price Range of Homes: $40 to $80 single, $45 to $110 double
Breakfast Included in Price: Juice, fresh fruit, home-baked goods, tea and coffee. About 30% of the hosts serve a full breakfast, many of which are gourmet (Belgian waffles, quiche, fruited specialties, oven pancakes).
Brochure Available: Free; a host directory is also available for $2.
Reservations Should Be Made: 2 weeks in advance (last-minute reservations accepted when possible, but guests may not always stay in the desired area)

Scenic Attractions Near the B&B Homes: Newport mansions and historic homes, yachting and sailing center, Colt State Park (Bristol), lighthouses and windmills, Slate Mill (Pawtucket), Providence's historic East Side, ocean beaches
Major Schools, Universities Near the B&B Homes: Brown, Rhode Island College, Providence College, Rhode Island School of Design, Johnson & Wales, U. of Rhode Island, Bryant, Salve Regina, St. George's School, Portsmouth Abbey

Best B&Bs

■ See their "50 Best B&Bs" winner in Part III.

■ Federal house in Hope, Rhode Island. This home is right out of a Colonial print—gabled roof, center chimney, five-bay façade—even a fanlight doorway. Cannon balls were once made in this area for the Revolutionary War (when it was known as Hope Furnace). You will have breakfast in the kitchen which has been decorated with blue-and-white Dutch tiles. Behind the old fireplace in the sitting room is an old smokehouse. An old blacksmith shop and two classic barns are on the property. Each room has its own fireplace.

CASTLE KEEP BED & BREAKFAST REGISTRY
44 EVERETT ST., NEWPORT, RI 02840

Offers B&B Homes In: Newport, Middletown, and Portsmouth
Reservations Phone: 401/846-0362
Phone Hours: 8 a.m. to 8 p.m. daily in season
Price Range of Homes: $40 single, $55 to $90 double
Breakfast Included in Price: Continental to full American, and various special dishes, at the hosts' discretion
Brochure Available: Free
Reservations Should Be Made: 2 weeks in advance, 3 weeks in summer (last-minute reservations accepted if possible)

Scenic Attractions Near the B&B Homes: Naval War College, Topiary Gardens, at least five major boat shows a year, and the summer "cottages" of the rich and famous of yesteryear, yours to explore on fabulous Bellevue Avenue
Major Schools, Universities Near the B&B Homes: St. George's, Portsmouth Abbey prep schools, Salve Regina, Roger Williams

GUEST HOUSE ASSOCIATION OF NEWPORT
P.O. BOX 981, NEWPORT, RI 02840

Offers B&B Homes In: Newport only
Reservations Phone: Each home on their list must be called directly for reservations; call 401/846-ROOM (846-7666) for other information
Price Range of Homes: $35 to $120 single, $35 to $120 double
Breakfast Included in Price: Continental (juice, roll or toast, coffee)
Brochure Available: Free
Reservations Should Be Made: 2 weeks in advance in winter, a month or more in summer or fall (last-minute reservations accepted if possible)

Scenic Attractions Near the B&B Homes: National Historic Landmarks, Victorian "gilded age" mansions, Touro Synagogue (first in America), Cliff Walk, beaches, wharf dining and shopping areas
Major Schools, Universities Near the B&B Homes: Naval War College, Salve Regina, St. George's Prep, St. Michael's, Portsmouth Abbey

_____ B&B Inns _____

WILLIAM FLUDDER HOUSE
30 BELLEVUE AVE., NEWPORT, RI 02840

Reservations Phone: 401/849-4220 or 401/846-2229
Description: With four rooms on the "Walking Tour of Newport,"
the guesthouse is a short walk to the waterfront for shopping
and some of Newport's finest restaurants. Note that breakfast
is not served.

Nearby Attractions: Million Dollar Drive and the stately "cottages" of Newport, the Newport Folk Festival, the Tennis Museum
Rates: $55 in summer

VERMONT

VERMONT BED & BREAKFAST
P.O. BOX 1, EAST FAIRFIELD, VT 05448

Offers B&B Homes In: Vermont
Reservations Phone: 802/827-3827
Phone Hours: 11 a.m. to 7 p.m. Monday through Friday and 9
a.m. to noon on Saturday
Price Range of Homes: $35 to $150
Breakfast Included in Price: Full or continental plus
Brochure Available: Free with stamped, self-addressed envelope
Reservations Should Be Made: Telephone reservations are high-
ly recommended

Scenic Attractions Near the B&B Homes: Green Mountain National Forest; Mount Independence; Stephen A. Douglas Birthplace
Major Schools, Universities Near the B&B Homes: U.V.M.,

Middlebury College, Green Mountain College, St. Michaels, Johnson State College

Best B&Bs

▪ Victorian home in Bennington, Vermont. This turn-of-the-century home has ten-foot ceilings and raised-plaster moldings. A special treat in winter is the massive mahogany fireplace in the library. The library is decorated in Italianate style.

▪ An 18th-century home in Brandon, Vermont. This white Colonial offers five guest rooms, all with private baths. You are only minutes from the Green Mountain National Forest.

▪ Farmhouse in Waterbury, Vermont. Relax in an 1830s farmhouse with a two-section common room. Each of the guest rooms is air-conditioned with individual temperature controls. *Insider's Tip:* Come home in the afternoon and the host will serve wine and cheese.

▪ Colonial "cottage" in Barton, Vermont. This is a restored revival mansion located right on the shore of Lake Willoughby, a beautiful lake. Guests have full use of the facilities, which include swimming, windsurfing, canoeing, paddleboats, volleyball, and croquet.

B&B Inns

THE EVERGREEN
SANDGATE ROAD, ARLINGTON, VT 05250

Reservations Phone: 802/375-2272
Description: Set in the Green Mountains, the inn can accommodate 40 guests in comfortable rooms surrounded by spacious lawns.
Amenities: Full breakfast served to guests

Nearby Attractions: Bennington Museum, Southern Vermont Art Center, Dorset Playhouse, Skyline Drive
Special Services: Bus pickups, kitchen open in the evening for cookies and cakes, coffee or tea
Rates: $28 to $32 single, $56 to $64 double, in summer; $23 to $27 single, $46 to $54 double, in fall

GREENHURST INN
R.D. 2, BOX 60, BETHEL, VT 05032

Reservations Phone: 802/234-9474
Description: This 1890 inn, listed on the National Register of
Historic Places, is located in the geographic center of Vermont.
It has eight fireplaces, a library of 3,000 volumes, and a
Victrola and piano in the parlor.
Amenities: Choice of juice, hot muffins, quick bread, fresh fruit,
and Colombian coffee

Nearby Attractions: Mountains, ski areas, outdoor sports
Special Services: Perrier in every room, mints on your pillow,
game cupboard, electric blankets
Rates: $40 to $80 double

THE BLACK BEAR INN
MOUNTAIN ROAD, BOLTON, VT 05477

Reservations Phone: 802/434-2126 or 802/434-2920
Description: In a unique mountaintop setting, many of the inn's
rooms enjoy mountain views from balconies, and all rooms have
private bath and color TV. Guests are welcome to enjoy all the
sports and recreation facilities of the Bolton Valley Resort.

Nearby Attractions: Shelburne Museum, many ski areas
Special Services: Outdoor heated pool
Rates: $89 double in summer and fall, $59 double in winter

VILLAGE INN OF BRADFORD
MAIN STREET (U.S. 5), BRADFORD, VT 05033

Reservations Phone: 802/222-9303
Description: Built in 1826, this inn is a mix of several styles,
Federal/Victorian outside, Colonial/Victorian inside. Rooms and
a suite with private or shared bath are available.
Amenities: Continental breakfast during the week, full breakfast
on Sunday

Nearby Attractions: Connecticut River, golf course, historic restored mill, waterfall, horses, canoeing
Rates: $35 single, $40 to $60 double

TULIP TREE INN
CHITTENDEN DAM ROAD, CHITTENDEN, VT 05737

Reservations Phone: 802/483-6213
Description: In this gracious, rambling country house, a variety of antiques furnishes the eight guest rooms. The paneled den has a stone fireplace.
Amenities: Full breakfast served

Nearby Attractions: Green Mountain Forest, hiking trails, Killington (for skiing), canoeing, fishing, golf
Special Services: Hot tub
Rates: $65 to $90 per person with breakfast and dinner

ECHO LEDGE FARM INN
RTE. 2 (P.O. BOX 77), EAST ST. JOHNSBURY, VT 05838

Reservations Phone: 802/748-4750
Description: "The Dwelling House of Phineas Page" was built in 1793. Rooms have been freshly papered or stenciled, and have private baths.

Nearby Attractions: Maple Grove Museum and Factory, Fairbanks Museum and Planetarium, most outdoor sports
Rates: $60 double in fall, $38 to $45 double in summer

THE HIGHLAND LODGE
R.R. 1, BOX 1290, GREENSBORO, VT 05841

Reservations Phone: 802/533-2647
Description: This restored 1850s farmhouse is situated just above Caspian Lake in Vermont's Northeast Kingdom. The rooms and cottages are tastefully decorated and afford good views of the mountains. A large porch overlooks the perennial gardens.
Amenities: Full breakfast and dinner using local products

Nearby Attractions: The Green Mountains, complete range of outdoor sports
Special Services: Playroom, tennis courts, beachhouse, canoes, rowboats, paddleboat, and 40 miles of trails for cross-country skiing available for guests
Rates: $60 to $75 single, $105 to $135 double

MOUNTAIN MEADOWS LODGE
RTE. 1, BOX 2080, KILLINGTON, VT 05751

Reservations Phone: 802/775-1010
Description: This converted 130-year-old farmhouse and barn can accommodate 40 guests in summer. Most of the large rooms have private baths. The lodge is set on a 110-acre lake in a country setting.
Amenities: Full Vermont home-style breakfast

Nearby Attractions: Summer theater, Alpine slide, and Killington Gondola
Special Services: TV, games room, and pool; tennis, golf, and health clubs nearby
Rates: $55 single, $90 double, April to November; $75 single, $110 double, November to May

NORDIC INN
RTE. 11, LANDGROVE, VT 05148

Reservations Phone: 802/824-6444
Description: The inn is surrounded by the Green Mountain National Forest. It features five individual guest rooms and three dining rooms, two with fireplaces
Amenities: Juices, home-baked biscuits and sweet breads, fresh fruits, coffee, tea, and hot chocolate are served in summer; a full breakfast with Swedish pancakes and Vermont products is served in winter

Nearby Attractions: Hapgood Pond; Bromley Alpine Slide; Hildene, Bromley, Magic and Stratton Mountain ski areas; Dorset and Weston Summer Theaters; ice skating and horse-drawn sleigh rides
Special Services: Cross-country skiing in 15 miles of groomed trails, rentals and instruction available

Rates: $135 double, Modified American Plan (breakfast and dinner included), December through March; $53 double, European Plan (B&B), May to December

BLACK LANTERN INN
RTE. 118, MONTGOMERY, VT 05470

Reservations Phone: 802/326-4507, or toll free 800/255-8661
Description: This restored Colonial building was built in 1803 as a stagecoach inn. The old brick building is less than ten miles from the Canadian border. The rooms are decorated with antiques, and the suite has a Jacuzzi and a fireplace.

Nearby Attractions: Jay Peak ski area, Hazen's Notch Cross-Country Ski Center, covered bridges
Special Services: Swimming, tennis
Rates: $50 to $75 double

NORTH HERO HOUSE
CHAMPLAIN ISLANDS, NORTH HERO, VT 05474

Reservations Phone: 802/372-8237
Description: This is a small country inn overlooking Lake Champlain. All rooms have private bath, and lake-view accommodations have screened porches to view Mount Mansfield across the lake.

Nearby Attractions: Burlington, Shelburne Museum, Stowe, Trapp Family Lodge, fishing, sailing, waterskiing, tennis, skiing
Special Services: Sauna, game room
Rates: $31 to $67 double in summer and fall

NORWICH INN
225 MAIN ST. (P.O. BOX 908), NORWICH, VT 05055

Reservations Phone: 802/649-1143
Description: The building, an inn since 1779, has 22 guest rooms each with private bath, telephone, and cable TV. Some of the rooms have canopied, rice-carved four-poster beds, while others are furnished with brass bedsteads.

Nearby Attractions: Swimming, hiking, fishing, canoeing, antiquing, downhill and cross-country skiing
Rates: $55 to $95 double

VALLEY HOUSE INN
4 MEMORIAL SQUARE, ORLEANS, VT 05860

Reservations Phone: 802/754-6665
Description: Built in the 1800s, the inn has a large porch going halfway around the building. There are 20 rooms in the inn, with a cocktail lounge facing the common.
Amenities: Hearty Vermont breakfast served

Nearby Attractions: Old Stone House Museum, three lakes within a three-mile radius, 18-hole golf course
Special Services: Live entertainment every Friday night
Rates: $20 to $39 single, $26 to $48 double; breakfast included with some rooms

CASTLE INN
P.O. BOX 157, PROCTORSVILLE, VT 05153

Reservations Phone: 802/226-7222
Description: This large stone castle built in 1904 contains elaborate public rooms like the Great Hall, with the family coat-of-arms carved into the woodwork, or the library, where cocktails are served. The guest rooms are done up in the style of the period.
Amenities: Rates include a full breakfast from the menu and dinner

Nearby Attractions: Black River Museum; Calvin Coolidge's Birthplace; Woodstock and Queechee Gorge; Robert Todd Lincoln's home, "Hildene"; major ski areas
Special Services: Swimming pool, tennis court, hot tub and sauna
Rates: $140 to $180 double, June to October and December to April

HARVEY MOUNTAIN VIEW FARM AND INN
ROCHESTER NORTH HOLLOW, ROCHESTER, VT 05767

Reservations Phone: 802/767-4273
Description: The inn was the subject of a full-page article by
Noel Perrin in the *New York Times* describing living on a farm
and petting and feeding the animals as a unique kind of
vacation. Besides accommodations in the inn there is a two-
bedroom chalet rented from Saturday to Saturday.
Amenities: Besides a full farm breakfast, dinner is included in the
rates

Nearby Attractions: Lake Dunmore, ski areas with gondola and
alpine slide, tennis courts, Texas Falls with nature walk
Special Services: Bus pickup, swimming pool, a pond for fishing,
animals to interact with, a pony to ride, lawn games
Rates: $38 to $45 double

GREEN MOUNTAIN TEA ROOM AND GUEST HOUSE
RTE. 7 (R.R. 1, BOX 400), SOUTH WALLINGFORD, VT 05773

Reservations Phone: 802/446-2611
Description: This former stagecoach stop was built in 1792. There
are five guest rooms. The Colonial house is on eight acres of
land bordering Otter Creek.

Nearby Attractions: Green Mountain National Park, Appalachian
Trail, ski areas, fishing, canoeing
Rates: $40 single, $50 double; $10 per extra person

KEDRON VALLEY INN
RTE. 106, SOUTH WOODSTOCK, VT 05071

Reservations Phone: 802/457-1473
Description: The building has been operating as an inn for over
150 years. The guest rooms have canopied beds, Franklin

stoves, fireplaces, private baths, and antique quilts. It's on a large lake with a beach.
Amenities: Full country breakfast

Nearby Attractions: Skiing; Silver Lake State Park; Vermont Institute of Natural Science; summer walking tours of historic Woodstock
Rates: $75 to $131 single, $80 to $136 double; midweek discounts available

SCARBOROUGH INN
RTE. 100, HC65 #23, STOCKBRIDGE, VT 05772

Reservations Phone: 802/746-8141
Description: This restored 1780 farmhouse is full of Chippendale, Sheraton, and other antiques, pewter, and Haviland china.
Amenities: Full country breakfast

Nearby Attractions: Long Trail
Rates: $40 to $60 per person, double occupancy

BUTTERNUT INN AT STOWE
MOUNTAIN ROAD (R.D. 1, BOX 950), STOWE, VT 05672

Reservations Phone: 802/253-4277, or toll free 800/3-BUTTER
Description: This three-diamond AAA bed-and-breakfast country inn is set on 8½ acres of landscaped grounds by a mountain stream. All rooms have private bath and are air-conditioned and furnished with antiques. This is a no-smoking inn.
Amenities: Breakfast (served poolside when possible) may include omelets, ham steak, quail, French toast with Vermont maple syrup

Nearby Attractions: Mount Mansfield ski resort, gondola ride, alpine slide
Special Services: Swimming pool, golf, tennis, horseback riding
Rates: $85 double, June to October; $95 double, December to April

FIDDLERS GREEN INN
MOUNTAIN ROAD (RTE. 108), STOWE, VT 05672

Reservations Phone: 802/253-8124
Description: This country inn in the Green Mountains was built in 1820 and is situated well off the highway next to a babbling brook.
Amenities: Breakfast specialties include home-grown blueberry and juneberry pancakes, Grand Marnier French toast, and cheese, mushroom, and herb omelets

Nearby Attractions: Mount Mansfield, alpine slide, gondola ride, tennis, golf, balloon and glider rides
Special Services: Picnic grove
Rates: $34 to $52 double

TIMBERHOLM INN
COTTAGE CLUB ROAD (R.R.1, BOX 810), STOWE, VT 05672

Reservations Phone: 802/253-7603 (8 a.m. to 8 p.m.)
Description: The inn has a view of Worcester Mountain. The living room has a large stone fireplace, picture windows, a deck, and family furniture.
Amenities: Breakfast

Nearby Attractions: Mount Mansfield ski area and State Park, Stowe Village, Trapp Family Lodge, biking, hiking, tennis, golf
Special Services: Complimentary soup, après-ski
Rates: $56 to $86 double

MAD RIVER BARN LODGE
RTE. 17, WAITSFIELD, VT 05673

Reservations Phone: 802/496-3310
Description: This is a traditional Vermont lodge filled with mementos of years gone by and the charm of country living. Rooms are furnished in simple but comfortable style.
Amenities: Continental and full breakfast

Nearby Attractions: Shelburne Museum, Lake Champlain, Audubon Society Nature Center, Rock of Ages Quarries, alpine slide
Special Services: Pool, golf, tennis, fishing, soaring, biking
Rates: $46 double with private bath, December to April; $28 double with private bath, May to November; children under 10 free in their parents' room

---

MILLBROOK LODGE
R.F.D. BOX 62, WAITSFIELD, VT 05673

Reservations Phone: 802/496-2405
Description: This Cape-style farmhouse dates to the 1850s. The seven guest rooms are decorated with hand-stenciling, antique bedsteads, and handmade quilts. There's a view of the Green Mountains.
Amenities: Full country breakfast including pancakes with fruit, French toast made with anadama bread, real Vermont maple syrup

Nearby Attractions: Some of the finest skiing in the East five minutes away, Sugarbush and Mad River Glen, 60 miles of groomed trails for the cross-country skier, golfing, canoeing, soaring, tennis, horseback riding, windsurfing
Rates: $60 to $330 single, $110 to $480 double, in winter; $40 to $50 single, $50 to $70 double, in summer

---

MOUNTAIN VIEW INN
R.F.D. BOX 69, WAITSFIELD, VT 05673

Reservations Phone: 802/496-2426
Description: Though built in 1826, the house has been an inn only for the last 40 years. The seven rooms, each with bath, are decorated in the Colonial style with antiques, quilts, and braided rugs.
Amenities: Breakfast begins with fruit and coffee or tea, and continues with bacon, eggs, and toast, or blueberry pancakes, or waffles, with bacon.
Nearby Attractions: Ski areas at Sugarbush, Mad River Glen, and the Long Trail; soaring, tennis, golf, horseback riding; Shelburne Museum, a Morgan horse farm
Rates: $120 double in winter, $110 double in summer

TUCKER HILL LODGE
RTE. 17 (R.D.1, BOX 147), WAITSFIELD, VT 05673

Reservations Phone: 802/496-3983, or toll free 800/451-4580
Description: The gray clapboard buildings are on a hillside setting surrounded by very elaborate flower gardens.
Amenities: Breakfast includes homemade bread and muffins, local berries, homemade jams, and maple syrup from the innkeeper's trees.

Nearby Attractions: Mad River for fishing and canoeing, Sugarbush and Mad River Glen ski areas, museums, craft galleries, Shelburne Museum
Special Services: Pool, two clay tennis courts, airport pickup, fresh flowers in guest rooms
Rates: $96 double with breakfast

VALLEY INN
RTE. 100 (BOX 8), WAITSFIELD, VT 05673

Reservations Phone: 802/496-3450
Description: The first inn built in the Mad River Valley, the all-wood structure is made of native timbers. The parlor has a large stone fireplace.
Amenities: Full breakfast with fresh berries and Vermont maple syrup

Nearby Attractions: Sugarbush Ski Resort, Historic Waitsfield Village, covered bridges
Special Services: Tennis, golf, soaring, ski packages, private airport
Rates: $120 double, MAP, in winter; $70 double, B&B, in summer

WINDHAM HILL INN
R.R.1, BOX 44, WEST TOWNSHEND, VT 05359

Reservations Phone: 802/874-4080 or 802/874-4976
Description: This restored 1825 farmhouse and barn has 15 antique-filled guest rooms and private baths set on 150 acres.
Amenities: Full breakfast and six-course gourmet dinner included in the rates

Nearby Attractions: Townshend State Park; Jamaica State Park; Marlboro Music Center; Stratton, Bromley, and Magic Mountain ski areas; Volvo International Tennis Tournament
Special Services: Sherry in room on arrival, chamber music
Rates: $75 per person, double occupancy

THE WHITE HOUSE OF WILMINGTON
RTE. 9, WILMINGTON, VT 05363

Reservations Phone: 802/464-2135
Description: This turn-of-the-century mansion set high on a hill has 12 distinctive rooms with private bath.
Amenities: Full breakfast and dinner included in the rates

Nearby Attractions: The Historic Molly Stark Trail, Bennington, lakes, horseback riding
Special Services: Pool, sauna, and whirlpool, cross-country skiing
Rates: $170 to $210 double

The Middle Atlantic States

B&B Reservation Services

BED & BREAKFAST OF DELAWARE

3650 SILVERSIDE RD. (P.O. BOX 177), WILMINGTON, DE 19810

Offers B&B Homes In: City and suburbs of Wilmington, Newark, Odessa, Lewes, in Delaware; Chadds Ford and other towns in nearby Pennsylvania and Maryland
Reservations Phone: 302/479-9500
Phone Hours: 9 a.m. to 9 p.m. daily (any hour on answering service)
Price Range of Homes: $30 to $35 single, $45 to $65 double (beach homes to $65 in summer)
Breakfast Included in Price: Full American (juice, eggs, bacon, toast, coffee)
Brochure Available: Free
Reservations Should Be Made: 2 weeks in advance (last-minute reservations accepted if possible)

Scenic Attractions Near the B&B Homes: Winterthur, Longwood Gardens, Brandywine River Museum, Hagley Museum, Nemours, Old New Castle, beach resorts, Philadelphia attractions
Major Schools, Universities Near the B&B Homes: U. of Delaware, Delaware Law School, West Chester U.

DISTRICT OF COLUMBIA

B&B Reservation Service

BED 'N' BREAKFAST LTD. OF WASHINGTON, D.C.
P.O. BOX 12011, WASHINGTON, DC 20005

Offers B&B Homes In: Washington, D.C., and nearby Maryland and Virginia
Reservations Phone: 202/328-3510
Phone Hours: 10 a.m. to 5 p.m. Monday through Friday, to 1 p.m. on Saturday
Price Range of Homes: $30 to $75 single, $45 to $85 double
Breakfast Included in Price: Continental breakfast included in B&B rooms; no breakfast included in one-bedroom apartments
Brochure Available: Free
Reservations Should Be Made: One month in advance if possible (will make last-minute reservations, subject to availability)

Scenic Attractions Near the B&B Homes: All major Washington, D.C., attractions
Major Schools, Universities Near the B&B Homes: Georgetown U., George Washington U., American U., Catholic U., Trinity College, Mount Vernon College, Johns Hopkins School of Economic and International Studies

Best B&Bs
■ Georgian-style home in Washington, D.C. Right on Tenley Circle, this home is located on a tree-lined avenue in a residential neighborhood. You have a choice of two large guest rooms with color TV, and private bathrooms with tile showers. *Insider's Tip:* For romantic evenings, ask for the guest room with a fireplace. Host no. 126.

■ Federal-style brick house in Washington, D.C. This Friendship Heights home was custom-designed by the owners just four years ago. It features a lovely stained-glass window, several fireplaces, a walled-in garden, and a heated outdoor swimming pool. *Insider's Tip:* The games room has a pool table, pinball machine, game table, and stereo. The house is convenient to many good restaurants and a short walk from the metro. Host no. 131.

■ A Victorian mansion in Washington, D.C. This home was built on Logan Circle over 100 years ago. Its present owner has added landscaping, gardens, a terrace, and fountains to the original town house. Each guest room has a color TV. Laundry facilities are available. *Insider's Tip:* You will certainly enjoy talking with your host. He is a former Fulbright Fellow and law clerk to Supreme Court Justice Tom Clark. He is now a senior partner of a prominent Washington law firm.

MARYLAND

——————— B&B Reservation Services ———————

THE TRAVELLER IN MARYLAND, INC.
P.O. BOX 2077, ANNAPOLIS, MD 21404

Offers B&B Homes In: Annapolis, Baltimore, and 45 other cities and towns throughout Maryland
Reservations Phone: 301/269-6232 or 301/261-2233
Phone Hours: 9 a.m. to 3 p.m. Monday through Thursday
Price Range of Homes: $55 to $75 single, $60 to $80 and up double (yachts, $100 and up)
Breakfast Included in Price: Continental
Brochure Available: No; please reserve by phone only
Reservations Should Be Made: As far in advance as possible; not less than 24 hours

Scenic Attractions Near the B&B Homes: Historic Annapolis, Baltimore Inner Harbor, Chesapeake Bay, U.S. Naval Academy, hiking and biking, major-league sports, horse racing, historic homes
Major Schools, Universities Near the B&B Homes: Johns Hopkins, Goucher, U.S. Naval Academy, St. John's, Washington College, U. of Maryland

Best B&Bs

■ See their "50 Best B&Bs" winner in Part III.

■ Detached town house in Annapolis, Maryland. This B&B is within walking distance of all the historic sights in the beautiful sea-oriented town. The hosts are friendly and like to give tips about walking tours. The room has twin beds and a private bath.

AMANDA'S BED & BREAKFAST RESERVATION SERVICE

1428 PARK AVE., BALTIMORE, MD 21217

Offers B&B Homes In: Baltimore area, Annapolis, Eastern Shore of Maryland, Gettysburg, Pennsylvania, and Washington, D.C.
Reservations Phone: 301/225-0001
Phone Hours: 8:30 a.m. to 5:30 p.m. Monday through Friday
Price Range of Homes: $40 to $100 single, $40 to $120 double
Breakfast Included in Price: Continental or full American; regional specialties sometimes served include shoo-fly pie and sausage bread
Brochure Available: Free
Reservations Should Be Made: 2 weeks in advance (last-minute reservations accepted when possible)

Scenic Attractions Near the B&B Homes: Baltimore Inner Harbor, the Aquarium, Science Center, Baltimore Museum of Art, Zoo, historic neighborhoods, beaches
Major Schools, Universities Near the B&B Homes: Johns Hopkins, Peabody, Loyola, U. of Maryland–Baltimore

Best B&Bs

■ Victorian country home near Baltimore, Maryland. Just 15 minutes from Baltimore's Inner Harbor. You have a choice of six guest rooms, two of them with private baths, the others with shared baths.

B&B Inns

THE ROSEBUD INN
4 N. MAIN ST., WOODSBORO, MD 21798

Reservations Phone: 301/845-2221
Description: Opened as an inn in 1981, it was once the home of
the founder of the Rosebud Perfume Co., which is still in
operation next door to the inn. A rose motif is carried throughout the interior, reflected in the rosebud designs in the leaded-
glass doors. There are five large air-conditioned rooms, two
with private bath. Marble mantels decorate the parlor and
living room fireplaces. There is a gift shop on the premises.
Amenities: Continental breakfast

Nearby Attractions: Tennis, ice skating, bicycling, fishing, hiking,
antique shops
Rates: $55 single, $65 double

NEW JERSEY

B&B Reservation Services

NORTHERN NEW JERSEY BED & BREAKFAST
11 SUNSET TRAIL, DENVILLE, NJ 07854

Offers B&B Homes In: Northern New Jersey
Reservations Phone: 201/625-5129
Phone Hours: 9 a.m. to noon and 4 to 6 p.m. Monday through
Friday
Price Range of Homes: $30 to $66 single, $40 to $66 double
Breakfast Included in Price: Continental or full American (de-
pending on the host)
Brochure Available: Free
Reservations Should Be Made: 2 weeks in advance

Scenic Attractions Near the B&B Homes: Washington's Headquarters, Waterloo Village, Meadowlands Sports Complex

Major Schools, Universities Near the B&B Homes: Drew, Fairleigh Dickinson, Montclair State

Best B&Bs

■ Home on Indian Lake, Denville, New Jersey. Offers private guest quarters on the first floor. Guests can obtain free beach passes. Take some time to enjoy the view of the bay from the outside deck. Wine and cheese are served in the afternoon.

■ Contemporary home in Bridgewater, New Jersey. On the side of a mountain in a wooded setting right next to a deer preserve. You can find many private nooks in this custom-built home for reading, conversation, and cable TV. The large sunken living room has a cathedral ceiling and fieldstone see-through fireplace.

BED & BREAKFAST OF NEW JERSEY, INC.
103 GODWIN AVE., SUITE 132, MIDLAND PARK, NJ 07432

Offers B&B Homes In: New Jersey (also in Pennsylvania and Florida); also reserves B&B inns.
Reservations Phone: 201/444-7409
Phone Hours: 9 a.m. to 3 p.m. Monday through Friday
Price Range of Homes: $50 to $60 single, $60 to $135 double
Breakfast Included in Price: Continental to full American
Brochure Available: Free; complete directory for $5
Reservations Should Be Made: As soon as travel dates are firm—two weeks preferred, but will attempt to handle last-minute requests

Scenic Attractions Near the B&B homes: Northeastern New Jersey offers beautiful natural terrain, from the Ramapo Mountains to the Palisades, as well as easy access to New York City.

Best B&Bs

■ Federal-style home in Columbus—Mount Holly, New Jersey. This home is famous, having been featured in many country magazines. It is located in a country setting of 12 acres. The three guest rooms on the third floor are furnished with period antiques and country décor. *Insider's Tip:* The third bedroom has a working fireplace. Animal lovers will enjoy meeting the dog, two cats, six Suffolk sheep, an Arabian horse, and a Welsh pony on the grounds.

BED & BREAKFAST OF PRINCETON
P.O. BOX 571, PRINCETON, NJ 08540

Offers B&B Homes In: Princeton
Reservations Phone: 609/924-3189
Phone Hours: 24 hours
Price Range of Homes: $30 to $60 single, $40 to $70 and up double
Breakfast Included in Price: Mostly continental, but some serve full breakfast
Brochure Available: Free with stamped, self-addressed no. 10 envelope
Reservations Should Be Made: As early as possible, but last-minute reservations accepted if possible

Scenic Attractions Near the B&B Homes: Historic homes, buildings, parks, downtown shopping and dining
Major Schools, Universities Near the B&B Homes: Princeton, Institute for Advanced Study, Princeton Theological Seminary, Rider College, Westminster Choir College

Best B&Bs
■ Victorian home in Princeton, New Jersey. This large home offers three double guest rooms just a few minutes from the university and center of town. The hostess is a longtime Princeton resident who can give you a lot of good local information about sights and restaurants.

B&B Inns

HOLLY HOUSE
20 JACKSON ST., CAPE MAY, NJ 08204

Reservations Phone: 609/884-7365
Description: The house (c. 1890) is one of seven Victorian cottages that are famous as Cape May's Seven Sisters. Renaissance Revival in style, it's the work of Stephen Decatur Button. It has six guest rooms with two shared baths, plus an ocean-view front porch with swing and rockers. The inn has achieved National Historic Landmark status.

Nearby Attractions: Physick House Victorian Museum, the Cold Spring Village restoration, a bird sanctuary and wildlife preserve, beach, shopping mall
Special Services: Parking permits and beach tags are supplied.
Rates: $55 double in summer, $50 double in winter

NORTH CAROLINA

B&B Reservation Services

BED AND BREAKFAST IN THE ALBEMARLE
P.O. BOX 248, EVERETTS, NC 27825

Offers B&B Homes In: Northeastern North Carolina
Reservations Phone: 919/792-4584
Phone Hours: 5:30 to 10:30 p.m. Monday through Friday; answering machine at other times
Price Range of Homes: $30 to $50 single, $35 to $100 double
Breakfast Included in Price: Continental (juice, roll or toast, coffee); some hosts also serve Carolina country ham, and most homes serve country biscuits.
Brochure Available: Free; a host listing is also available for $5
Reservations Should Be Made: 2 weeks in advance (can accept last-minute reservations for some locations)

Scenic Attractions Near the B&B Homes: Hope Plantation, Historic Edenton, Historic Bath, Museum of the Albemarle, Elizabeth City Historic District, Fort Branch Confederate Earthworks, Jockey's Ridge State Park, Outer Banks beaches, National Seashore Recreational Area, Merchants Mill Pond State Park, Sommerset Place State Historic Site
Major Schools, Universities Near the B&B Homes: East Carolina U., Chowan, Roanoke Bible College, College of the Albemarle

Best B&Bs _____

▪ Restored Federal country farm house in Everetts, North Carolina. Good stopover point on your way to the beach at Nags Head. This B&B is set in a large pecan grove, screened from the highway by pine trees. Breakfast is served family style in the dining room overlooking the woods. *Insider's Tip:* In September you can pick your own grapes from the old grape arbors right on the grounds. If you're on your honeymoon, don't be too bashful to say so. For an additional $10, you can get the honeymoon special: champagne and breakfast served from a teacart in the master bedroom. Home no. 105.

■ Georgian/Williamsburg-style estate in Elizabeth City, North Carolina. Available May 20 to August 15. This home has large rooms and a beautiful library. It's situated on large landscaped acres with a view of the Pasquotank River. Full breakfast is available for an extra charge. Home no. 114.

BED & BISCUITS
P.O. BOX 19664, RALEIGH, NC 27619

Offers B&B Homes In: North Carolina; also some in South Carolina, Virginia, and Delaware
Reservations Phone: 919/787-2109
Phone Hours: 9 a.m. to 6 p.m. Monday through Thursday, to 5 p.m. on Friday, 10 a.m. to 2 p.m. on Saturday; answering machine other hours
Price Range of Homes: $35 to $150 per room
Breakfast Included in Price: In most cases
Brochure Available: Free; listings directory, $1.50
Reservations Should Be Made: As far in advance as possible (at last minute subject to availability)

Scenic Attractions Near the B&B Homes: Mountains, coast, Piedmont attractions, Charleston
Major Schools, Universities Near the B&B Homes: U. of North Carolina system

Best B&Bs
■ Federalist southern homestead in Charlotte, North Carolina. Has five attractive guest rooms, three of them with private baths. In summer enjoy the screened-in porch and swimming pool. Full gourmet breakfast.

■ A 1775 manor house in Durham, North Carolina. The eight guest rooms are individually decorated in Colonial or Victorian themes. In the afternoon there is complimentary tea or sherry. You can visit historic areas. *Insider's Tip:* Business travelers will find this a convenient place to stay if they're visiting any of the research firms in this area.

_____ **B&B Inns** _____

WOMBLE INN
301 W. MAIN ST. (P.O. BOX 1441), BREVARD, NC 28712

Reservations Phone: 704/884-4770
Description: Furnished with 18th- and 19th-century antiques, all rooms have private baths. The seven guest rooms are air-conditioned.
Amenities: Breakfast is served on a silver tray in your room, or in the dining room

Nearby Attractions: Pisgah National Forest, Biltmore House, North Carolina State Theater, the Brevard Music Center
Special Services: Swimming pool, tennis, shuttle to the Music Center
Rates: $36 single, $42 double, in summer; $32 single, $38 double, in winter

NANTAHALA VILLAGE
P.O. DRAWER J, BRYSON CITY, NC 28713

Reservations Phone: Toll free 800/438-1507
Description: Built of stone and wormy chestnut, the inn dates back to 1949. The cottages and log cabins are earlier. They offer simple but comfortable rustic accommodations.
Amenities: Continental breakfast

Nearby Attractions: Great Smoky Mountain National Park, Cherokee Indian Reservation, white-water rafting, swimming, horseback riding, tennis, shuffleboard
Rates: $60 double in summer, $35 double off-season

THE COLONIAL INN

153 W. KING ST., HILLSBOROUGH, NC 27278

Reservations Phone: 919/732-2461
Description: One of the ten oldest inns in the country, the
Colonial has been in continuous operation since 1759. Lord
Cornwallis and Aaron Burr stayed here. The ten bedrooms all
have private baths and are air-conditioned.
Amenities: Country breakfast

Nearby Attractions: Historic museum, 100 historic buildings with-
in walking distance, near Durham and Chapel Hill Research
Triangle Park
Rates: $48 to $65 double

THE GREYSTONE INN

P.O. BOX 6, LAKE TOXAWAY, NC 28747

Reservations Phone: 704/966-4700, or toll free 800/824-5766
outside North Carolina
Description: Built in 1915, the Greystone offers complete resort
facilities: Five soft-surface and one all-weather tennis courts,
waterskiing (boat, skis, and driver provided), and sunset cruises
on a party boat, *Mountain Lily II*
Amenities: High-country breakfast

Nearby Attractions: Blue Ridge Mountains; Biltmore House; waterfalls; Brevard Music Festival; 18-hole, par-72 championship
golf course on North Carolina's largest lake
Special Services: White wicker sun porch, afternoon tea, library
Rates: $75 to $175 per person

OSCAR'S HOUSE

RTE. 12 (P.O. BOX 206), OCRACOKE ISLAND, NC 27960

Reservations Phone: 919/928-1311
Description: This island, to which Europeans first came in the
1500s, was later the home of Blackbeard the Pirate and retains

the feeling of its historical beginnings. Oscar's House, built in 1940 by the lighthouse keeper, now provides accommodations for island visitors. Single or double rooms are available with shared baths.

Amenities: Breakfast is liable to include fresh fruit, garden tomatoes, omelets, grits, cooked apples, French toast, muffins or breads

Nearby Attractions: The Lighthouse, British Cemetery, Pamlico Sound, Silver Lake Harbor, Coast Guard Station

Rates: $40 to $45 single, $50 to $55 double, in summer; $35 single, $45 double, in spring and fall, with full breakfast included

THE PINES COUNTRY INN
719 HART RD., PISGAH FOREST, NC 28768

Reservations Phone: 704/877-3131

Description: Accommodations in this 1883 inn include seven double rooms with private bath, and five cabins and cottages. A family room with cable TV is available to all guests.

Amenities: A full breakfast with eggs any way you'd like them

Nearby Attractions: Pisgah National Forest, Holmes State Park, Brevard Music Center, Biltmore House, Carl Sandburg's House, Flatrock Playhouse

Special Services: Airport pickup upon request; rates include full breakfast.

Rates: $48 single, $58 double

BLUE BOAR LODGE
200 SANTEELAH RD., ROBBINSVILLE, NC 28771

Reservations Phone: 704/479-8126

Description: The lodge is a mountain hideaway in the Nantahala Forest. The accommodations are rustic but comfortable. The wood-paneled rooms sit on the edge of a lake.

Amenities: Breakfast with country sausage and ham, grits, gravy, and homemade biscuits

Nearby Attractions: Nantahala National Forest, Great Smokies, white-water rafting, fishing, Joyce Kilmer Memorial Forest

Special Services: Breakfast and supper are included in the room rate. Picnic lunches can be arranged.
Rates: $45 single, $80 double

PINE CREST INN
200 PINE CREST LANE, TRYON, NC 28782

Reservations Phone: 704/859-9135, or toll free 800/633-3001
Description: The inn's ten buildings on a wooded knoll contain a variety of accommodations—rooms, suites, and cottages. A full-service restaurant is on the premises.

Nearby Attractions: Blue Ridge Parkway, waterfalls, Biltmore House
Special Services: Fox hunting in season, nearby tennis, golf, swimming pool
Rates: $53 to $90 double in spring and fall, $48 to $85 double in summer and winter

STONE HEDGE INN
P.O. BOX 366, TRYON, NC 28782

Reservations Phone: 704/859-9114
Description: Set at the base of Mount Tyron, the inn offers a cottage complete with fireplace next to the pool and three beautiful and spacious rooms in the main house. All rooms have private bath, color TV, air conditioning, and mountain views. One is a two-room suite.
Amenities: Full house breakfast included

Nearby Attractions: Swimming pool, tennis, golf, hiking
Rates: $56 to $74 double occupancy

B&B Reservation Services

BED & BREAKFAST OF SOUTHEAST PENNSYLVANIA

146 W. PHILADELPHIA AVE., BOYERTOWN, PA 19512

Offers B&B Homes In: Easton, west through Bethlehem, Allentown, Kutztown, Reading, to East Greenville, and Sumneytown
Reservations Phone: 215/367-4688
Phone Hours: 24 hours daily
Price Range of Homes: $15 to $35 single, $35 to $90 double
Breakfast included in Price: Continental or full American (one hostess serves a vegetarian, or macrobiotic breakfast)
Brochure Available: For $2
Reservations Should Be Made: 2 weeks in advance (last-minute reservations accepted if possible)

Scenic Attractions Near the B&B Homes: Pennsylvania Dutch Country, historic Bethlehem, Dorney Park, Lehigh County Velodrome, Hopewell Village, Kutztown Folk Festival, Reading shopping outlets
Major Schools, Universities Near the B&B Homes: Lehigh, Lafayette, Moravian, Allentown, Cedar Crest, Muhlenberg, Albright, and Alvernia colleges; Kutztown U., Perkiomen School

Best B&Bs

■ Town house in Bethlehem, Pennsylvania. Good starting point for a walking tour of this historic city. Your host is a professor of industrial engineering.

■ Cottage at the Quiltery in Landis Store, Pennsylvania. Staying here is like a trip to the English countryside. You're surrounded by woodland. The house has been decorated with antiques, handmade furniture, and quilts. How long has it been since you've seen a wood-burning stove? You'll find one in the living room here. Good antique shopping nearby.

BED & BREAKFAST OF PHILADELPHIA

P.O. BOX 630, CHESTER SPRINGS, PA 19425

Offers B&B Homes In: Center City Philadelphia, all four surrounding counties of Bucks, Chester, Montgomery, and Delaware, including Main Line, New Hope, Doylestown Valley Forge, West Chester, Chadds Ford, and Chestnut Hill

Reservations Phone: 215/827-9650

Phone Hours: 9 a.m. to 5 p.m. Monday through Friday and noon to 4 p.m. on Saturday

Price Range of Homes: $25 to $35 single, $35 to $110 double (family rates in some specific homes)

Breakfast Included in Price: "Gourmet" continental or full breakfasts, which may include quiches, Philadelphia sticky buns, scrapple, other host specialties and regional fare

Brochure Available: Free

Reservations Should Be Made: 1 week in advance or sooner (last-minute reservations accepted, according to availability).

Scenic Attractions Near the B&B Homes: Valley Forge National Park, Independence Hall and National Park, Philadelphia Museum of Art, Franklin Institute, Rodin Museum, Longwood Gardens, Winterthur Museum and Gardens, Hagley Museum, Brandywine River Museum (Wyeth paintings), Skippack Village, Mennonite and Amish country, Sesame Place, New Hope

Major Schools, Universities Near the B&B Homes: U. of Pennsylvania, Drexel, Temple, Haverford, Bryn Mawr, Villanova, Swarthmore, Eastern, Beaver, Cabrini, St. Josephs, La Salle, Rosemont, Philadelphia Textile College, Jefferson Medical School, Wills Eye Hospital, American College of Physicians, Presbyterian Hospital, Dufreye Medical Center.

Best B&Bs

■ See their "50 Best B&Bs" winner in Part III.

■ An 1807 Society Hill rowhouse in Philadelphia, Pennsylvania. Easy walking distance of Independence Hall and Penn's Landing. City buses stop nearby. There are three double, air-conditioned B&B bedrooms. Third-floor room has a private powder room.

■ Suburban home at Rosemont, Pennsylvania. This attractive B&B is surrounded by tall trees. You will be greeted by the hostess and one large but friendly Great Dane. A swimming pool is available to guests. This home is very convenient to Main Line colleges.

BED & BREAKFAST CONNECTIONS
P.O. BOX 21, DEVON, PA 19333

Offers B&B Homes In: Philadelphia, Chestnut Hill, Mount Airy,
Germantown, Valley Forge, King of Prussia, Main Line communities
Reservations Phone: 215/687-3565
Phone Hours: 9 a.m. to 9 p.m. Monday through Saturday and 1
to 9 p.m. on Sunday
Price Range of Homes: $25 to $110
Breakfast Included in Price: Continental or full American
Brochure Available: Free directory
Reservations Should Be Made: By phone only, preferably 2
weeks in advance

Scenic Attractions Near the B&B Homes: Historic Philadelphia,
Independence National Park, Valley Forge National Historical
Park, Brandywine Valley, Longwood Gardens, Winterthur
Major Schools, Universities Near the B&B Homes: U. of Pennsylvania, Swarthmore College, Drexel U., Bryn Mawr, Temple
U., Villanova, Haverford College, Valley Forge Military Academy

Best B&Bs

■ Each B&B is personally inspected by this reservation-service
organization each year for cleanliness, comfort, and safety.

■ Suburban home in Newtown Square, Pennsylvania. Centrally
located to historic Philadelphia, the Brandywine Valley, and Valley
Forge Park, this lovely home overlooks five acres of rolling hunt
country. You may want to talk history with the host, who is a buff.
The host will also serve a full breakfast either in the garden room
or on the terrace overlooking the Pennsylvania countryside. This
home is equipped for handicapped guests, with a chair lift to the
second floor.

■ Historic home in Valley Forge, Pennsylvania. This stone Colonial
from the pre-Revolutionary period is nestled on four acres of
wooded land. The first part of the house was built before 1700.
Two more "recent" additions were made over 200 years ago.
Insider's Tip: You have a choice of rooms (based on availability).
You may want to choose the room with a lovely view of the stream

in front and the woods in back. It offers a unique cast-iron double bed. The private adjoining bath has a marble antique washbasin and a footed bathtub, with hand-held shower. That really is "new" (from the early 1900s).

■ Victorian town house in Philadelphia. Very reasonable prices with single occupancy as low as $25; double, $35. Within walking distance of Children's Hospital and the University of Pennsylvania. The hostess is a retired schoolteacher who serves a full breakfast family style in the kitchen.

HERSHEY BED & BREAKFAST RESERVATION SERVICE
P.O. BOX 208, HERSHEY, PA 17033

Offers B&B Homes In: Lancaster County (Lancaster, Manheim, Lititz); Dauphin County (Hershey, Harrisburg); Lebanon County (Annville, Palmyra); southeastern Pennsylvania
Reservations Phone: 717/533-2928
Phone Hours: 7 a.m. to 10 p.m. daily
Price Range of Homes: $45 to $50 single, $45 to $75 double
Breakfast Included in Price: Continental or full American; many Lancaster-area farm homes provide Pennsylvania Dutch country breakfasts, with their own cured hams and sausages, and breads and rolls baked early in the same morning; special gourmet breakfasts are served at a historic home in Annville.
Brochure Available: Free if you send a stamped, self-addressed no. 10 envelope
Reservations Should be Made: 2 weeks in advance preferred, 1 week accepted (no last-minute reservations accepted)

Scenic Attractions Near the B&B Homes: Pennsylvania Farm Museum, Amish Homestead, Strasburg Railroad, Dutch Wonderland, Hershey Park, Hershey Museum of American Life, Hershey Rose Gardens, William Penn Museum, Antique Automobile Club of America, Zoo America, Chocolate World, many shopping outlets
Major Schools, Universities Near the B&B Homes: Franklin and Marshall, Millersville, Elizabethtown College, Lebanon Valley College, Capitol Campus of Penn State, M.S. Hershey Medical Center of Penn State, Harrisburg Area Community College

Best B&Bs

■ Victorian mansion in Annville, Pennsylvania. This home was built in 1860 and borders the Swatara Creek on four acres. Every room is different, with period furnishings, including canopy beds. A full Pennsylvania Dutch breakfast is served in the family dining room.

■ Large brick home (Country Pines Farm) in Manheim, Pennsylvania. Built in 1817, this home offers a front porch for warm summer evenings or a walk-in fireplace for cold winter nights. This is a working dairy farm on 100 acres. You're close to the attractions of Hershey and Lancaster when you stay here.

■ An 1800 log cabin in Hershey, Pennsylvania. Located on Stonelock Farm, this cabin offers you country charm. On cold winter evenings you can warm up with some hot cider by a pot-belly stove. Close to Hershey Park.

BED AND BREAKFAST OF CHESTER COUNTY
P.O. BOX 825, KENNETT SQUARE, PA 19348

Offers B&B Homes In: Brandywine Valley, from the Philadelphia suburbs and Wilmington, Delaware, to Pennsylvania Dutch country
Reservations Phone: 215/444-1367
Phone Hours: Anytime daily
Price Range of Homes: $30 and up single, $45 to $125 double
Breakfast Included in Price: Continental or full American, depending on individual home; many feature gourmet cooking with homemade specialties.
Brochure Available: For $3
Reservations Should Be Made: At least 1 week in advance preferred—"We try to accommodate immediately, or as soon as possible."

Scenic Attractions Near the B&B Homes: Longwood Gardens, Winterthur, Brandywine River Museum (Wyeth paintings), Delaware Natural History Museum, Valley Forge, Brandywine Battlefield, Phillips Mushroom Museum, Pennsylvania Dutch Country
Major Schools, Universities Near the B&B Homes: West Chester U., Lincoln, Widener, U. of Delaware, Penn State at Lima

Best B&Bs _____

■ An 18th-century home near Longwood Gardens, Pennsylvania. The owner is an antiques dealer, as you can quickly tell as you walk through this B&B. A swimming pool is available to guests.

BED & BREAKFAST OF LANCASTER COUNTY
P.O. BOX 19, MOUNTVILLE, PA 17554

Offers B&B Homes In: Lancaster County, Gettysburg, Harrisburg, York, Hershey, Reading
Reservations Phone: 717/285-7200
Phone Hours: 9 a.m. to 2 p.m. and 4 to 9 p.m. every day
Price Range of Homes: $35 to $100 single, $55 to $100 double
Breakfast Included in Price: Continental to full American
Brochure Available: Free with stamped, self-addressed no. 10 envelope
Reservations Should Be Made: 1 week in advance recommended (last-minute reservations accepted if possible)

Scenic Attractions Near the B&B Homes: Pennsylvania Dutch Country, Hershey, Gettysburg, state parks
Major Schools, Universities Near the B&B Homes: Franklin Marshal, Millersville U., Lititz School for Girls, St. Anne School for Girls, Stevens Trade School

Best B&Bs _____

■ A 1738 farmhouse B&B inn in Lancaster County, Pennsylvania. This old home has been carefully restored. You can enjoy one of the six working fireplaces.

CENTER CITY BED & BREAKFAST
1804 PINE ST., PHILADELPHIA, PA 19103.

Offers B&B Homes In: Center City Philadelphia, plus some outside the city
Reservations Phone: 215/735-1137
Phone Hours: 9 a.m. to 5 p.m. Monday through Saturday, except holidays
Price Range of Homes: $20 to $45 single, $35 to $65 double
Breakfast Included in Price: Continental or full American (juice,

eggs, bacon, toast, coffee); full breakfast served at certain homes

Brochure Available: Free

Reservations Should Be Made: 2 weeks in advance (last-minute reservations accepted if possible)

Scenic Attractions Near the B&B Homes: Independence Hall, Betsy Ross House, Liberty Bell, Fairmount Park, Carpenters' Hall, Rodin Museum, Franklin Museum, Amish Country, Philadelphia Art Museum, Philadelphia Zoo

Major Schools, Universities Near the B&B Homes: U. of Pennsylvania, Temple, Drexel Institute, Moore College of Art, largest number of medical schools in mid-Atlantic area

REST & REPAST BED & BREAKFAST SERVICE
P.O. BOX 126, PINE GROVE MILLS, PA 16868

Offers B&B Homes In: Central Pennsylvania

Reservations Phone: 814/238-1484

Phone Hours: 9 a.m. to noon on Monday, Wednesday, and Saturday; 6:30 to 9:30 p.m. on Monday, Tuesday, Wednesday, and Friday; other hours, answering machine

Price Range of Homes: $25 to $30 single, $30 to $45 double (on football weekends, $40 to $65 double, and a $7 surcharge for one-night stays; two-night minimum on Homecoming and Parents Weekends)

Breakfast Included in Price: Continental or full American; almost half the hosts serve full breakfasts, including Pennsylvania Dutch specialties, fresh-gathered eggs and homemade jams

Brochure Available: Free; directory available for $3.50

Reservations Should Be Made: 2 weeks in advance (last-minute reservations accepted if possible); 3 to 6 months in advance for football weekends, and especially Homecoming Weekend

Scenic Attractions Near the B&B Homes: Penns Cave, Indian Caverns, Woodward Cave, 28th Division Military Shrine and Museum, Governor Curtin Mansion Village, four wineries, Belleville Amish Market, Baalsburg (home of Memorial Day)

Major Schools, Universities Near the B&B Homes: Penn State, Bucknell, Juniata College, Greer Girls School

Best B&Bs

■ Modern, unique home in Port Matilda, Pennsylvania. Imagine stepping into an octagonal house with skylight windows, a woodstove, with a deck overlooking acres of woodland. This is a great spot for privacy. There are a number of trails into the woods. Breakfast includes home-baked muffins and fresh fruit. *Insider's Tip:* Tell the host the night before that you like pancakes and you'll get them in the morning.

■ An 1800s home in Bellefonte, Pennsylvania. This home has been carefully restored by its hosts. Once it was a rain-soaked, fire-gutted mess. Now it has been transformed once more into a beautiful Victorian home with a formal dining room and a Victorian parlor with its own 1830s square grand piano. The B&B is called Rebecca's House. It was built for the young woman who was the wife of the former president of Penn State.

PITTSBURGH BED AND BREAKFAST SERVICE
2190 BEN FRANKLIN DR., PITTSBURGH, PA 15237

Offers B&B Homes In: Pittsburgh, Laurel Highlands, Mercer, Cranberry, Washington, Shellsburg, and the Northeast
Reservations Phone: 412/367-8080
Phone Hours: 9 a.m. to 5 p.m. Monday through Friday, to noon on weekends
Price Range of Homes: $25 to $48 single, $34 to $65 double
Breakfast Included in Price: Continental; some hosts prepare special muffins or rolls and herb teas (you can pick your own home-grown herbs)
Brochure Available: Free if you send a stamped, self-addressed no. 10 envelope
Reservations Should Be Made: 2 weeks in advance (last-minute reservations accepted when possible)

Scenic Attractions Near the B&B Homes: Amish antique shopping, Lake Erie
Major Schools, Universities Near the B&B Homes: U. of Pittsburgh, Carnegie-Mellon, Duquesne, Washington and Jefferson College

Best B&Bs
■ A 100-year-old home in Cownsville, Pennsylvania. Located about an hour's drive from Pittsburgh in 40 acres of rolling hills and gardens. Known as Garrotts Bed & Breakfast, this home offers guest rooms furnished with antiques. "The entire home is a showcase of heirlooms and collectibles." Your choice of three guest rooms. *Insider's Tip:* Because of the altitude and dark nights in this

area, this is an ideal spot for an amateur astronomer to watch the stars.

■ "Foursquare" home in Indiana, Pennsylvania. This B&B is an excellent example of a restored 1920 "Foursquare" home. The beds are particularly comfortable—feather beds with down pillows and handmade quilts. You can visit an Amish community and a vineyard just a few miles away.

BED & BREAKFAST OF VALLEY FORGE
P.O. BOX 562, VALLEY FORGE, PA 19481

Offers B&B Homes In: Valley Forge, Philadelphia, Phoenixville, Skippack, Chestnut Hill, Berwyn, Strafford, Newtown Square, Malvern, Bucks County, Lancaster County (all in Pennsylvania)
Reservations Phone: 215/783-7838
Phone Hours: 9 a.m. to 9 p.m. daily
Price Range of Homes: $25 to $70 single, $35 to $100 double
Breakfast Included in Price: Continental or full American (depending on the hostess)
Brochure Available: Free
Reservations Should Be Made: At your convenience; last-minute reservations accepted

Scenic Attractions Near the B&B Homes: Valley Forge National Park, many historic homes, hiking and horse trails in the park; Pennsylvania Dutch Country; Reading factory discount shopping; Longwood Gardens; Andrew Wyeth Art Museum; King of Prussia (largest shopping center in the U.S.); Devon Horse Show
Major Schools, Universities Near the B&B Homes: West Chester U., Villanova, Rosemont, Immaculata College, Ursinus, Eastern College, Valley Forge Military Academy, Bryn Mawr, Harcum, Penn State Graduate School

Best B&Bs
■ A 1720 house in Valley Forge, Pennsylvania. "The Great Valley House" is a 15-room Pennsylvania stone farmhouse. The white pillared front overlooks acres of fields. The oldest part of the house is the summer kitchen. This is where guests gather to enjoy a full country breakfast. The title deeds to this land can be traced back to William Penn in 1681. A secluded swimming pool surrounded by evergreen trees is available to guests. *Insider's Tip:* Your hosts are members of the local historical society and good

sources of information about the history of the house and the area.

■ Brownstone mansion in Collegeville area, Pennsylvania. This house was built in 1901. In addition to the main building, there is a hay barn that has been converted to two apartments. The Victorian parlor has a woodstove, and is furnished with two rococo sofas and a hand-cranked Victrola that plays 78-rpm records (remember those?). This B&B is about 30 minutes from Valley Forge and an hour from Lancaster County Amish country.

GUESTHOUSES
P.O. BOX 2137, WEST CHESTER, PA 19380

Offers B&B Homes In: Pennsylvania, Delaware, New Jersey, Maryland
Reservations Phone: 215/692-4575
Phone Hours: Noon to 4 p.m. Monday through Friday
Price Range of Homes: $35 to $150 per night, double occupancy
Breakfast Included in Price: Yes
Brochure Available: Descriptive sampling and "package" brochures
Reservations Should Be Made: Ideally 8 or more days in advance

Scenic Attractions Near the B&B Homes: Winterthur, Longwood Gardens, Hagley Museum, Brandywine River Museum (Wyeth), Brandywine Battlefield, Valley Forge
Major Schools, Universities Near the B&B Homes: U. of Delaware, Swarthmore, Villanova, Bryn Mawr, Hoverford, U. of Pennsylvania

Best B&Bs
■ Ask about "Guest Yachts" (30 air-conditioned sailing yachts berthed on the upper banks of the Chesapeake Bay's Eastern Shore) and Great Country Weekend packages

■ Log House located on a restored historic estate, Battle Hill, in "Wyeth Country," on the Brandywine Battlefield, Pennsylvania. Newly restored, the Log House offers a complete kitchen, living room, bedroom, and bath. Wonderful old trees surround you. A swimming pool is open seasonally.

■ Leni is located on a landmark site between West Chester, Pennsylvania, and Wilmington, Delaware. It's an Italianate serpentine-stone country manor house that dates back to the mid-1800s. Ask for one of the guest quarters with a fireplace.

B&B Inns

THE OVERLOOK INN
DUTCH HILL ROAD, CANADENSIS, PA 18325

Reservations Phone: 717/595-7519
Description: The inn has 20 rooms furnished with individually chosen antiques and decorated with a mixture of prints, plants, and country crafts. There are also accommodations in the carriage house and in the lodge. Six rooms have fireplaces.
Amenities: Fresh-squeezed orange juice, farm-fresh eggs, pop-overs, muffins, fruit pancakes, homemade sausage, scrapple, coffee and tea are served; dinner is included in the price.

Nearby Attractions: Downhill and cross-country skiing
Special Services: Library stocked with books, games, and color TV; shuffleboard, bocci, badminton; pool; high tea at 4 p.m., iced tea by the pool
Rates: $85 single, $150 double

CEDAR RUN INN
CEDAR RUN, CEDAR RUN, PA 17727

Reservations Phone: 717/353-6241
Description: Situated in Pennsylvania's Grand Canyon, the inn is 100 years old and furnished with the original furniture. The chef/owner is from the Culinary Institute of America.
Amenities: Full breakfast (choice of blueberry pancakes, French toast, eggs, or fruit and yogurt plate)

Nearby Attractions: Trout trophy streams, Black Forest hiking and skiing trails, Pine Creek directly in front of inn for swimming, fishing, or canoeing
Rates: $39 per person, MAP; $20 per person for room only

CENTER BRIDGE INN
BOX 74, STAR ROUTE, NEW HOPE, PA 18938

Reservations Phone: 215/862-9139
Description: This Williamsburg Colonial overlooks the Delaware River. Guest rooms have 2 canopy beds and private baths.
Amenities: Continental breakfast

Nearby Attractions: Canoeing, tubing, fishing, horseback riding, swimming, summer theater
Rates: $70 to $125 double on weekends; $60 to $100 double on weekdays

THE INN AT PHILLIPS MILL
NORTH RIVER ROAD, NEW HOPE, PA 18938

Reservations Phone: 215/862-2984
Description: Aaron Phillips built a grist mill here in 1756. Over the years an art colony formed around the mill and organized art exhibitions, concerts, dances, and theatrical productions, and it's still a cultural center. There are now five comfortable bedrooms with private bath and three dining rooms. Each bedroom is furnished with antiques, quilts on four-poster beds, and embroidered cloths.

Nearby Attractions: Swimming pool, craft shows, an annual play production
Rates: $65 to $75 double

────────── B&B Reservation Services ──────────

CHARLESTON SOCIETY BED & BREAKFAST
84 MURRAY BLVD., CHARLESTON, SC 29401

Offers B&B Homes In: The historic area of Charleston
Reservations Phone: 803/723-4948
Phone Hours: 9 a.m. to 5 p.m. daily
Price Range of Homes: $60 to $70 single, $70 to $100 double
Breakfast Included in Price: Continental (juice, roll or toast, coffee)
Brochure Available: Free
Reservations Should Be Made: 2 or 3 weeks in advance (last-minute reservations accepted if possible)

Scenic Attractions Near the B&B Homes: All the Historic District homes and other historic points of interest are within easy walking distance
Major Schools, Universities Near the B&B Homes: The Citadel, the College at Charleston, Baptist College

Best B&Bs ─────────────────────────────

■ Carriage house in Charleston, South Carolina. You'll have your own private entrance to this attractive home which has a living room with fireplace. Located in Charleston's Historic District.

■ Historic home on Battery, Charleston, South Carolina. This home offers a beautiful view of Charleston Harbor and a swimming pool. The two bedrooms have double beds.

HISTORIC CHARLESTON BED AND BREAKFAST
43 LEGARE ST., CHARLESTON, SC 29401

Offers B&B Homes In: The Historic District of Charleston
Reservations Phone: 803/722-6606
Phone Hours: 24 hours daily
Price Range of Homes: $50 to $100 single, $50 to $115 double
Breakfast Included in Price: Continental (juice, roll or toast, coffee)
Brochure Available: Free
Reservations Should Be Made: 2 weeks in advance; for the period March to June, 2 to 3 months in advance (last-minute reservations accepted if possible)

Scenic Attractions Near the B&B Homes: Historic homes, museums, harbor tours, famous gardens, beaches
Major Schools, Universities Near the B&B Homes: The Citadel, College of Charleston, Medical University of South Carolina

Best B&Bs

■ See their "50 Best B&Bs" winner in Part III.

■ Williamsburg-style house built before 1715, Charleston, South Carolina. You can stay in the oldest frame house in Charleston. Once this was the oldest drugstore in the U.S., but now it has been restored to its original use as a private residence. "The rooms have cypress floors, heavy beams, and antique furnishings." *Insider's Tip:* Ask for the room with a fireplace.

■ Greek Revival home in Charleston, South Carolina. This B&B was built in 1838. As you approach you can see its impressive façade with four columns and a large classic garden. The home is furnished with 18th-century American antiques. It's an easy stroll from here to the Historic District. Interested in restoring your own home? Talk with your hosts. They are retired interior decorators who have brought many plantations and historic houses back to their original grandeur.

■ A 1770s house in Charleston, South Carolina. This home was originally built in an orange grove. You can still see its 18th-century moldings and paneling. The original kitchen building behind the house has now become the B&B self-contained unit. It has a sitting room, a built-in kitchen unit, and an upstairs bedroom and bath. The furnishings are southern antiques. For breakfast you can expect homemade coffee cakes and breads. The refrigerator is stocked with breakfast staples (eggs, milk, butter). Your host's hobbies include travel, cooking, interior design, and gardening.

B&B Inns

EVERGREEN INN
1103 S. MAIN ST., ANDERSON, SC 29621

Reservations Phone: 803/225-1109
Description: The inn located in Anderson's Historic District is one of the oldest mansions. The accommodations consist of seven rooms, six baths, and eight fireplaces. The house is on the National Register.
Amenities: Continental breakfast with fresh fruit, yogurt, and cheeses

Nearby Attractions: Jane Hartwell Park, Anderson Historic District
Rates: $52 single, $65 double

OLD POINT INN
212 NEW ST., BEAUFORT, SC 29902

Reservations Phone: 803/524-3177 or 803/525-6104
Description: This 1898 Victorian in the "Beaufort Style," with double porches, front and side, is located in the Historic District half a block from the Beaufort River.
Amenities: Breakfast includes juice, fruit, homemade muffins.

Nearby Attractions: Hunting Island State Park, Hilton Head Island
Special Services: Mints and flowers in the rooms, bicycles
Rates: $55 double

INDIGO INN
ONE MAIDEN LANE, CHARLESTON, SC 29401

Reservations Phone: Toll free 800/845-7639, 800/922-1340 in South Carolina
Description: Located in historic downtown Charleston, the Indigo Inn has 18th-century décor, a courtyard, down pillows and comforters, one or two queen-size beds in each room, and facilities for the handicapped. Pets are allowed.
Amenities: "Hunt breakfast" (ham biscuits, homemade breads, fresh fruits, coffee, and juice), daily Charleston newspaper, private parking

Nearby Attractions: Within walking distance of the open-air market, historic churches and mansions, and fine restaurants
Rates: $95 to $105 double in summer, $75 to $105 double in winter

THE JASMINE HOUSE
64 HASELL ST., CHARLESTON, SC 29401

Reservations Phone: Toll free 800/845-7639, 800/922-1340 in South Carolina
Description: The inn has pre–Civil War Greek Revival architecture, 14-foot ceilings, fireplaces, and Oriental rugs.
Amenities: "Hunt breakfast" (ham biscuits, homemade breads, fresh fruit, coffee, and juice), complimentary wine

Nearby Attractions: Within walking distance of open-air markets, historic churches, and fine restaurants
Special Services: Jacuzzi and daily periodicals
Rates: $105 to $150 double

MEETING STREET INN
173 MEETING ST., CHARLESTON, SC 29401

Reservations Phone: 803/723-1882, or toll free 800/845-7638
Description: Located in the center of the historic district, the inn

has 55 rooms plus a conference suite. Some parts of the building date back to 1871.

Amenities: Continental breakfast, silver service

Nearby Attractions: Fort Sumter, Patriot's Point Museum, White Point Gardens, the Battery
Special Services: Heated Jacuzzi in courtyard, a bottle of wine in each guest room, afternoon chamber music concert
Rates: $98 to $115 double

THE JOHN LAWTON HOUSE
159 3RD ST. EAST, ESTILL, SC 29918

Reservations Phone: 803/625-3240 or 803/625-2586
Description: Built around the turn of the century from lumber and materials brought by mule and wagon from nearby Jericho Plantation, and extensively renovated in 1985, the inn is decorated with antiques, rich woods, Oriental rugs, and painted porcelains. Original family oil portraits are softly lit by crystal chandeliers. The draperies, wall coverings, and fabrics are period reproductions.
Amenities: Specialties include pear pie and homemade sausage served on silver, crystal, and fine china

Nearby Attractions: Charleston, Columbia, Hilton Head Island, and the South Carolina coast all less than two hours away
Special Services: A small kitchen and private entrance are available to guests, and there's parking on the premises for cars and campers
Rates: $40 double

CASSENA INN
P.O. BOX 5, PAWLEY'S ISLAND, SC 29585

Reservations Phone: 803/787-4556
Description: Rooms are located in three beachfront cottages. All cottages have rocking chairs and tables on the large porches. Some rooms have air conditioning and private bath.
Amenities: Full country breakfast

Nearby Attractions: Bellefield Nature Center, Rice Museum, Huntington Beach

Special Services: Airport pickup, golf, tennis
Rates: $67 to $86.50 double

LIBERTY HALL INN
S.C. BUSINESS HWY. 28, PENDLETON, SC 29670

Reservations Phone: 803/646-7500
Description: The inn is a restored Piedmont farmhouse with private baths, air conditioning, and TVs in rooms furnished with period antiques.
Amenities: Continental breakfast

Nearby Attractions: Woodburn Plantation, Clemson University, John Calhoun's Home, lakes for boating and fishing, golf
Rates: $55 to $65 double

CHAUGA RIVER HOUSE
COBB'S BRIDGE ROAD, WESTMINSTER, SC 29691

Reservations Phone: 803/647-9587
Description: Located directly on the rapids of the Chauga River in the center of the Sumter National Forest, the inn has five guest rooms decorated with French country antiques.
Amenities: Continental breakfast plus cereal and fruit

Nearby Attractions: Whitewater Falls, Clemson University
Special Services: Barbecue area, swimming, TV lounge, white-water rafting packages
Rates: $36 to $52 double

---------- B&B Reservation Services ----------

PRINCELY BED & BREAKFAST LTD.
819 PRINCE ST., ALEXANDRIA, VA 22314

Offers B&B Homes In: Alexandria
Reservations Phone: 703/683-2159
Phone Hours: 10 a.m. to 6 p.m. Monday through Friday
Price Range of Homes: $65 to $75 double
Breakfast Included in Price: Continental (juice, fresh fruit, home-baked breads, coffee or tea)
Reservations Should Be Made: 2 weeks in advance (no last-minute reservations accepted)

Scenic Attractions Near the B&B Homes: Washington, D.C.; Mount Vernon

BED & BREAKFAST OF TIDEWATER VIRGINIA
P.O. BOX 3343, NORFOLK, VA 23514

Offers B&B Homes In: Norfolk, Virginia Beach, Portsmouth, Chesapeake, the Eastern Shore and Northern Neck of Virginia
Reservations Phone: 804/627-1983 or 804/627-9409
Phone Hours: 8 a.m. to 8 p.m. daily (answering service 24 hours a day)
Price Range of Homes: $30 to $60 single, $35 to $75 double
Breakfast Included in Price: Continental or full breakfast, which may include spoonbread, country sausage, Smithfield ham, and homemade muffins. Fresh fruit and regional seafood dishes may also be served when in season.
Brochure Available: Free
Reservations Should Be Made: At least 2 weeks in advance, but the earlier the better (last-minute reservations accepted if possible)

Scenic Attractions Near the B&B Homes: Norfolk Naval Station, Chrysler Museum, MacArthur Memorial, Waterside Marketplace, fishing and water sports, Virginia Beach oceanfront, Harbor tours

Major Schools, Universities Near the B&B Homes: Old Dominion, Eastern Virginia Medical School, Virginia Wesleyan

Best B&Bs

■ Shingle house in Virginia Beach, Virginia. Located just a block and a half from the ocean, this attractive B&B has the charm of "Old Virginia Beach." The entire upstairs (two double rooms, a single room and bath) is available for guests.

■ Country house near Accomac, Virginia. This B&B is located on Virginia's Eastern Shore. The architecture is typical of this part of Virginia—big house, little house, colonnade, and kitchen. You're a short drive from Chincoteague, that beautiful wildlife preserve where you can view hundreds of birds from your car and meet wild ponies (now quite tame) on the trails.

BENSONHOUSE OF RICHMOND AND WILLIAMSBURG

2036 MONUMENT AVE., RICHMOND, VA 23220

Offers B&B Homes In: Richmond, Williamsburg, and Fredericksburg

Reservations Phone: 804/648-7560

Phone Hours: 10:30 a.m. to 5 p.m. Monday through Friday (24-hour answering service)

Price Range of Homes: $46 to $84 single, $48 to $95 double, $105 suites

Breakfast Included in Price: Continental or full American, depending on individual home; many homes serve home-baked breads and muffins.

Brochure Available: $2 with a stamped, self-addressed no. 10 envelope

Reservations Should Be Made: 3 or more weeks in advance (last-minute reservations accepted if accommodations available)

Scenic Attractions Near the B&B Homes: St. John's Church, Edgar Allan Poe Museum, Museum of the Confederacy, John Marshall House, State Archives, Virginia Historical Society, Science Museum of Virginia, Virginia Museum, and Virginia Theater for the Performing Arts; within a short drive of Colonial

Williamsburg, Busch Gardens, Kings Dominion, and James River Plantations

Major Schools, Universities Near the B&B Homes: U. of Richmond, Medical College of Virginia, Virginia Commonwealth U., Randolph Macon, Union Theological Seminary, St. Catherine's School, St. Christopher's School; in Williamsburg adjacent to the College of William and Mary

Best B&Bs

■ A 1908 house in Richmond, Virginia. Known as the "Summerhouse," this residence has been carefully restored. You'll enjoy the brightly colored walls, fireplaces, and detailed windows. *Insider's Tip:* Ask about the honeymoon or anniversary package. It includes breakfast in bed (on silver trays no less), wine or champagne, fruit and cheese, and enough fresh flowers to prove that romance can still be wonderful.

■ "Sheldon's Ordinary" home in Williamsburg, Virginia. This house is a copy of the 18th-century Sheldon's tavern in Litchfield, Connecticut. Yet it was built just a few years ago, in 1983. Many unusual decorative touches, such as hand-painted tiles from the Caribbean in the living room fireplace, and antique heart of pine wide-plank floors, and beautiful oak paneling from an old church in Indiana. This unique house is in a wooded area near William and Mary and one mile from the Colonial Williamsburg restored area. The host provides a full continental breakfast which includes homemade ham, rolls, apple coffee cake, and fresh fruit.

THE TRAVEL TREE

P.O. BOX 838, WILLIAMSBURG, VA 23187

Offers B&B Homes In: Williamsburg
Reservations Phone: 804/253-1571
Phone Hours: 6 to 9 p.m. Monday through Thursday
Price Range of Homes: $36 to $60 single, $45 to $75 double
Breakfast Included in Price: Continental (juice, breads or pastries, coffee)
Brochure Available: Free
Reservations Should Be Made: Several weeks in advance

Scenic Attractions Near the B&B Homes: Colonial Williamsburg, Busch Gardens, Yorktown, Jamestown
Major Schools, Universities Near the B&B Homes: College of William and Mary

Best B&Bs

■ New replica of an 18th-century home in Williamsburg, Virginia. You can walk to the Historic District. This B&B is furnished with period pieces and each of the two double guest rooms has a private bath.

■ Large brick home in Williamsburg, Virginia. Sits on a beautifully landscaped property in a wooded residential area. The guest room is large, with a private bath and private entrance. You can park off the street.

B&B Inns

THE CEDARS
616 JAMESTOWN RD., WILLIAMSBURG, VA 23185

Reservations Phone: 804/229-3591
Description: This stately three-story brick Colonial is within a ten-minute walk of the restored area. It has a lovely sitting room and porch, plus nine rooms and a cottage.
Amenities: Blueberry muffins, juice, coffee and tea; afternoon tea

Nearby Attractions: Colonial Williamsburg, Busch Gardens, Yorktown, Jamestown, Colonial Parkway
Rates: $40 to $55 double

WEST VIRGINIA

B&B Inns

MOUNTAIN VILLAGE INN AND CABIN LODGE
RTE. 219, HORSE SHOE, WV 26769

Reservations Phone: 304/735-3563
Description: A spruce-log lodge surrounded by a forest set beside a mountain stream, the inn has three bedrooms tucked up under

the eaves with a shared bath. The building is board and batten, and the guest rooms share a sitting room and a large enclosed porch.

Amenities: A full country breakfast including flapjacks, buckwheats, and Mexican specialties; dinner is included in the tariff

Nearby Attractions: Canaan State Park, Cathedral State Park, Blackwater Falls State Park, tennis, skiing, swimming
Special Services: A menagerie of farm animals on the grounds
Rates: $90 double

The Great Lakes Area

B&B Reservation Services

BED & BREAKFAST/CHICAGO, INC.
P.O. BOX 14088, CHICAGO, IL 60614

Offers B&B Homes in: Chicago, North Shore suburbs
Reservations Phone: 312/951-0085.
Phone Hours: 9 a.m. to 5 p.m. Monday through Friday
Price Range of Homes: $40 to $65 single, $50 to $75 double
Breakfast Included in Price: Continental
Brochure Available: Free
Reservations Should Be Made: 2 weeks in advance (last-minute
reservations accepted if possible)

Scenic attractions Near the B&B homes: Lake Michigan, Mc-
Cormick Place, Glencoe Botanic Garden, Ravinia Festival, Old
Town, Wrigley Field
Major Schools, Universities Near the B&B Homes: Northwest-
ern, Loyola, U. of Chicago, U. of Illinois at Chicago, DePaul

Best B&Bs

■ Studio apartment in Chicago, Illinois. This is an unhosted B&B in
a prime high-rise building complex which has its own restaurants,
dry cleaners, and grocery store. The air-conditioned apartment
has a double bed, sleeper sofa, TV, telephone, and a magnificent
skyline view. A self-serve continental breakfast is provided. You
can walk to business appointments, excellent shopping, and the
trendy art gallery district.

■ Apartment on the Magnificent Mile, Chicago, Illinois. This B&B
is in the heart of the city's premier shopping area, only a few
steps from the Water Tower Place. It's located in a luxury high-rise
and is furnished with antiques. The guest room has a single bed,
air conditioning, TV, telephone, and private attached bath. Your
host is a congenial semi-retired businessman who is active in
community affairs.

■ Old Town in Chicago, Illinois. Ever think of living in a garage? You may when you see the beautiful restoration job done by the current owner on a 1920s chauffeur's garage. A catwalk on the second level allows open space between the first and second floors. The home is furnished with antiques and features skylights, recessed lighting, Oriental rugs, and TV. You have a choice of two air-conditioned guest rooms, one with twin beds and the other with a double bed. Weather permitting, a continental breakfast is served in the garden. You are close to Lincoln Park and its famous zoo, the beach, and miles of lakefront.

MICHIGAN

———— B&B Reservation Services ————

BED & BREAKFAST IN MICHIGAN
P.O. BOX 1731, DEARBORN, MI 48121

Offers B&B Homes In: All over the state of Michigan, including the Upper Peninsula
Reservations Phone: 313/561-6041
Phone Hours: After 6 p.m. weekdays, or weekends
Price Range of Homes: $35 to $55 single, $40 to $80 double
Breakfast Included in Price: Some homes serve continental, but many offer a full breakfast, featuring special dishes. There is also a "Howell Festival" celebrating the Howell melons and hand-blended coffee in one of the homes.
Brochure Available: Free if you send a stamped, self-addressed no. 10 envelope
Reservations Should Be Made: 2 weeks in advance (last-minute reservations accepted if possible)

Scenic Attractions Near the B&B Homes: Henry Ford Museum, Greenfield Village, Fisher Theater, Cranbook Art Museum, Sleeping Bear Dunes National Park, Marshall Homes Tour, Meadow Brook Hall, Michigan Space Center, Ethnic Festivals Downtown Detroit, Grand Prix racing, Convention Center, Detroit Zoo, Irish Hills, resort areas
Major Schools, Universities Near the B&B Homes: U. of Michi-

gan, Michigan State, Wayne State, Albion, Cranbrook Schools, Oakland

Best B&Bs

- See their "50 Best B&Bs" winner in Part III.

- Farmhouse on the National Historic Register near Troy, Michigan. This home is 145 years old, and filled with antiques. After breakfast you can enjoy the walking trail along Paint Creek. Or on cooler days you may want to watch all the varieties of birds that gather at the feeder right outside the living room picture window. Home R-2.

- Estate home on the shore of a bay, Northport, Michigan. Every afternoon guests are served complimentary beverages in the Common Room with a bay window overlooking the water. You have a choice of four guest rooms. *Insider's Tip:* If you'd like some space, choose the suite with its own kitchen and private bath.

BED & BREAKFAST OF GRAND RAPIDS

455 COLLEGE AVE. SE, GRAND RAPIDS, MI 49503

Offers B&B Homes In: Heritage Hill Historic District in downtown Grand Rapids
Reservations Phone: 616/451-4849 or 616/459-7055
Phone Hours: 9 a.m. to 9 p.m. daily
Price Range of Homes: $45 single, $55 double
Breakfast Included in Price: Deluxe continental
Brochure Available: Free
Reservations Should Be Made: 2 weeks in advance (last-minute reservations accepted if possible)

Scenic Attractions Near the B&B Homes: Gerald R. Ford Museum, Holland Tulip Festival, Lake Michigan, Heritage Hill District
Major Schools, Universities Near the B&B Homes: Grand Rapids Junior College, Davenport Business College, Grand Valley State, Kendall School of Design, Calvin College

Best B&Bs

- Turn-of-the-century home in Grand Rapids, Michigan. Grand Rapids is world famous as a furniture manufacturer. When you stay in this grand house (known as the Barber House), you'll see much of his original Mission-style furniture in the main living areas. The living room has a copper-hooded fireplace and love seats.

Every sleeping room is extra-large. At night you can sink into one of those antique clawfoot bathtubs.

■ Victorian home in Grand Rapids, Michigan. This B&B is known as the Heald Lear House, and it's big! The 17 rooms with many decorative touches, such as a parquet floor in the foyer, leaded-glass windows, and a gurgling fountain in the solarium. Guests are welcome to relax in the living room or the library.

B&B Inns

WICKWOOD INN
510 BUTLER ST., SAUGATUCK, MI 49453

Reservations Phone: 616/857-1097
Description: An English country manor with several common rooms with Laura Ashley papers and fabrics and antiques, the inn has 11 air-conditioned rooms with private bath.
Amenities: Homemade coffee cake, fruit in season, coffee. Brunch is served on Sunday, and hot and cold hors d'oeuvres are served each night in the library bar.

Nearby Attractions: Cross-country ski area with 200 miles of mapped trails, charter fishing boats, two blocks from quaint Victorian Village
Special Services: "Our London taxi is at our door to drive guests to dinner or town." Crabtree & Evelyn soaps and shampoo are in each bath.
Rates: $80 to $115 double, May 1 to December 31; $65 to $100 January 1 to April 30

CLIFFORD LAKE HOTEL
561 CLIFFORD LAKE DR., STANTON, MI 48888

Reservations Phone: 517/831-5151
Description: A Michigan historic site overlooking Clifford Lake, the inn contains rooms in the hotel and cottages with two, three, and four bedrooms. The rooms are furnished with antiques, and have corner sinks and country furniture.
Amenities: Continental breakfast; complete food and beverage service

Nearby Attractions: Crystal Speedway, Morelands Moto-Cross, swimming, paddleboats, snowmobiles, fishing-boat rentals
Rates: $55 single, $65 double, in summer; $45 single, $55 double, in fall and winter

---

OHIO

B&B Reservation Services

COLUMBUS BED & BREAKFAST
769 S. 3RD ST., COLUMBUS, OH 43206

Offers B&B Homes In: Columbus, Ohio, area
Reservations Phone: 614/443-3680 or 614/444-8888
Phone Hours: 8 a.m. to 11 p.m. daily (closed in January)
Price Range of Homes: $35 single, $55 double
Breakfast Included in Price: Continental (juice, roll or toast, coffee)
Brochure Available: Free
Reservations Should Be Made: 2 weeks in advance (last-minute reservations accepted if possible)

Scenic Attractions Near the B&B Homes: German Village, restored residential area listed in the National Register
Major Schools, Universities Near the B&B Homes: Ohio State, Franklin, Denison, Otterbein, Kenyon, Capital

---

BUCKEYE BED & BREAKFAST
P.O. BOX 130, POWELL, OH 43065

Offers B&B Homes In: Akron, Athens, Belmont, Canton, Bethel, New Richmond, Tipp City, West Milton, Vandalia, Troy, Piqua, Poland, DeGraft, Peninsula, Port Clinton, Johnstown, Columbus, Cincinnati, Delaware, Cambridge, Spring Valley, Dublin, Muirfield, Westerville, Worthington, Marietta, Dayton, Logan, North Olmstead, and Seville, all in Ohio
Reservations Phone: 614/548-4555
Phone Hours: 24 hours daily

Price Range of Homes: $22 to $30 single, $30 to $65 double
Breakfast Included in Price: Some homes serve continental; others, full American. Many hosts who are gardeners and "nutrition-oriented" serve organically grown specialties.
Brochure Available: Free
Reservations Should Be Made: 10 days in advance (last-minute reservations accepted if possible)

Scenic Attractions Near the B&B Homes: Kings Island, Cincinnati Opera/Zoo, Ohio Historical Center, Muirfield Golf Course, Mound Builders' Sites, Little Brown Jug Harness Classic, Vandalia Trap Shoot, Marietta River Festival
Major Schools, Universities Near the B&B Homes: Ohio State, Ohio U., Ohio Wesleyan, Otterbien, Capital, Kenyon, Muckingum, Marietta, Wilmington, Wright State, U. of Cincinnati, Wittenberg, Concordia College, Antioch, U. of Dayton, Columbus Tech, Ohio Dominican

Best B&Bs

■ Manor house in Delaware, Ohio. Located just north of Columbus is a lovely old home known as Delaware Manor. Built in 1906, it offers a parlor crammed with books and games. Or you can play games outdoors under the maple trees. Mallets are available for croquet on the lawn. Breakfast is really special, with home-baked breads and muffins, Ohio honey, and maple syrup (with Ohio apple cider in season). *Insider's Tip:* Want to watch a great movie? *Out of Africa, The Wizard of Oz,* and *The Sound of Music,* among other classics, are available for guest showings on the VCR.

■ Rural home in Spring Valley, Ohio. The hosts of this B&B have traveled in Germany, France, and India—and the decorations reflect their purchases along the way. It's located between Dayton and Cincinnati in the rolling countryside of the Miami Valley. Many craft shops, antique stores, and fine restaurants are nearby. *Insider's Tip:* Visit neighboring Waynesville; your hosts call it an "antique browser's paradise."

---------- B&B Reservation Services ----------

BED & BREAKFAST GUEST HOMES
RTE. 2, ALGOMA, WI 54201

Offers B&B Homes In: Wisconsin, particularly Door County
Reservations Phone: 414/743-9742
Phone Hours: 7 a.m. to 9 p.m. daily
Price Range of Homes: $30 to $60 single, $40 to $80 double
Breakfast Included in Price: "Practically all hosts serve a gener-
ous full breakfast."
Brochure Available: Free if you send a stamped, self-addressed
no. 10 envelope
Reservations Should Be Made: Preferably 1 or more weeks in
advance (last-minute reservations filled if possible)

Scenic Attractions Near the B&B Homes: State parks, fishing,
villages, cherry orchards, farms, urban and rural settings

Best B&Bs

■ See their "50 Best B&Bs" winner in Part III.

■ Stone farmhouse in Mequon, Wisconsin. Only 20 miles north of
Milwaukee and centuries away in flavor. Each of the three guest
rooms is decorated in Early American antiques and reproduction
furniture.

■ Brick farmhouse in Manitowoc, Wisconsin. Great area for an
outdoors vacation—fishing, skiing, horseback riding. You have a
choice of four guest rooms. Your host is certainly an interesting
person. He builds sailboats and once studied to be a concert
pianist.

■ New home in Lake Delton, Wisconsin. This place was built
especially as a B&B, and is close to all the water activities of
Wisconsin Dells. Each of the four guest rooms has a private bath.
It is furnished not only with antiques but with an unusual collection
of old gas station memorabilia.

WISCONSIN SOUTHERN LAKES BED & BREAKFAST RESERVATION SERVICE
P.O. BOX 322, FONTANA-ON-GENEVA LAKE, WI 53125

Offers B&B Homes In: Southeastern Wisconsin, primarily Walworth County
Reservations Phone: 414/275-2266
Phone Hours: 3 to 10 p.m. daily
Price Range of Homes: $30 to $50 single, $40 to $60 double
Breakfast Included in Price: Full country-style breakfast of beverage, juice, fresh fruit, specialty, and meat. The specialty might be pineapple crêpes with sherry cream, creamed mushrooms on toast, buttermilk pancakes, or French toast; most hosts offer afternoon refreshments
Brochure Available: Free with stamped, self-addressed envelope
Reservations Should Be Made: 2 to 3 weeks in advance; last-minute reservations accepted if guaranteed with a credit card

Scenic Attractions Near the B&B Homes: Cruises, Yerkes Observatory, Outdoor Ethnic Museum, Clown Hall of Fame, Electric Railroad Museum, Southern Kettle Morraine State Forest
Major Schools, Universities Near the B&B Homes: Northwestern Military & Naval Academy in Fontana, Wisconsin School for the Deaf, George Williams College, U. of Wisconsin at Whitewater

Best B&Bs
▪ Emerald View House in the hills above Geneva Lake, Wisconsin. The home overlooks soft rolling hills and a golf course. The family suite is particularly spacious with a bedroom decorated with a country geese motif and a private bath. "Emerald Cream coffee is served at breakfast, along with fruit juice, seasonal fresh fruits, and specialties such as blueberry buttermilk pancakes with bacon, and ham and cheese blended into great scrambled eggs, and French toast with Canadian bacon." *Insider's Tip:* Be sure to see the rose garden. It recently won top honors from the local garden club.

▪ Small country home in Fontana, Wisconsin. This home is surrounded by gardens and sits right on a golf course. The hosts have visited many B&Bs in Europe, and guests benefit from their experience. Breakfast is definitely a gourmet affair. *Insider's Tip:* This is the B&B that serves pineapple crêpes—as described above.

BED & BREAKFAST OF MILWAUKEE, INC.
320 E. BUFFALO ST., WAUKESHA, WI 53202

Offers B&B Homes In: Milwaukee, and southeastern Wisconsin
Reservations Phone: 414/271-2337
Phone Hours: 9 a.m. to 7 p.m. Monday through Saturday
Price Range of Homes: $35 to $75 single, $45 to $85 double, up to $125 for deluxe suites
Breakfast Included in Price: Varies from hearty continental (fruit yogurt, granola) to full American, which might include Belgian waffles, herb and cheese omelets, or custard French toast
Brochure Available: Free if you send a stamped, self-addressed envelope
Reservations Should Be Made: 2 weeks in advance (last-minute reservations accepted if possible)

Scenic Attractions Near the B&B Homes: Botanical Gardens, Zoo, Grand Avenue Mall, Audubon Center, Lake Michigan, museums, city parks, ethnic restaurants, major-league baseball, symphony, ballet, repertory theater, Summerfest, ethnic festivals
Major Schools, Universities Near the B&B Homes: U. of Wisconsin, Marquette, Medical College of Wisconsin

Best B&Bs

■ See their "50 Best B&Bs" winner in Part III.

■ Penthouse in Milwaukee, Wisconsin. Right in the downtown area, with spectacular views of the city skyline and Lake Michigan. You can walk to downtown activities. There's a solarium with a large whirlpool spa, a roof garden, and deck. This secured building has a private elevator and heated indoor parking.

■ Tudor home in Milwaukee, Wisconsin. This B&B features leaded-glass windows and natural woodwork. The British hosts offer their special touch of a traditional B&B in America. The host is a language professor at the nearby university. The second-floor guest room has twin beds and a private bath.

─────────────────── **B&B Inns** ───────────────────

LOUE HOUSE

1111 S. MAIN ST., ALMA, WI 54610

Reservations Phone: 608/685-4923

Description: This Italianate house was designed by Charles Maybury in 1853 and is on the National Register of Historic Places. There are sinks in most rooms, and baths down the hall.

Amenities: Continental breakfast: "Help yourself—toast your own muffin."

Nearby Attractions: Beautiful swamp, canoeing, excellent fishing, tennis, and golf

Special Services: Coffee in rooms, fish-cleaning facilities, gas grill and picnic table

Rates: $16 single, $30 double

The Northwest & Great Plains

IDAHO

INDIAN CREEK GUEST RANCH
RTE. 2 (P.O. BOX 105), NORTH FORK, ID 83466

Reservations Phone: Ask the Salmon operator for 24F-211.
Description: The rustic main lodge with three cabins is hidden in a mountain valley. A fishing stream runs through the front yard.
Amenities: Juice, eggs, hotcakes, sausage, hash-browns, coffee or tea

Nearby Attractions: Ride on horseback to the old ghost town of Ulysses, the scenic Salmon River
Special Services: Pickups from the airport or from Salmon
Rates: $25 single, $50 double

SAWTOOTH HOTEL
P.O. BOX 52, STANLEY, ID 83278

Reservations Phone: 208/774-9947
Description: Each room is decorated with a lodgepole double bed and old-fashioned furnishings.
Amenities: Breakfast highlights include sourdough pancakes, cinnamon rolls, and country sausage.

Nearby Attractions: Sawtooth Recreation Area, Salmon River, Sawtooth National Fish Hatchery, rafting, field trips, horseback riding
Special Services: Will serve predawn breakfast and pack a lunch for day-trippers.
Rates: $20 to $25 single, $25 to $40 double

─────────── B&B Reservation Services ───────────

BED & BREAKFAST IN IOWA LTD.
P.O. BOX 430, PRESTON, IA 52069

Offers B&B In: Iowa
Reservations Phone: 319/689-4222
Phone Hours: Anytime in person or via an answering machine
Price Range of Homes: $25 to $50 single, $35 to $65 double
Breakfast Included in Price: Full, with Iowa breakfast specialties, or continental
Brochure Available: Send $1 for a directory of homes
Reservations Should Be Made: 2 weeks in advance; short notice also accepted by most homes when space is available

Scenic Attractions Near the B&B Homes: Iowa Great Lakes, historic homes, Iowa farms
Major Schools, Universities Near the B&B Homes: Drake, U. of Northern Iowa, Iowa State, U. of Iowa, Grand View

Best B&Bs ─────────────────────────────────

■ An 1854 brick home in Burlington, Iowa. Known as the Roads-Gardner House, this building is perched right at the top of Heritage Hill. It is furnished with antiques. *Insider's Tip:* One of the guest rooms has a marble fireplace. So does the library.

■ Edwardian mansion in Dubuque, Iowa. Looking for a romantic retreat? You may have found it. Each of the five guest rooms in this historic home is based on a different theme: travel, weddings, flowers. The flowered wallpaper and stained-glass windows will carry you back to a simpler time.

■ Working farm in Ogden, Iowa. Here's your chance to introduce your children to farmlife. You may want to visit Boone, about 20 miles away, birthplace of Mamie Eisenhower.

B&B Inns

THE REDSTONE INN
504 BLUFF, DUBUQUE, IA 52001

Reservations Phone: 319/582-1894
Description: This restored Victorian mansion is in the heart of the city and has undergone extensive renovations in the last few years. It is furnished in antiques, and has a plaster crown molding with gold-leaf cherubs in the parlor. The four double suites have whirlpool baths.
Amenities: Continental breakfast; with suites only, full valet and room service

Nearby Attractions: River rides, Woodward Riverboat Museum, the Fenelon Rivers Hall of Fame, arboretum, cross-country and downhill skiing
Special Services: Turn-down service and morning coffee
Rates: $60 to $140, double occupancy

STOUT HOUSE
1105 LOCUST, DUBUQUE, IA 52001

Reservations Phone: 319/582-1894
Description: Purchased in 1985 from the archdiocese of Dubuque, the house was built in the Richardsonian Romanesque style by lumber baron F.D. Stout. It is a massive red sandstone home with a hexagonal tower and stone archways, now an elegant accommodation for guests.
Amenities: Continental breakfast

Nearby Attractions: Dubuque Greyhound Park, National Rivers Hall of Fame, Fenelon Place Elevator, skiing
Special Services: Complimentary beverages
Rates: $65 to $80 double

B&B Inns

GUNFLINT LODGE
GT100, GRAND MARAIS, MN 55604

Reservations Phone: Toll free 800/328-3325, 800/328-3362 in Minnesota
Description: This rustic lodge and cottages are set in Minnesota's North Woods on a glacial lake surrounded by towering bluffs.
Amenities: Full breakfast

Nearby Attractions: Gunflint Trail, Boundary Waters Canoe Wilderness Area
Rates: $48 single, $96 double

MONTANA

B&B Reservation Services

BED & BREAKFAST WESTERN ADVENTURE
P.O. BOX 20972, BILLINGS, MT 59104

Offers B&B Homes In: Montana and Wyoming
Reservations Phone: 406/259-7993
Phone Hours: Weekdays from noon to 5 p.m. in winter, 9 a.m. to 5 p.m. in summer; answering machine always on
Price Range of Homes: $25 to $95, single and double
Breakfast Included in Price: "Full breakfast in 90% of the homes"; continental in others

Brochure Available: Free; directory available for $4.50
Reservations Should Be Made: 2 weeks in advance

Scenic Attractions Near the B&B Homes: Most are located in the Rocky Mountain range near Yellowstone and Glacier National Parks
Major Schools, Universities Near the B&B Homes: U. of Montana, Carroll College, Rocky Mountain College, U. of Wyoming
Scenic Attractions Near the B&B Homes: Most are located in the Rocky Mountain Range near Yellowstone and Glacier National Parks. Many are on the blue-ribbon trout streams and rivers for which the two states are famous. They are also located on ranches and in historic districts.
Major Schools, Universities Near the B&B Homes: U. of Montana, Montana State U., Carroll College, Rocky Mountain College, Eastern Montana College

Best B&Bs

■ See their "50 Best B&Bs" winner in Part III.

■ An 1875 Victorian home in Helena, Montana. This B&B is known as Sanders. It offers seven spacious guest rooms that have been restored to reflect turn-of-the-century living in the state's capital. All have private baths and are furnished with canopied beds, tiger oak armoires, clawfoot tubs, and many other of the original furnishings. This home is located within three blocks of the original Governor's Mansion, St. Helena's Cathedral, and the historic Last Chance Gulch. Says Paula Diegert, head of the reservation service, "Whenever I travel to Helena, I enjoy the company of these gracious and interesting hosts while entering a part of Montana's elegant history. It's an honor to recommend them as an exceptional bed-and-breakfast."

■ Lodge in Polson, Montana. Borchers of Finley Point is a B&B lodge located on the edge of Finley Point between Bootleggers Cover and Stavaston Bay on the shore of Flathead Lake. This is the largest natural freshwater lake west of the Mississippi. The huge living room features a ten-foot-long fireplace made from the local quarried rock, and an open beamed ceiling with hand-hewn timbers. Activities include water sports, visits to nearby museums, summer theater, and hiking in Glacier Park. *Insider's Tip:* This is a good area for viewing birds—everything from soaring osprey and eagles to hummingbirds.

—————————————— **B&B Inns** ——————————————

IZAAK WALTON INN
P.O. BOX 653, ESSEX, MT 59916

Reservations Phone: 406/888-5700
Description: Built in 1939 by the Great Northern Railway, the inn
  is now listed on the National Register of Historic Places. The
  inn's walls are lined with railroad pictures and memorabilia,
  and some rooms have private bath.

Nearby Attractions: Cross-country skiing, fishing, annual eagle
  migration, railfanning, Glacier National Park with the Bob
  Marshall and Great Bear Wilderness
Special Services: Sauna
Rates: $35 to $64 single, $40 to $69 double

FOXWOOD INN
P.O. BOX 404, WHITE SULPHUR SPRINGS, MT 59645

Reservations Phone: 406/547-3918
Description: The Foxwood Inn is a renovated 1890 Montana poor
  farm. Situated in the Smith River Valley between the Crazy
  Castle, Big Belt, and Little Belt Mountains, the inn has 28
  rooms.
Amenities: Breakfast is farm style, and consists of six to ten
  different foods each morning.

Nearby Attractions: Castle Museum, two ghost towns (Diamond
  City and Castle Town) the inn is located halfway between
  Glacier and Yellowstone National Parks.
Special Services: Fishing and floating guide service
Rates: $26 to $34 double

NORTH DAKOTA

B&B Reservation Services

OH WEST B&B
P.O. BOX 211, REGENT, ND 58650

Offers B&B Homes In: North Dakota
Reservations Phone: No phone listed
Price Range of Homes: $20 to $45 single, $25 to $50 double
Breakfast Included in Price: Full American breakfast, with specialties including Swedish and Ukrainian breads, and home-processed maple syrup
Brochure Available: Send a stamped, self-addressed envelope for a directory
Reservations Should Be Made: 2 weeks in advance

Scenic Attractions Near the B&B Homes: State and national parks, Badlands, State Capitol
Major Schools, Universities Near the B&B Homes: Minot State College, U. of North Dakota

OREGON

B&B Reservation Services

GALLUCCI HOSTS HOSTEL, BED & BREAKFAST
P.O. BOX 1303, LAKE OSWEGO, OR 97035

Offers B&B Homes In: Oregon
Reservations Phone: 503/636-6933
Phone Hours: 10 a.m. to 6 p.m. daily

Price Range of Homes: $12 to $35 single, $15 to $50 double
Breakfast Included in Price: Continental (juice, roll or toast, coffee)
Brochure Available: For a $1 fee, plus a stamped, self-addressed no. 10 envelope
Reservations Should Be Made: 3 days in advance (last-minute reservations accepted if possible)

Scenic Attractions Near the B&B Homes: Mount St. Helens, Fort Vancouver, state parks, zoos, historic homes

---

————————— **B&B Inns** —————————

THE AUBURN STREET COTTAGE
549 AUBURN ST., ASHLAND, OR 97520

Reservations Phone: 503/482-3004
Description: The inn is newly built in 1900s style, with separate cottages in a quiet garden setting. Each cottage contains a kitchenette (with microwave oven), skylights, and large windows, and sleeps four.

Nearby Attractions: Shakespeare Festival Theater, Britt Garden Music Festival, mountain lakes, many rafting rivers, Crater Lake Park, Oregon Caves
Rates: $66 double in summer, $56 double in winter

OREGON CAVES CHÂTEAU
20,000 CAVES HWY., CAVE JUNCTION, OR 97523

Reservations Phone: 503/592-3400
Description: This six-story structure (no elevator) was built in 1934 in rustic style. The rooms are comfortable, and the lobby is framed with fir timber, with two large marble fireplaces. There's also a campground.

Nearby Attractions: Redwood National Park, Crater Lake National Park, Illinois and Rogue Rivers
Special Services: Cave tours, hiking trails
Rates: $50 to $53 double

PARADISE RANCH INN
7000 MONUMENT DR., GRANTS PASS, OR 97526

Reservations Phone: 503/479-4333
Description: Set in the Rogue River Valley, the inn has comfortably furnished rooms and an indoor recreation center.

Nearby Attractions: Crater Lake, Oregon Caves, Ashland Shakespeare Theater, Peter Britt Music Festival, salmon and steelhead fishing, rafting on the Rogue River
Special Services: Heated pool and spa, lighted tennis courts, triangular golf, hot tub, recreational facility, mountain bikes, jogging trails, fishing
Rates: $69 to $84 single, $74 to $89 double, in summer; $44 to $54 single, $49 to $59 double, in winter

---

WASHINGTON

B&B Reservation Services

TRAVELLER'S BED & BREAKFAST
P.O. BOX 492, MERCER ISLAND, WA 98040

Offers B&B Homes In: Washington State, northern Oregon, and Vancouver and Victoria, British Columbia
Reservations Phone: 206/232-2345
Phone Hours: 8:30 a.m. to 4:30 p.m. Monday through Friday
Price Range of Homes: From $35 single, $45 to $120 double
Breakfast Included in Price: Varies; some may include regional and gourmet specialties
Brochure Available: Free; $6 for a descriptive directory with maps and photos
Reservations Should Be Made: As early as possible (last-minute reservations dealt with on an availability-only basis)

Scenic Attractions Near the B&B Homes: Mount Rainier National Park, Olympic National Park (includes Rain Forest), Mount St. Helens tours, San Juan Island, Snoqualmie Falls, North Cascades loop, Columbia River Gorge, Grand Coulee Dam, Lake Chelan, 1986 Expo site, Grouse Mountain, Provincial Museum, and Butchart Gardens in Victoria

Major Schools, Universities Near the B&B Homes: U. of Washington, Seattle College, Seattle Pacific College, U. of British Columbia

Best B&Bs

■ Tudor mansion in Seattle, Washington. You'll stay in a beautifully decorated suite with a private bath, your own deck, and a four-poster bed. Your hosts are avid travelers who fly their own plane. Breakfast is festive, even including champagne.

■ Cottage on Lake Washington, Washington. Here's a hideaway for privacy lovers. This two-bedroom B&B is completely self-contained with TV, telephone, and a well-stocked refrigerator for a make-your-own breakfast.

■ Mansion in Seattle, Washington. A millionaire lumber baron built this home, and it shows. There is extensive handcrafted woodwork throughout. The furniture is custom-made and dates back to the early 1900s. But there are some modern touches too—a spa room with Jacuzzi and sauna, and your choice of five bedrooms, all with private bath.

■ Hillside home in West Linn, Oregon. This B&B near Portland offers a spectacular view—the Tualitin River rushing through green hills. You can view this scenery through the high cathedral windows, from a willow swing on the lower level, and from an upper deck. The den on the lower floor is available to guests and offers TV/VCR and an old-movie collection. *Insider's Tip:* This is a great place for bird lovers/watchers. It's surrounded by bird feeders. You'll often see herons, mallards, geese, and hawks flying overhead. Home no. SP213.

■ Brick Colonial in Seattle, Washington. This house sits on top of Queen Anne Hill with a great view of Seattle, the water, and those wonderful mountains. It's surrounded by formal English gardens and only a short walk to bus lines and the Seattle Center. Each room has fine period furniture. On arrival you'll find fresh flowers and fruit in your room (much nicer than the typical motel room welcome). During the week, breakfast is self-catering. On weekends the hostess offers a great home-cooked breakfast. Home QA-3.

■ An 1890 Victorian home in Seattle, Washington. This is a true Victorian: stained-glass windows, original woodwork, fine refinished furniture. One writer/guest published this account in a national magazine: "The skylight view from the shower will make your spirits soar." Home CH-2.

PACIFIC BED & BREAKFAST
701 N.W. 60TH ST., SEATTLE, WA 98107

Offers B&B Homes In: Greater Metropolitan Seattle area and throughout the state of Washington, including Mount Rainier and the San Juan Islands; all of Oregon; also British Columbia, Canada
Reservations Phone: 206/784-0539
Phone Hours: 9 a.m. to 5 p.m. Monday through Friday
Price Range of Homes: $35 to $50 single, $40 to $85 double
Breakfast Included in Price: "Gourmet" continental or full American (homemade breads, muffins, and croissants a specialty)
Brochure Available: Free if you send a stamped, self-addressed no. 10 envelope (or $5 for the listing directory)
Reservations Should Be Made: 3 weeks in advance (last-minute reservations accepted if possible)

Scenic Attractions Near the B&B Homes: City and national parks, museums, theaters, opera house, ferry rides
Major Schools, Universities Near the B&B Homes: U. of Washington and more than eight other universities and colleges (inquire about a specific school when you call for reservations)

―――――――――――― **B&B Inns** ――――――――――――

HAUS ROHRBACH PENSION
12882 RANGER RD., LEAVENWORTH, WA 98826

Reservations Phone: 509/548-7024
Description: In the foothills of the Washington Cascades, the inn has ten comfortable rooms (six with private bath) and a separate chalet with kitchen and accommodations for six.

Amenities: In fine weather, breakfast and desserts are served on the deck.

Nearby Attractions: The Bavarian village of Leavenworth, skiing, tobogganing, sleigh rides
Special Services: Heated pool, hot tub
Rates: $50 to $70 single, $60 to $80 double; $98 for the chalet (no breakfast)

PALACE HOTEL
1004 WATER ST., PORT TOWNSEND, WA 98368

Reservations Phone: 206/385-0773 or toll free 800/962-0741 in Washington
Description: In this three-story restored Victorian building over-looking the harbor in historic downtown Port Townsend are 15 units, 12 with private bath, several with kitchens. Children are welcome. The hotel is listed on the National Historic Register.
Amenities: Continental breakfast

Nearby Attractions: Fort Worden State Park, biking, fishing, beachcombing, boating
Special Services: Coffee and tea in each room
Rates: $40 to $79 double in spring and summer, $36 to $72 double in fall and winter

The Southeastern States

B&B Reservation Services

BED & BREAKFAST BIRMINGHAM
P.O. BOX 43190, BIRMINGHAM, AL 35243

Offers B&B Homes In: Alabama
Reservations Phone: 205/933-2487
Phone Hours: 9 a.m. to 5 p.m. Monday through Friday
Price Range of Homes: $35 single to $75 double
Breakfast Included in Price: Continental
Brochure Available: Free.
Reservations Should Be Made: 2 weeks in advance with a $40
  deposit or VISA or MasterCard advance payment

Scenic Attractions Near the B&B Homes: Lakes, Space Center,
  historic sites
Major Schools, Universities Near the B&B Homes: Auburn U.,
  U. of Alabama at Birmingham

Best B&Bs

■ A-frame at the edge of Bankhead National Forest, Alabama.
This two-bedroom brick-and-wood home offers almost complete
privacy. It is hidden by a stand of pines and a high hedge and is
out of sight of the main house. There is a spacious great room in
the center of this A-frame with several conversation areas and a
large brick fireplace. Activities include picnics, hiking, and jogging. *Insider's Tip:* A half-mile jogging track winds around the
pasture. The backroads in this area are a good challenge for
cyclists.

■ An 1890 Methodist Parsonage, Prattville, Alabama. Located ten
miles north of Montgomery, this home is one of three former
Methodist parsonages located in the historic district of Prattville.
It's a one-story cottage of large proportions that served as a
residence for Methodist pastors from the early 1880s until 1935. It
is furnished with family heirlooms and furniture. The Miss Julia

Suite has its own private sitting room, bedroom, and bathroom. *Insider's Tip:* Good place to stay if you plan to visit the Shakespeare Theatre (only 20 minutes away).

BED & BREAKFAST MONTGOMERY
P.O. BOX 886, MILLBROOK, AL 36054

Offers B&B Homes In: Montgomery
Reservations Phone: 205/285-5421
Phone Hours: 7 a.m. to 9 p.m. daily
Price Range of Homes: $32 to $65 single, $40 to $75 double
Breakfast Included in Price: Continental (juice, roll or toast, coffee); hosts serve full breakfasts if guests desire, and at least two will serve dinner (for a fee) if requested
Brochure Available: Free
Reservations Should Be Made: 1 to 2 weeks in advance (last-minute reservations accepted if possible)

Scenic Attractions Near the B&B Homes: Montgomery, the capital and a pre—Civil War city on the Alabama River; many beautiful antebellum homes in nearby Lowndesboro; home of nationally famous Alabama Shakespeare Theater, first White House of the Confederacy
Major Schools, Universities Near the B&B Homes: Auburn, U. of Montgomery, Huntingdon College, Alabama State, Faulkner U.

Best B&Bs

■ "Red Bluff Cottage" in Montgomery, Alabama. This is a newly built home in one of the city's oldest historical districts, conveniently located to I-65, I-85, and downtown. Choice of four guest rooms with private baths. *Insider's Tip:* You can get a great view of the Alabama River from the deep upstairs porch.

■ Restored farmhouse near Montgomery, Alabama. The specialty of the house is a great breakfast. After breakfast you can take a walk by the red barn and take some pictures of the pastoral scenes.

■ A country contemporary near Montgomery, Alabama. Located on 60 acres, East Fork Farm offers four guest rooms and private entrances opening to a covered pool and terrace.

B&B Inns

THE MENTONE INN

P.O. BOX 284, MENTONE, AL 35984

Reservations Phone: 205/634-4836
Description: This rustic inn on top of Lookout Mountain offers 12 guest rooms. Rooms are furnished simply but comfortably. One of the popular activities is watching the sunset from the big front porch (there's a beautiful view of the valleys).
Amenities: Full breakfasts are served. The fare is varied and can include eggs, country ham, waffles (if there aren't too many guests), pancakes, and French toast.

Nearby Attractions: An old log church, St. Joseph's on the Mountain, DeSoto State Park and Falls, many antique shops
Rates: $40 single, $55 to $65 double (plus 7% room tax)

FLORIDA

B&B Reservation Services

BED & BREAKFAST OF THE FLORIDA KEYS, INC.

5 MAN-O-WAR DR., MARATHON, FL 33050

Offers B&B Homes In: The Florida Keys and along the east coast of Florida
Reservations Phone: 305/743-4118
Phone Hours: 8 a.m. to 5 p.m. Monday through Friday, on Saturday and Sunday to noon
Price Range of Homes: $40 to $50 single, $45 to $75 double
Breakfast Included in Price: Continental (juice, roll or toast, coffee) or full American; banana bread is one of the specials served
Brochure Available: Free
Reservations Should Be Made: 2 weeks in advance (last-minute reservations accepted if possible)

Scenic Attractions Near the B&B Homes: John Pennekamp State Park, Bahia Honda State Park, Theater of the Sea, Seven Mile Bridge

Major Schools, Universities Near the B&B Homes: Florida Atlantic U.

Best B&Bs

■ Home in the heart of the Keys, Florida. The room has a king-size bed, private bath, and its own private deck overlooking the ocean.

BED & BREAKFAST CO. TROPICAL FLORIDA
P.O. BOX 262, SOUTH MIAMI, FL 33243

Offers B&B Homes In: Florida (also the Caribbean and London)
Reservations Phone: 305/661-3270
Phone Hours: 9 a.m. to 5 p.m. Monday through Friday, plus an answering machine to 10 p.m. and on weekends
Price Range of Homes: $30 to $80; some guest houses higher
Breakfast Included in Price: Continental to full American
Brochure Available: Free with stamped, self-addressed envelope
Reservations Should Be Made: 2 weeks in advance (last-minute reservations accommodated when possible)

Scenic Attractions Near the B&B Homes: State parks of Florida, Everglades National Park, John Pennekamp Coral Reef State Park, Cape Canaveral, St. Augustine historic area, Orlando, state forests

Major Schools, Universities Near the B&B Homes: U. of Miami, Florida State U., U. of Southern Florida, Nova U.

Best B&Bs

■ Restored home in West Palm Beach, Florida. This B&B is located in the historic district of large homes formerly occupied by prosperous professionals. The floors and woodwork shine. You'll find interesting antiques all over this house, and attractive plantings (bougainvillea, palms) in the garden, grouped around a small swimming pool. *Insider's Tip:* The host is a former New Yorker who enjoys meeting and talking with people about travel, antiques, and gardening.

■ Oceanfront home on Summerland Key, Florida. What a nice place to relax—in a swimming pool or hot tub, with a view of the ocean. The home has an attractive garden. You're close to Bia

Honda State Park—"best sand swimming beach in the Keys." There is no beach in front of the house, but you can swim, fish, and snorkle from a private dock. *Insider's Tip:* Tell the hostess if you're on your honeymoon and she'll break out the champagne.

■ Mansion on a residential island in Biscayne Bay, Florida. From this home you're within a five-minute drive of Atlantic Ocean beaches and some excellent restaurants and shops. The home is decorated with mementos of the host family's world travels. The family is originally from Denmark. They are very interested in the arts and enjoy talking about plays, music, and ballet. When you break bread (homemade) with this hostess, she may also talk about another family passion, sailing.

BED & BREAKFAST REGISTRY
P.O. BOX 3025, PALM BEACH, FL 33480

Offers B&B Homes In: Palm Beach County
Reservations Phone: 407/842-5190
Phone Hours: Evenings and weekends
Price Range of Homes: $35 to $65, single and double
Breakfast Included in Price: Continental to full American
Brochure Available: Free
Reservations Should Be Made: As soon as possible

Scenic Attractions Near the B&B Homes: Lion Country Safari, Palm Beach Polo and Country Club, Worth Avenue in Palm Beach (renowned shopper's paradise)
Major Schools, Universities Near the B&B Homes: Florida Atlantic U., Palm Beach Jr. College

SUNCOAST ACCOMMODATIONS
8690 GULF BLVD., ST. PETERSBURG, FL 33706

Offers B&B Homes In: Florida, specializing in the Gulf Coast
Reservations Phone: 813/360-1753
Phone Hours: 9 a.m. to 10 p.m. daily
Price Range of Homes: $30 to $60 single, $45 to $80 double
Breakfast Included in Price: Continental (juice, roll or toast, coffee); "But a few hosts are gourmet cooks and enjoy whipping up a full, delicious breakfast"; many breakfasts are "Help yourself."

Brochure Available: Free for Florida ($3 for listings throughout the U.S. and foreign countries); send a stamped, self-addressed envelope
Reservations Should Be Made: 2 weeks to 1 month in advance (last-minute reservations accepted in the St. Petersburg area)

Scenic Attractions Near the B&B Homes: Walt Disney World, Sea World, Sunken Gardens, Dali Museum
Major Schools, Universities Near the B&B Homes: St. Petersburg Jr. College, Eckard College, U. of Florida, Tampa College, Stetson Law School, Bay Pines VA Hospital

Best B&Bs _____
▪ See their "50 Best B&Bs" winner in Part III.

A & A BED & BREAKFAST OF FLORIDA, INC.
P.O. BOX 1316, WINTER PARK, FL 32790

Offers B&B Homes In: Orlando, Winter Park, St. Augustine, Kissimmee, Longwood, Deland, Tampa, Fort Meyers, Del Ray Beach, Miami
Reservations Phone: 407/628-3233
Phone Hours: 9 a.m. to 6 p.m. Monday through Saturday
Price Range of Homes: $35 to $45 single, $45 to $65 double
Breakfast Included in Price: Most hosts provide full breakfast.
Brochure Available: Free, with samples
Reservations Should Be Made: In advance; deposits should be made before arrival.

Scenic Attractions Near the B&B Homes: Walt Disney World, EPCOT, Sea World, Kennedy Space Center, Busch Gardens
Major Schools, Universities Near the B&B Homes: U. of Central Florida, Rollins College, Stetson, Naval Training Center

Best B&Bs _____
▪ Victorian home in St. Augustine, Florida. Right in the heart of the historic district, this 1883 home is within one to four blocks of the waterfront and some excellent restaurants. The Victorian Porch is a good place to people-watch.

B&B Inns

CABBAGE KEY, INC.
P.O. BOX 200, PINELAND, FL 33945

Reservations Phone: 813/283-2278
Description: On a unique hideaway island, the main house was constructed in 1930 by novelist Mary Roberts Rinehart. There are rooms with private or shared bath, a suite for four, and three cottages.

Nearby Attractions: Intracoastal Waterway, the islands of Sanibel and Captiva, Fort Myers, fishing, sailing, water sports
Rates: $45 to $125 double

SEMINOLE COUNTRY INN
15885 WARFIELD BLVD. (P.O. BOX 625), INDIANTOWN, FL 33456

Reservations Phone: 407/597-3777
Description: The historic inn was built by the uncle of the Duchess of Windsor, and the lobby has an open fireplace, twin white staircases, pecky cypress ceilings, and brass chandeliers molded with the crest of royalty.

Nearby Attractions: Indiantown with its $1-million marina; the largest citrus grove in Florida, four miles away; Lake Okeechobee, less than ten miles from the inn
Special Services: Grass airfield, tennis courts, racquetball courts, 18-hole golf course, swimming pool, restaurant
Rates: $40 single, $45 to $60 double, in winter; $35 single, $40 to $55 double, in summer

---

B&B Reservation Services

ATLANTA HOSPITALITY—A B&B RESERVATION SERVICE

2472 LAUDERDALE DR. NE, ATLANTA, GA 30345

Offers B&B Homes In: Atlanta (Georgia), Massachusetts, Barbados (West Indies)
Reservations Phone: 404/493-1930
Phone Hours: 9 a.m. to 10 p.m. daily
Price Range of Homes: $20 to $30 single, $35 to $55 double
Breakfast Included in Price: Mostly continental, but may include grits and country ham, pecan rolls, red-eye gravy
Brochure Available: Free
Reservations Should Be Made: 2 weeks in advance (last-minute reservations accepted if possible)

Scenic Attractions Near the B&B Homes: Martin Luther King Memorial Site, High Museum, Stone Mountain Park, largest shopping mall in the Southeast
Major Schools, Universities Near the B&B Homes: Emory, Atlanta U., Mercer

Best B&Bs

■ Home near downtown Atlanta, Georgia. Each guest room has a private bath. You'll like talking with your hostess, a charming lady who is a professor of sociology at a local college. She has traveled extensively.

■ Home in northeast Atlanta, Georgia. This B&B is about 35 minutes by car from downtown Atlanta. You reach the house via a long winding driveway flanked by beautiful landscaping. A collie may greet you on arrival. The guest room has a private bath and a private entrance.

BED & BREAKFAST ATLANTA
1801 PIEDMONT AVE. NE, ATLANTA, GA 30324

Offers B&B Homes In: Metropolitan Atlanta, Stone Mountain, Marietta, Decatur, Roswell, McDonough, Smyrna, and other retreat areas around the state
Reservations Phone: 404/875-0525
Phone Hours: 9 a.m. to noon and 2 to 5 p.m. Monday through Friday
Price Range of Homes: $32 to $70 double; $48 to $100 double for guesthouses, suites, condominiums, and B&B inns; monthly rates starting at $750
Breakfast Included in Price: Continental or full American; southern breakfasts sometimes served at the discretion of the individual hosts
Brochure Available: Free if you send a stamped, self-addressed no. 10 envelope
Reservations Should Be Made: 2 weeks or more in advance (last-minute reservations accepted on a space-available basis)

Scenic Attractions Near the B&B Homes: Stone Mountain, Cyclorama, Civil War monuments, World Congress Center, the High Museum of Art, Six Flags, Atlanta Historical Society
Major Schools, Universities Near the B&B Homes: Emory, Georgia Institute of Technology, Atlanta U., Oglethorpe, Georgia State, Agnes Scott

Best B&Bs

▪ See their "50 Best B&Bs" winner in Part III.

▪ Contemporary home in Atlanta, Georgia. This house is convenient to Atlanta-Emory University, Executive Park, and the Fernbank Science Center. Your hosts are a real estate appraiser and his teenage son. Two guest rooms are available, each with a private bath. *Insider's Tip:* For more room, ask for the Master Suite. You get a huge bedroom with a king-size bed, a dressing area, and a spacious bath. Your balcony overlooks the private pool on the rear terrace. There is a phone and TV in every room. Guests are welcome to use the pool and the sauna.

▪ Guesthouse in Atlanta, Georgia. Located behind the home of the owners in northwest Atlanta, this cottage is a self-contained B&B in the woods. It's furnished with a sleep sofa, chairs, desk, and a refrigerator stocked with breakfast treats for a self-catered breakfast. The cottage is also air-conditioned and equipped with telephone and TV. *Insider's Tip:* For good ideas on what to see, talk with your host—he's the editor of a local tourist publication.

■ Home in Atlanta, Georgia. This B&B is close to Virginia Highland, downtown Atlanta, and Piedmont Park. Many trendsetters have bought homes in this older neighborhood which is filled with good restaurants, shops, and galleries. The guest room features a queen-size bed and a huge walk-in closet. Your host is an avid music lover and world traveler.

R.S.V.P. SAVANNAH BED & BREAKFAST RESERVATION SERVICE
417 E. CHARLTON ST., SAVANNAH, GA 31401

Offers B&B Homes In: Historic Savannah, Tybee Island, St. Simons Island, Brunswick, in Georgia; Historic Charleston, Beaufort, Daufuski Island, South Carolina
Reservations Phone: 912/232-7787
Phone Hours: 9 a.m. to 5 p.m. weekdays and most weekends
Price Range of Homes: $50 to $175 per room
Breakfast Included in Price: Provided in many different ways: sit-down, tray service in room, guests self-serve in their own kitchens
Brochure Available: Free
Reservations Should Be Made: As far in advance as possible. Minimum one-night's deposit required with all reservations. Personal checks and traveler's checks preferred; some credit cards accepted.

Scenic Attractions Near the B&B Homes: National Historic Districts, Atlantic Ocean and coastline, barrier islands along the Intra-Coastal Waterway
Major Schools, Universities Near the B&B Homes: College of Art and Design, Armstrong State College, Savannah State College, The Citadel, The College of Charleston

Best B&Bs
■ Brick town house in Savannah, Georgia. Built in 1854, this elegant home has antique furnishings. Did you ever hear harp music at breakfast? You may well at this B&B. The hostess is a famous concert harpist, and she enjoys playing for guests.

■ Town house in the Central Savannah Historic District. You can have a complete suite of rooms in this 1872 home. A family could occupy two bedrooms, a living room with working fireplace, and a full country kitchen. Breakfast is in the refrigerator and you fix your own. If the house looks familiar, you may have seen it featured in various national magazines.

QUAIL COUNTRY BED & BREAKFAST, LTD.
1104 OLD MONTICELLO RD., THOMASVILLE, GA 31792

Offers B&B Homes In: Thomasville, Georgia (city and country)
Reservations Phone: 912/226-7218 or 912/226-6882
Phone Hours: 8 a.m. to 10 p.m. daily
Price Range of Homes: $30 to $40 single, $40 to $50 double
Breakfast Included in Price: Continental (juice, roll or toast, coffee)
Brochure Available: Free if you send a stamped, self-addressed no. 10 envelope
Reservations Should Be Made: 1 week in advance (last-minute reservations accepted if possible)

Best B&Bs

■ Neoclassical home in Thomasville, Georgia. Located in pecan groves, this house has large columns on three sides. Each bedroom has its own bath and fireplace. The floors throughout are heart of pine and the rooms are furnished with antiques.

■ Williamsburg-style guesthouse in Thomasville, Georgia. Take a trip back to the 18th century as you walk through this B&B's garden and dependencies (early buildings constructed to provide services to the main house). Guests are welcome to use the swimming pool.

■ A 100-year-old farmhouse in Thomasville, Georgia. It's furnished with antiques and wicker, and located amid 20 acres of scenic woods across from the country club and just minutes from downtown. The private upstairs wing has a sitting area with three bedrooms and two baths.

B&B Inns

THE SMITH HOUSE, INC.
202 S. CHESTATEE ST., DAHLONEGA, GA 30533

Reservations Phone: 404/864-3566
Description: This 100-year-old home has rooms with color-coordinated furnishings, tile baths, and wide porches with rockers.

Nearby Attractions: Amicalola DeSoto Falls, Vogel State Park, Dockery Lake, the Gold Museum, rafting, canoeing, tennis, panning for gold
Special Services: Air conditioning, cable TV
Rates: $30 to $75 per room

LAKE RABUN HOTEL
LAKE RABUN ROAD (RTE. 1, BOX 2090), LAKEMONT, GA 30552

Reservations Phone: 404/782-4946
Description: This rustic hotel is built of wood and stone, the lobby furnished in handmade rhododendron and mountain laurel furniture. It's across the street from one of Georgia's most beautiful lakes.
Amenities: Self-serve continental breakfast

Nearby Attractions: Chattahoochee National Forest, Dahlonega Gold Museum, Anna Ruby Falls
Rates: $28 single, $36 double

SUSINA PLANTATION INN
RTE. 3 (P.O. BOX 1010), THOMASVILLE, GA 31792

Reservations Phone: 912/377-9644
Description: This antebellum mansion built in the Greek Revival style was the plantation house for a cotton farmer who employed 100 slaves. This gracious inn still has 115 acres of lawns and woodlands as an attractive setting. There are eight bedroom suites for guests.
Amenities: Full breakfast and dinner with wine included

Nearby Attractions: Pebble Hill Historic Plantation House, Annual Arts and Crafts Fair, Rose Test Gardens
Special Services: Swimming pool, tennis court, stocked fish pond, jogging trails, conference rooms, screened veranda
Rates: $100 single, $150 double

────────── B&B Reservation Services ──────────

OHIO VALLEY BED & BREAKFAST
6876 TAYLOR MILL RD., INDEPENDENCE, KY 41051

Offers B&B Homes In: Southern Ohio, southeastern Indiana, and northern Kentucky
Reservations Phone: 606/356-7865
Phone Hours: 9 a.m. to 9 p.m. Monday through Friday; answering machine at other times
Price Range of Homes: $30 to $40 single, $35 to $60 double
Breakfast Included in Price: Continental (juice, roll or toast, coffee), full American (juice, eggs, bacon, toast, coffee), and homemade breads, biscuits, yogurt
Brochure Available: Free if you send a stamped, self-addressed envelope
Reservations Should Be Made: 2 weeks in advance (last-minute reservations accepted if possible)

Scenic Attractions Near the B&B Homes: Major-league sports, zoo, Kings Island Park, College Football Hall of Fame, symphony, opera, ballet, repertory theater, state parks, recreational lakes
Major Schools, Universities Near the B&B Homes: U. of Cincinnati, Northern Kentucky, Xavier, Mount St. Joseph, Thomas More

Best B&Bs ──────────────────────────────

■ See their "50 Best B&Bs" winner in Part III.

■ Restored farmhouse in Lebanon, Ohio. Close to Cincinnati, "White Tor" B&B was built during the Civil War. It overlooks the Miami River Valley. The private suite includes a private bath and a guest room with a queen-size bed, and a private sitting room with a daybed and a trundle bed. A full breakfast is served. When you stay here you'll be close to King's Island, Caesar Creek State Park, and many antique stores.

■ Gregorian country home in Batesville, Indiana. Known as the Beechwood Inn, this B&B features three wood-burning fireplaces and some original Romweber custom-made furniture. The two-story home high atop a hill is in the heart of historic southern Indiana. A buffet breakfast is served in the dining room or on the outside brick terrace. *Insider's Tip:* Some of Indiana's most famous fishing spots are nearby.

■ Restored farmhouse in New Richmond, Ohio. Natural surroundings: pond, wildlife, sheep. Private suite available. It includes a private bath and sitting room with TV and a fireplace. Breakfast is big—seven courses—and served on the outside patio or in the cozy kitchen. The hostess will make reservations for nearby restaurants and attractions.

BLUEGRASS BED & BREAKFAST
RTE. 1, BOX 263, VERSAILLES, KY 40383

Offers B&B Homes In: Central Kentucky (Lexington)
Reservations Phone: 606/873-3208
Phone Hours: 8 a.m. to 8 p.m. daily
Price Range of Homes: $40 to $80 double
Breakfast Included in Price: Full American (juice, eggs, bacon, toast, coffee)
Brochure Available: Free
Reservations Should Be Made: 2 weeks in advance (last-minute reservations discouraged)

Scenic Attractions Near the B&B Homes: Kentucky Horse Park, Mary Todd Lincoln House, Mammoth Cave, Lake Cumberland, Henry Clay's home, Shakertown
Major Schools, Universities Near the B&B Homes: U. of Kentucky, Transylvania U.

Best B&Bs
■ See their "50 Best B&Bs" winner in Part III.

■ An 1829 home (Peacham) near Lexington, Kentucky. Count 'em, nine fireplaces in this charming old home. The brick that built this B&B was fired right on the farm. The private first-floor suite includes a living room, bedroom, and private bath. The second-floor room has twin beds and a private bath.

■ Artist's studio near Lexington, Kentucky. Polly Place has been described as a "dream studio—beautiful, comfortable, yet with touches of whimsy." The first level is one great room oriented around a huge fireplace. Above are open balconied bedrooms and bath with Jacuzzi. The studio itself was built on a shaded knoll on a 200-acre farm. Four people can sleep here comfortably, "six in a pinch." The whole place can be taken over by couples traveling together or a family.

MISSISSIPPI

—————— B&B Reservation Services ——————

LINCOLN LTD. BED & BREAKFAST; MISSISSIPPI RESERVATION SERVICE
P.O. BOX 3479, MERIDIAN, MS 39303

Offers B&B Homes In: The whole state of Mississippi, from Holly Springs in the north to Pass Christian in the south
Reservations Phone: 601/482-5483
Phone Hours: 8:30 a.m. to 4:30 p.m. Monday through Friday, and also Saturday mornings (answering service on weekends)
Price Range of Homes: $45 to $95 single, $45 to $150 double
Breakfast Included in Price: Full American (juice, eggs, bacon, toast, coffee), served simply or elegantly according to guest's preference
Brochure Available: Free; host list available for $3
Reservations Should Be Made: 1 or 2 weeks in advance (no last-minute reservations accepted)

Scenic Attractions Near the B&B Homes: National Civil War Park and historic homes in Vicksburg, Natchez, Jackson State Capitol, Columbus Pilgrimage, Holly Springs Pilgrimage, William Faulkner home in Oxford, Jimmy Rodgers Festival, Meridian, Natchez Trace Parkway
Major Schools, Universities Near the B&B Homes: U. of Mississippi at Oxford, Mississippi State, Millsaps, Mississippi College, Mississippi U. for Women, Belhaven

Best B&Bs

- See their "50 Best B&Bs" winner in Part III.

- Victorian home in Aberdeen, Mississippi. High on a hill over-looking the Tombigbee River is one of the outstanding examples of Victorian architecture in Mississippi. The home is filled with antiques and is decorated in a style typical of the Victorian period: an 1840s square grand piano, a stereoscope with a stack of cards, beautiful woodwork. Home Aberdeen no. 43.

- Small cottage in historic Natchez, Mississippi. The cottage has a skylight vaulted ceiling and heart-of-pine floors. There's a fireplace for warmth and romance. The small kitchen is stocked with the ingredients for a do-it-yourself breakfast. The hosts have traveled widely and speak Japanese, German, and French. Home Natchez no. 31.

TENNESSEE

B&B Reservation Services

BED & BREAKFAST IN MEMPHIS
P.O. BOX 41621, MEMPHIS, TN 38174

Offers B&B Homes In: Memphis, Nashville, New Orleans, and other areas of the South
Reservations Phone: 901/726-5920
Phone Hours: 8 a.m. to 6 p.m. Monday through Friday, 1 to 4 p.m. on Saturday, 2 to 6 p.m. on Sunday
Price Range of Homes: $26 to $55 and up single, $32 to $55 and up double; weekly and monthly rates available
Breakfast Included in Price: Continental, though a few hosts serve a full American breakfast; specialties include blueberry muffins, homemade jams, and grits
Brochure Available: Free if you send a stamped, self-addressed no. 10 envelope
Reservations Should Be Made: 2 weeks in advance, 3 weeks or more from April through November (last-minute reservations can sometimes be accepted)

Scenic Attractions Near the B&B Homes: Mud Island, famous Beale Street, Victorian Village, Pink Palace Museum of Natural History, Memphis Convention Center, Dixon Gallery and Gardens, Graceland

Major Schools, Universities Near the B&B Homes: Rhodes College, U. of Tennessee Medical School, Memphis State, U. of Mississippi

Best B&Bs

■ Contemporary two-bedroom apartment in Memphis, Tennessee. This B&B is unhosted. You will have plenty of things to do. The reservation service waxes poetic: "Wake up to the mighty Mississippi. Save spectacular sunsets from your balcony on the river." The apartment is furnished with elegant country English items. You have a choice of pools indoor and out, and tennis and racquetball courts. You can walk to great restaurants and jazz on Beale Street. B&B no. D-0303.

■ Lakeside cottage near Grand Junction, Tennessee. About 80 miles east of Memphis. The sleeping alcove overlooks the lake. There is a wood-burning stove for chilly fall days, and a spacious galley kitchen. *Insider's Tip:* Stay here for a month and you can get a very special rate, just $21.75 per night for one or two people.

■ Modern condominium in Memphis, Tennessee. Located on the bluff overlooking the Mississippi River. You'll have great views of the river from the plant-filled patio. The skylighted guest room has a queen-size bed.

BED AND BREAKFAST HOST HOMES OF TENNESSEE
P.O. BOX 110227, NASHVILLE, TN 37222

Offers B&B Homes In: Throughout Tennessee, including Memphis, Nashville, Knoxville, and Chattanooga
Reservations Phone: 615/331-5244
Phone Hours: 9 a.m. to 5 p.m. Monday through Friday (answering machine available other times)
Price Range of Homes: $28 to $75 single, $38 to $120 double
Breakfast Included in Price: Continental plus
Brochure Available: $2
Reservations Should Be Made: 2 weeks in advance (for written confirmation); immediately by telephone

Scenic Attractions Near the B&B Homes: All the state parks, lakes, and hunting areas in the state, Opryland

Major Schools, Universities Near the B&B Homes: Vanderbilt, Austin Peay, Memphis State

Best B&Bs

▪ Restored church in West Nashville, Tennessee. A suite is available with an antique double bed with sitting area and private bath. Another guest room offers a Louis XIV double bed with private bath. A contemporary loft can sleep four, and has the added plus of a Jacuzzi.

The Southwest & South-Central Area

ARKANSAS

B&B Reservation Services

BED AND BREAKFAST RESERVATION SERVICES AND TOURIST ACCOMMODATIONS
11 SINGLETON, EUREKA SPRINGS, AR 72632

Offers B&B Homes In: Eureka Springs and northwestern Arkansas
Reservations Phone: 501/253-9111
Phone Hours: 24 hours daily
Price Range of Homes: $45 to $125
Breakfast Included in Price: Continental to full American
Brochure Available: In progress
Reservations Should Be Made: As early as possible (last-minute reservations accepted if possible)

Scenic Attractions Near the B&B Homes: The Pasion Plan, Thorncrown Chapel, Miles Musical Museum, Silver Dollar City
Major Schools, Universities Near the B&B Homes: U. of Arkansas

Best B&Bs

■ Restored Victorian in Eureka Springs, Arkansas. This is described as "an old-fashioned place with a touch of magic." It's located in the historic district, and decorated with a whimsical collection of items. The guest rooms have ceiling fans and handmade quilts on antique brass-and-iron bedsteads. Breakfast is served on the balcony overlooking a garden. *Insider's Tip:* Take a closer look at this garden. It has wildflowers, curious birdhouses, and a lily-filled fish pond.

ARKANSAS & OZARKS BED & BREAKFAST
RTE. 1, BOX 38, CALICO ROCK, AR 72519

Offers B&B Homes In: Batesville, Calico Rock, Des Arc, Eureka Springs, Fayetteville, Fort Smith, Mountain View, Norfork, Rogers, and Yellville (all in Arkansas)

Reservations Phone: 501/297-8211 days, 501/297-8764 evenings

Phone Hours: 9 a.m. to 5 p.m. and evenings Monday through Saturday

Price Range of Homes: $28 to $50 single, $30 to $65 double

Breakfast Included in Price: Continental to full American, many serving lavish spreads

Brochure Available: Free if you send a stamped, self-addressed envelope

Reservations Should Be Made: As much in advance as possible; $20 deposit

Scenic Attractions Near the B&B Homes: Blanchard Caverns, Ozark National Forest, White River

Major Schools, Universities Near the B&B Homes: Arkansas College, U. of Arkansas

Best B&Bs

■ Log cabins in Calico Rock, Arkansas. You may feel a little like a pioneer gone soft with modern comforts. Each cabin has a sleeping loft which sleeps two, plus a main sleeping area with a hide-a-bed or double bed, kitchen, bath (showers only), and a fireplace or stove. You have to fix your own breakfast, but all the fixings—cereal, homemade fruit bread, milk, coffee—are in the cabin. *Insider's Tip:* Save some time just to sit on the front porch. You will have either a panoramic view of the river or of the woods. Host no. ACR02.

■ Colonial Revival home in Des Arc, Arkansas. This unusual home, recorded on the National Register of Historical Places, is halfway between Memphis and Little Rock. Nearby are wildlife management areas and lakes. *Insider's Tip:* Like to talk about science? The host is a retired petroleum engineer; the hostess, a retired science teacher. Even the breakfast is scientific, healthful, and (on request) made to accommodate special dietary needs. Host no. ADA01.

■ Country home in Calico Rock, Arkansas. High on a 500-foot bluff overlooking the spectacular White River. The three-manual organ in the living room is available to musical guests. The host is a retired marine officer who can arrange trout fishing and river float trips. Host no. ACR01.

—————————— B&B Inns ——————————

THE GREAT SOUTHERN HOTEL
127 W. CEDAR, BRINKLEY, AR 72021

Reservations Phone: 501/734-4955
Description: The three-story brick hotel has 61 rooms with baths,
  mosaic-tile floors, and pressed-tin patterned ceilings 15 feet
  tall. Restored in a turn-of-the-century style, the bedrooms have
  antique double beds and furnishings. The ground-floor rooms
  have ceiling fans, air conditioning, and cable TV.
Amenities: Continental breakfast

Nearby Attractions: Louisiana State Park, Mississippi Fly Way
Special Services: Airport pickup
Rates: $37.75 to $42.50 double

COLORADO

—————— B&B Reservation Services ——————

BED & BREAKFAST COLORADO, LTD.
P.O. BOX 6061 BOULDER, CO 80306

Offers B&B Homes In: Throughout Colorado
Reservations Phone: 303/494-4994
Phone Hours: 8:30 a.m. to 5 p.m. Monday through Friday
  (closed Saturday, Sunday, and major holidays)
Price Range of Homes: $30 to $55 single, $40 to $95 double
Breakfast Included in Price: Continental or full American (juice,
  eggs, bacon, toast, coffee); breakfasts vary with each home:
  some may offer continental during the week with full breakfast
  on weekends; special diets accommodated
Brochure Available: Free; directory costs $2.

Reservations Should Be Made: 2 weeks in advance (last-minute reservations accepted if possible, but no placements after sundown); $5 add-on for one-night stays

Scenic Attractions Near the B&B Homes: Rocky Mountain National Park, Coors International Bicycle Race, Shakespeare Festival, World Affairs Conference, skiing, all mountain areas
Major Schools, Universities Near the B&B Homes: U. of Colorado, Naropa Institute, U. of Denver, Colorado College of Mines

Best B&Bs

■ A 1902 Victorian in Colorado Springs, Colorado. Each of the guest rooms here is named after an early Colorado mining town—Cripple Creek, Leadville, and Silverton. All are decorated with heirloom quilts and antiques. Historic "Old Colorado City" is only minutes away. *Insider's Tip:* Stay for Sunday breakfast. It's a treat served with champagne.

■ William's Fork Ranch in Hot Sulphur Springs, Colorado. If you want a secluded place, this could be it. The ranch is located 4½ miles from the nearest paved road and borders the Arapahoe National Forest. This is one of the state's premier fishing areas. When you want to go cross-country skiing in the winter, you just step into your skis right outside the door. You'll sleep in a cabin with a queen-size bed and one bunk. Shower only. The owners add a rather whimsical touch to their invitation: "Horses and llamas welcome."

BED & BREAKFAST ROCKY MOUNTAINS
P.O. BOX 804, COLORADO SPRINGS, CO 80901

Offers B&B Homes In: Colorado, New Mexico, Utah
Reservations Phone: 719/630-3433
Phone Hours: 9 a.m. to 5 p.m. in summer, or noon to 5 p.m. in winter, Monday through Friday
Price Range of Homes: $30 to $68 single, $35 to $125 double
Breakfast Included in Price: Over half the hosts serve a full American breakfast, often including homemade delicacies.
Brochure Available: Free; descriptive directory updated quarterly listing 100 approved B&B homes and inns costs $4.50; an annual subscription is $9.50.
Reservations Should Be Made: 2 weeks in advance to avoid

special booking fees; MasterCard and VISA accepted on last-minute bookings only

Scenic Attractions Near the B&B Homes: National forests, 30 state parks, skiing, hiking, gold panning, white-water rafting, ballooning, snowmobiling, horseback riding, Jeep tours, sleigh rides, hay rides, fishing, 53 mountain peaks over 24,000 feet high, ghost towns, and mining towns

Major Schools, Universities Near the B&B Homes: Colorado State U., Colorado College, Colorado School of Mines, U. of Colorado, U. of Denver, Colorado Mountain College, U.S. Air Force Academy; and all universities in northern New Mexico and Utah

Best B&Bs

■ See their "50 Best B&Bs" winner in Part III.

■ A 200-year-old adobe hacienda in Taos, New Mexico. An elegant location with wonderful amenities: a king-size bed, a hot tub in your room for bubbling yourself under a skylight, with a fireplace in the room (four out of the five guest rooms have fireplaces). *Insider's Tip:* The hosts are semi-retired award-winning restaurateurs—so you can expect some great breakfasts.

■ Tudor mansion in Colorado Springs, Colorado. Located in the historic district of the city, this B&B is beautifully landscaped with half-century-old spruce trees and native wildflowers. The sunporch has great views of the Cheyenne Mountain. The library has a fireplace, TV, and railroad memorabilia. The host enjoys gourmet cooking, fishing, and traveling. Two nights minimum.

BED & BREAKFAST VAIL VALLEY
P.O. 491, VAIL, CO 81658

Offers B&B Homes In: Vail/Beaver Creek, Aspen, Steamboat, Summit County, Breckenridge and Keystone, and Copper Mountain ski areas
Reservations Phone: 303/949-1212
Phone Hours: 9 a.m. to 5 p.m. Monday through Friday; answering machine other times
Price Range of Homes: $45 to $55 single, $65 and up double, in winter; $35 and up single, $45 and up double, in summer
Breakfast Included in Price: Continental or full American, specialties available at most homes
Brochure Available: $2

Reservations Should Be Made: As far in advance as possible, especially for winter holidays (last-minute reservations honored subject to availability)

Scenic Attractions Near the B&B Homes: Vail and Beaver Creek ski areas with annual average snowfall of 300 to 350 inches, ten square miles of skiing terrain

Best B&Bs

■ Private home in East Vail, Colorado. The hosts live upstairs in this mountain hideaway known as Cotton Falls. You can join them in the morning for such house specialties as eggs Benedict. You are located on a free bus route that takes you to ski areas. You will enjoy such nice touches as a rock fireplace and a private entrance.

■ Private home in Frisco, Colorado. The amenities include a delightful summer breakfast served by a backyard creek. It should be quite a treat—the hostess is a local baker. On cold winter days after a day on the ski slopes, you can come home to an inside hot tub in the atrium. It is on a bike path. A free shuttle bus will take you to the nearby ski areas.

B&B Inns

TIPPLE INN
747 S. GALENA ST., ASPEN, CO 81611

Reservations Phone: Toll free 800/321-7025
Description: This small, cozy inn is located in downtown Aspen at the base of Aspen Mountain, near the gondola and between the two chair lifts. The building is built out of heavy timber from an old Aspen silver mine. The studio or two-bedroom apartments have a fully equipped kitchen and TV, and in most apartments, a fireplace.

Nearby Attractions: Aspen Highlands, Snowmass, and Buttermilk
Special Services: Redwood hot tub, daily maid service, cable color TV
Rates: $140 to $185 double in February and March, $90 to $125 double in December, January, and April

FIRESIDE INN
114 FRENCH ST. (P.O. BOX 2252), BRECKENRIDGE, CO 80424

Reservations Phone: 303/453-6456
Description: The accommodations at this Victorian inn range from dormitory space to private rooms and even a private suite. All are tastefully decorated and comfortable

Nearby Attractions: Ski area
Special Services: Hot tub, free shuttle to town and ski areas
Rates: $17 in a dorm, $52 double, in fall and winter; $10 in a dorm, $29 double, in spring and summer

THE HOME RANCH
P.O. BOX 822FB, CLARK, CO 80428

Reservations Phone: 303/879-1780
Description: This small guest ranch is located in the mountains of northwestern Colorado. The seven cabins range from a studio to a two-bedroom/two-bath with a living room. They are furnished with antiques and original wall hangings, with down comforters on the beds. Outside on the porch stands your own private spa.
Amenities: The full breakfast is served family style in the lodge dining room. Three meals a day are included in the rates.

Nearby Attractions: Mount Zirkel Wilderness Area, Steamboat and Pearl Lakes State Parks, Continental Divide, horseback riding (the specialty here, and lots of it), fishing, bathing, boating, hiking
Special Services: Airport pickup, heated pool, hot tub and sauna, coffee maker and refrigerator stocked with cheeses, crackers, and homemade cookies
Rates: $175 single, $325 double

PURPLE MOUNTAIN LODGE

714 GOTHIC AVE. (P.O. BOX 897), CRESTED BUTTE, CO 81224

Reservations Phone: 303/349-5888

Description: This small lodge with six guest rooms and two shared baths has a view of the ski mountain and surrounding peaks.

Amenities: Full breakfast during the ski season

Nearby Attractions: Crested Butte is a National Historic Town full of interesting buildings, shops, and restaurants.

Special Services: Free shuttle bus, package ski rates available

Rates: $44 double

THE ASPEN LODGE

LONGS PEAK ROUTE, ESTES PARK, CO 80517

Reservations Phone: 303/586-8133, or toll free 800/332-MTNS

Description: This handcrafted log lodge has 36 rooms, individual cabins, and a separate dining facility with three meals a day included in the rate.

Amenities: Breakfast featuring homemade sweet rolls and huevos rancheros

Nearby Attractions: Rocky Mountain National Park, Estes Park, Hidden Valley ski area

Special Services: Racquetball, horseback riding, tennis, skiing, fishing, snowmobiling, heated pool, sleigh and hay rides

Rates: $80 per person per day in summer, $60 to $80 per double room in winter

KANSAS

────────── B&B Reservation Services ──────────

BED & BREAKFAST KANSAS CITY

P.O. BOX 14781, LENEXA, KS 66215

Offers B&B Homes In: Kansas City, Parkville, Lee's Summit, Independence, Liberty, Grandview, St. Joseph, Weston, and Warrensburg (in Missouri); Lenexa, Overland Park, Leawood, and Kansas City (in Kansas)
Reservations Phone: 913/888-3636
Phone Hours: daily, evenings and weekends
Price Range of Homes: $30 to $60 single, $35 to $90 double
Breakfast Included in Price: Some continental, but most homes serve a full breakfast.
Brochure Available: "Homes Directory" for $1 if you send a stamped, self-addressed no. 10 envelope
Reservations Should Be Made: 2 weeks in advance (last-minute reservations usually accepted)

Scenic Attractions Near the B&B Homes: Truman Library, Worlds of Fun, Crown Center Plaza, Kansas City Zoo, Nelson Art Gallery, Kansas City Museum, American Royal, Country Club Plaza, Stadium
Major Schools, Universities Near the B&B Homes: U. of Missouri, Avila College, U. of Kansas, Central Missouri State

Best B&Bs

■ Spacious home in Independence, Missouri. This B&B is private, adjacent to the host's home. It overlooks the Missouri River and has a good view of the Kansas City skyline. There is a fireplace in the master bedroom. Home WO12.

■ Contemporary geodesic dome home near Kansas City, Missouri. Located on nine acres, this B&B has 2,000 square feet of deck. It has been described as a "treehouse in the woods." Two guest rooms are available. Breakfast specialty: Belgian waffles. Home FA28.

LOUISIANA

B&B Reservation Services

SOUTHERN COMFORT BED & BREAKFAST RESERVATION SERVICE
2856 HUNDRED OAKS, BATON ROUGE, LA 70808

Offers B&B Homes In: 20 cities in Louisiana, Mississippi, New Mexico, Florida, and Acapulco

Reservations Phone: 504/346-1928 or 504/928-9815

Phone Hours: 8 a.m. to 8 p.m. daily (no collect calls)

Price Range of Homes: $32 to $125 single, $37 to $150 double (depending on the number of additional people)

Breakfast Included in Price: Continental or full American (except in a few unhosted apartments); some homes serve "plantation breakfasts" which can include various meats, grits and gravy, hot breads, and native preserves

Brochure Available: "Directory of Host Homes" and toll-free telephone number available for $3

Reservations Should Be Made: 2 weeks in advance (last-minute reservations accepted if possible)

Scenic Attractions Near the B&B Homes: In Louisiana: in New Orleans, Audubon Park and Zoo, French Quarter, famous restaurants and museums; in Baton Rouge, old and new state capitols, historic sites; in Cajun country, bayous, sugarcane fields, swamp tours, Cajun music and food. In Mississippi: antebellum homes, plantations, Civil War battle sites, museums, Gulf Coast. In New Mexico: desert, mountains, and art colonies. In Florida, Walt Disney World, Sea World, EPCOT, and Silver Springs.

Major Schools, Universities Near the B&B Homes: Louisiana State, Southern U., Tulane, Loyola, Xavier, Dillard, U. of Mississippi, Mississippi Southern, U. of New Mexico

Best B&Bs

■ See their "50 Best B&Bs" winner in Part III.

■ Raised cottage in Franklin, Louisiana. You will have full use of the home and can enjoy the Bayou Room overlooking Bayou Teche. This is a good headquarters while you visit antebellum homes, take bayou tours, or take in some of the excellent restaurants. The host is an authority on history and local activities.

■ An 1830 home in the French Quarter, New Orleans, Louisiana. This B&B is listed on the National Register of Historic Places. It's just a three-minute walk from Jackson Square and the St. Louis Cathedral. It represents some of the best French/Spanish architecture in the Quarter and received an Honor Award of the Vieux

Carré Commission for outstanding restoration. Every room opens onto a gallery, balcony, or the courtyard with a fountain. *Insider's Tip:* The butler did it! When the hostess is not in residence, a butler brings coffee to your room and serves a full breakfast in the dining room. Ask for a complete tour of the house—it's something to see.

BED & BREAKFAST, INC., RESERVATION SERVICE

1360 MOSS ST. (P.O. BOX 52257), NEW ORLEANS, LA 70152

Offers B&B Homes In: New Orleans and surrounding areas
Reservations Phone: 504/525-4640, or toll free 800/228-9711, wait for dial tone, then ext. 184
Phone Hours: 24 hours daily
Price Range of Homes: $25 to $110 single, $35 to $110 double (some rates may go up seasonally)
Breakfast Included in Price: Continental (juice, roll or toast, coffee or tea)
Brochure Available: Free
Reservations Should Be Made: Anytime (last-minute reservations accepted if possible)

Scenic Attractions Near the B&B Homes: French Quarter, Mississippi River, Superdome, Audubon Zoo, New Orleans Museum of Art, Jazz Halls, world-famous restaurants, antique stores, historic St. Charles Avenue streetcar, Jackson Square artists
Major Schools, Universities Near the B&B Homes: Tulane, Loyola, U. of New Orleans, Dominican College, Tulane Medical School, LSU Dental School, French Quarter

Best B&Bs

■ Quaint guest cottages in New Orleans, Louisiana. Three private guest cottages sit behind an 1876 home. They have wonderful decorative touches: leaded-glass windows, French doors, cypress staircases, and a brick courtyard. Guests are only minutes away from major New Orleans attractions, including the French Quarter, the Superdome, and the Mississippi River. Each cottage has a telephone, tea and coffee pot, TV, stereo, queen-size and/or twin bed. *Insider's Tip:* These cottages have many repeat guests. The staff of CNN (Cable Network News) stayed here during the Republican National Convention.

■ Queen Anne Victorian home in New Orleans, Louisiana. Right in the Garden District, this home typifies past life in the Deep South with its wide veranda, tall French windows, high ceilings, and detailed woodwork. The home is decorated with original artwork. Just at the corner the St. Charles Avenue streetcar can take you to the downtown convention center and the French Quarter. The hosts are music and food enthusiasts.

PEGGY LINDSAY ENTERPRISES
4431 ST. CHARLES AVE., NEW ORLEANS, LA 70115

Offers B&B Homes In: New Orleans area
Reservations Phone: 504/897-3867
Phone Hours: 7 a.m. to 11 p.m. Monday through Friday (accept calls on weekends)
Price Range of Homes: $40 single, $50 to $75 double (rates 20% more during Mardi Gras and Super Bowl periods, and about 20% less during the summer)
Breakfast Included in Price: Continental (juice, roll or toast, coffee)
Brochure Available: Free
Reservations Should Be Made: 2 weeks in advance (last-minute reservations accepted when possible)

Scenic Attractions Near the B&B Homes: Historic areas (French Quarter, Garden District), St. Charles Avenue streetcar, Audubon Zoo, battlefields, many five-star restaurants
Major Schools, Universities Near the B&B Homes: Tulane, Loyola

Best B&Bs

■ Tudor mansion in New Orleans, Louisiana. Located right on glamorous oak-lined St. Charles Avenue. This home has large guest rooms with 13-foot-high ceilings. You can walk to several fine restaurants or take the trolley to the French Quarter. You can have breakfast in your room or on the patio.

■ One-bedroom apartment in New Orleans, Louisiana. Located in the beautiful Garden District of the city. Two couples could share this apartment which has a newly renovated living-dining area with a complete kitchen.

NEW ORLEANS BED & BREAKFAST
2714 CANAL ST., ROOM 404B, NEW ORLEANS, LA 70119

Offers B&B Homes In: New Orleans and surrounding area, "Cajun country," plantations
Reservations Phone: 504/822-5046 or 504/822-5038
Phone Hours: 8 a.m. to 5 p.m. daily
Price Range of Homes: $30 to $75 single, $35 to $150 double
Breakfast Included in Price: Continental (juice, roll or toast, coffee)
Brochure Available: Free if you send a stamped, self-addressed no. 10 envelope
Reservations Should Be Made: As early as possible for special events and best selection (last-minute reservations accepted if available)

Scenic Attractions Near the B&B Homes: Historic homes, Audubon Park Zoo, plantation tours and river cruises, Cajun bayou tours, Gulf Coast, Acadian Country, French Quarter, New Orleans nightlife, Longvue Gardens, Magazine Street antique shops, West End Yacht Club and restaurants on Lake Pontchartrain
Major Schools, Universities Near the B&B Homes: Tulane, Loyola, U. of New Orleans, Dillard, New Orleans Baptist Seminary

Best B&Bs

■ West Indies—style plantation home on Lake Vista, Louisiana. This home was built from the remains of an old plantation mansion. It's filled with antiques, Mardi Gras mementos, and giant Audubon prints. Two guest bedrooms on the second floor have private baths and a back gallery overlooking the lake. On the levee you can jog, ride bikes, or just stroll. Fresh coffee is waiting at your door in the morning. Later, the works—a full plantation breakfast in the family dining room.

■ Courtyard apartment in New Orleans, Louisiana. In the French Quarter. The living room has a sofa bed, and there's a dining area with a kitchenette. Upstairs is a bedroom with a double bed and a balcony overlooking the courtyard. Your continental breakfast is in the refrigerator. *Insider's Tip:* You can also stay right next door in a handsome French Quarter home with exposed brick, hand-hewn cypress, and French doors. A continental breakfast is served in the sun room overlooking the patio.

──────────────── **B&B Inns** ────────────────

TEZCUCO
3138 HWY. 44, DARROW, LA 70725

Reservations Phone: 504/562-3929
Description: This 1855 Greek Revival plantation house is set
  beneath majestic live oaks. It has individual cottages with bedroom, sitting room, and bath, plus formal gardens, a chapel,
  dollhouse, blacksmith shop, carriage house, and a commissary.
Amenities: Country Créole breakfast served in your cottage on a
  silver tray consists of juice, eggs, grits, sausage or bacon,
  biscuits, jellies, coffee or tea

Nearby Attractions: Center of plantation country on a historic
  Mississippi road
Special Services: Hot tub, complimentary wine, tour of the
  plantation
Rates: $60 to $185 double

NINE-O-FIVE ROYAL HOTEL
905 ROYAL ST., NEW ORLEANS, LA 70116

Reservations Phone: 504/523-0219
Description: This quaint European-style hotel built in the 1980s is
  located in the heart of the French Quarter. The rooms are
  furnished with kitchenettes and balconies overlooking Royal
  Street.

Nearby Attractions: The French Market, Jackson Square, river-
  boat rides, famous restaurants
Special Services: Color TV, daily maid service
Rates: $35 to $65 double, $95 for suites

MARQUETTE HOUSE HOSTEL
2253 CARONDELET ST., NEW ORLEANS, LA 70130

Reservations Phone: 504/523-3014
Description: You'll find clean, simple, basic accommodation for
  the budget traveler in this 100-year-old antebellum home lo-

cated a block off the historic St. Charles Avenue streetcar line next to the Garden District, 22 blocks from the French Quarter. All rooms are with hall bath.

Nearby Attractions: Chalmette National Historic site commemorating the Battle of New Orleans, the Mississippi River with its steamboats, Jean Lafitte National Park
Special Services: Guest kitchen, garden patio, picnic tables, arrangements for tours
Rates: $21 single, $25 double, $9.50 to $12.50 in dormitories

---

MISSOURI

────────── B&B Reservation Services ──────────

OZARK MOUNTAIN COUNTRY BED & BREAKFAST
P.O. BOX 295, BRANSON, MO 65616

Offers B&B Homes In: Southwest Missouri, Northwest Arkansas, and Northeast Oklahoma
Reservations Phone: 417/334-4720 or 334-5077
Phone Hours: Anytime, daily
Price Range of Homes: $25 to $80 single, $30 to $85 double
Breakfast Included in Price: Continental (juice, roll or toast, coffee); most homes also offer gourmet or hearty country breakfasts
Brochure Available: Free if you send a stamped, self-addressed no. 10 envelope
Reservations Should Be Made: 2 weeks in advance (last-minute reservations accepted if possible)

Scenic Attractions Near the B&B Homes: Mountain Music Shows, Shepherd at the Hills, Silver Dollar City, White Water Fun Park, trout fishing in Taneycomo and Table Rock Lakes

Best B&Bs ────────────────────────────────
■ Contemporary home in Branson, Missouri. This B&B offers four guest rooms. You can enjoy the large sitting area with fireplace

and TV. In summer join other guests on the patio or around the swimming pool. Home OMC 118.

■ Victorian home in Hartville, Missouri. This area was a Civil War battle site, and is the crossroads of scenic routes and Rtes. 5 and 38 (transcontinental bicycle route). It's close to Mansfield (Laura Ingalls Wilder home and museum). The home is decorated with antiques of the Victorian era. Home OMC-202.

NEW MEXICO

B&B Reservation Services

BED & BREAKFAST OF SANTA FE
436 SUNSET, SANTA FE, NM 87501

Offers B&B Homes In: Santa Fe only
Reservations Phone: 505/982-3332
Phone Hours: 9 a.m. to 5 p.m.
Price Range of Homes: $50 to $65 double
Breakfast Included in Price: Continental
Reservations Should Be Made: 2 weeks in advance (last-minute reservations accepted if possible)

Scenic Attractions Near the B&B Homes: Annual Indian Market (third week of August), cliff dwellings, pueblo and Spanish church ruins, colorful adobe architecture, major art center, ski basin, opera, Chamber Music Festival, Arts Festival

---

B&B Inns

PRESTON HOUSE
106 FAITHWAY ST., SANTA FE, NM 87501

Reservations Phone: 505/982-3465
Description: This Queen Anne–style building was built in 1886 and is listed on the National Historic Register. It provides the

comfort of the present in a turn-of-the-century setting. Most rooms have private baths and fireplaces.
Amenities: Continental breakfast

Nearby Attractions: Skiing, museums, art galleries, hiking, fishing, opera, Indian pueblos
Special Services: Afternoon refreshments, help with trip planning
Rates: $55 to $125 double

HOTEL EDELWEISS
TAOS SKI VALLEY, TAOS, NM 87571

Reservations Phone: 505/776-2301
Description: In the winter season this is a high-mountain resort hotel. The comfortable accommodations afford spectacular views. *Note:* Open only from Thanksgiving to Easter.
Amenities: Breakfast specialties include a variety of egg dishes and special sauces.

Nearby Attractions: Indian ruins, pueblos, art galleries, craft fairs, music and theater
Special Services: Jacuzzi, sauna, tennis, ski packages, week-long cooking schools
Rates: $95 single, $120 double

TEXAS

———— B&B Reservation Services ————

SAND DOLLAR HOSPITALITY/BED & BREAKFAST
3605 MENDENHALL, CORPUS CHRISTI, TX 78415

Offers B&B Homes In: Texas Coastal Bend, primarily Corpus Christi
Reservations Phone: 512/853-1222
Phone Hours: 8 a.m. to 8 p.m. daily

Price Range of Homes: $27 to $54 single, $30 to $60 double
Breakfast Included in Price: Continental or full American, depending on individual home, plus some Mexican specialties, such as breakfast taquitos and Mexican sweet breads
Brochure Available: Free
Reservations Should Be Made: 3 days in advance preferred (last-minute reservations accepted if possible)

Scenic Attractions Near the B&B Homes: Padre Island, King Ranch, Aransas Wildlife Refuge (home of the whooping crane), Rockport Art Colony, Japanese Art Museum, Corpus Christi Art Museum, Natural History Museum
Major Schools, Universities Near the B&B Homes: Corpus Christi State, Del Mar Jr. College

Best B&Bs

■ Home in Corpus Christi, Texas. Your choice of two bedrooms, one with a double bed, the other with a queen-size bed. The rooms share a full bath. In fair weather you can have your morning coffee on a covered patio. Well-behaved pets are acceptable.

■ Home near downtown Corpus Christi, Texas. Close to town but still only a block from the water. This B&B, Blue Heron, has three guest rooms and a backyard pool, plus a new paneled indoor hot tub.

BED & BREAKFAST TEXAS STYLE, INC.
4224 W. RED BIRD LANE, DALLAS, TX 75237

Offers B&B Homes In: Austin, Arlington, Amarillo, Aledo, Belton, Big Sandy, Brownsville, Burnet, Burton-Brenham, Canyon, Cedar Creek Lake, Center, Chappell Hill, Cleburne, Dallas, El Paso, Fort Worth, Fredericksburg, Fort Stockton, Galveston, Garland, Georgetown, Houston, Jacksonville, Jefferson, Lake Ray Hubbard, Lampasas, Midland, Marshall, Waco
Reservations Phone: 214/298-8586 or 214/298-5433
Phone Hours: 8:30 a.m. to 5:30 p.m. Monday through Friday; answering machine other hours
Price Range of Homes: $20 to $60 single, $25 to $85 double; some higher
Breakfast Included in Price: Continental to full American, but sometimes left in the refrigerator for unhosted accommodations
Brochure Available: Free; directory for $3.50

Reservations Should Be Made: 1 week in advance preferred, but last-minute reservations accepted

Scenic Attractions Near the B&B Homes: Rivers, state fairs, Six Flags, Ranger Games, Gulf of Mexico, Oil Museum in Midland, Kimball Museum

Major Schools, Universities Near the B&B Homes: SMU, U. of Texas, Rice, U. of Houston, Baylor, Texas Christian U., U. of Texas at Arlington, Midwestern U.

Best B&Bs

■ Spanish-style mansion in El Paso, Texas. You can have a room with a view in this beautiful home. Ask for the room that gives you a king-size waterbed and a view of Mexico, three U.S. states, and two cities (El Paso and Juárez)! Or a good second choice would be the sun-view room which has a sofa daybed and has a view of the large swimming pool and patio in the rear of the home. Breakfast is served in a secluded nook or in the landscaped courtyard. Host also serves High Tea.

■ Red-brick home in Houston, Texas. Close to the Galleria Mall, this home has the charm of the Victorian era with many antiques, lace, doilies, and pillows. Breakfast is served in the atrium room next to a flowing fountain. Good place for a romantic honeymoon.

■ Home on White Rock Lake in Dallas, Texas. Each guest room has a private bath. Guests have access to the great outdoors, and the hostess will even lend a bicycle to those who'd like to peddle around the attractive lake. Breakfast is more than filling: eggs, or blueberry pancakes, or oatmeal with raisins and fresh fruit. *Insider's Tip:* The hostess, on request, will make dinner reservations at some choice restaurants.

■ Dome home in Temple, Texas. This B&B really is a dome with a living room that looks like a cathedral. The dome was specially designed for the semi-retired host and hostess by their architect son. Each guest bedroom has a king-size bed and private bath. *Insider's Tip:* Your hosts will be glad to show you pictures of how the dome was constructed. The hostess also likes to talk gardening; she tends over 200 houseplants.

BED & BREAKFAST OF FREDERICKSBURG
102 S. CHERRY, FREDERICKSBURG, TX 78624

Offers B&B Homes In: Fredericksburg area
Reservations Phone: 512/997-4712
Phone Hours: 8 a.m. to 9 p.m. daily
Price Range of Homes: $55 to $75 double
Breakfast Included in Price: Continental to full American
Brochure Available: For $2
Reservations Should Be Made: 1 week to 2 or 3 months in advance, depending on event

Scenic Attractions Near the B&B Homes: Admiral Nimitz State Historical Park; Pioneer Museum; Enchanted Rock State Park

Best B&Bs

■ Two-story guest cottage in Fredericksburg, Texas. Located in a rural area, this cottage offers guests a large room with two twin beds, a fully equipped kitchen area, and one of those wonderful old clawfoot bathtubs. Breakfast is German style, and "fix your own" with ingredients from the refrigerator. Request house no. 4B when reserving this B&B.

■ "Sunday House" in Fredericksburg, Texas. This 1905 restored house has been carefully restored by a retired couple. They've found unique antiques ranging from iron beds to light fixtures from the local Admiral Nimitz Hotel. *Insider's Tip:* Ask the hosts if you'd like to browse their excellent collection of books on antique toys. Request house no. 10 when reserving this B&B.

BED & BREAKFAST HOSTS OF SAN ANTONIO
166 ROCKHILL, SAN ANTONIO, TX 78209

Offers B&B Homes In: San Antonio and outlying area
Reservations Phone: 512/824-8036
Phone Hours: 9 a.m. to 5 p.m. weekdays
Price Range of Homes: $36.50 to $94 per room, tax included
Breakfast Included in Price: Continental to full American
Brochure Available: Free
Reservations Should Be Made: As early as possible; last-minute reservations may be made at inns

Scenic Attractions Near the B&B Homes: Sea World, the Alamo, the Missions, the Riverwalk, Mexican Market, zoo, Botanical Gardens, museums, historic King William District, La Villita

Major Schools, Universities Near the B&B Homes: U. of Texas at San Antonio, Trinity U., Our Lady of the Lake, U.T. Health Science Center Medical and Dental Schools

Best B&Bs

■ Terrell Castle in San Antonio, Texas. A rock built in 1894 for $16,500 and worth hundreds of thousands of dollars today. Your choice of unique rooms, such as the Yellow Rose Room, "furnished with a high antique double bed with a lace canopy." The Giles Suite has a king-size bed under a canopy, TV, fireplace, wet bar, and private bath. *Insider's Tip:* Be sure to visit the library, a beautiful room with a molded-brick fireplace. Then take a complete tour of this beautiful "castle."

■ A Cape Cod guesthouse in Alamo Heights, San Antonio, Texas. This home offers comfortable rooms furnished with many antiques. The cathedral ceilings and fireplace add to the charm. A large sundeck looks out over a swimming pool. *Insider's Tip:* Musicians can try the grand piano in the Music Room.

B&B Inns

BULLIS HOUSE INN
621 PIERCE ST. (P.O. BOX 8059), SAN ANTONIO, TX 78208

Reservations Phone: 512/223-9426

Description: This historic white mansion is only minutes from the Alamo, Riverwalk, and downtown. The interior is decorated with chandeliers, fireplaces, 14-foot ceilings, and geometrically patterned floors of fine woods. Built in 1906 for Gen. John Bullis, a noted cavalry officer famous for his efforts in taming the Texas frontier, it's a registered Texas Historic Landmark.

Amenities: Continental breakfast with a variety of muffins

Nearby Attractions: Fort Sam Houston and Old Army Museum, Botanical Gardens and Brackenridge Park and Zoo, Institute of Texas Culture, San Antonio Art Museum, Spanish Missions National Park, McNay Art Museum, Sea World

Rates: $24 to $73 single, $31 to $79 double

California & the West

ARIZONA

———————— B&B Reservation Services ————————

BED & BREAKFAST IN ARIZONA
P.O. BOX 8628, SCOTTSDALE, AZ 85252

Offers B&B Homes In: Arizona (homes, ranches, guesthouses, and inns)
Reservations Phone: 602/995-2831
Phone Hours: 10 a.m. to 1 p.m. and 2 p.m. to 6 p.m. Monday through Friday and 10 a.m. to 2 p.m. on Saturday and Sunday (no holidays)
Price Range of Homes: $25 to $75 single, $35 to $150 double
Breakfast Included in Price: Continental or full American; many hosts are gourmet cooks.
Brochure Available: Free if you phone in or send a stamped, self-addressed no. 10 envelope; directory available for $3
Reservations Should Be Made: 2 weeks' advance notice preferred, but will attempt late reservations up to 24 hours in advance; VISA, MasterCard, and American Express accepted

Scenic Attractions Near the B&B Homes: Grand Canyon, Indian monuments, Phoenix and Tucson Zoos, Zane Grey home, national forests, 19 state parks, Lake Havasu, Lake Powell, Lowell Observatory, Kitt Peak Observatory, botanical gardens and art museums
Major Schools, Universities Near the B&B Homes: American Graduate School of Business, U. of Arizona at Tucson, Northern Arizona U. at Flagstaff, Arizona State U. at Tempe, Orme and Judson private schools

Best B&Bs ————————————————————————
■ See their "50 Best B&Bs" winner in Part III.

■ Home in Pinetop, Arizona. Says the reservation service, "This bed-and-breakfast is a delight! The very friendly hostess is a dynamo who has done every piece of needlework, every piece of ceramic craftwork in the house, and cooks a breakfast that simply won't quit—biscuits cooked from scratch, with sausage gravy, two kinds of muffins, three kinds of breakfast meats, eggs cooked to your order, fruit compote with cream sauce." This home is located right on the Fort Apache Indian Reservation boundary, a half mile from Zane Grey's famous Mogollon Rim. Hiking and cross-country ski trails are right out the door. Home LS101.

■ Famous home in Phoenix, Arizona. You may have seen this B&B featured in a number of national and local articles on interior design. The hostess is a tour guide at the Phoenix art museum as well as a gourmet chef. The backyard has a gazebo and open-pit fireplace and a Jacuzzi.

BED & BREAKFAST SCOTTSDALE AND THE WEST

P.O. BOX 3999, PRESCOTT, AZ 86302

Offers B&B Homes In: Scottsdale
Reservations Phone: 602/776-1102
Phone Hours: 9 a.m. to 6 p.m. daily
Price Range of Homes: $40 to $75 single, $65 to $150 double
Breakfast Included in Price: Continental (juice, roll or toast, coffee), and full American with specialties (pecan rolls, chili and eggs); pick your own breakfast fruit from some hosts' orchards.
Brochure Available: Free
Reservations Should Be Made: 2 to 3 weeks in advance, 1 month in advance for February reservations (last-minute reservations accepted when possible)

Scenic Attractions Near the B&B Homes: Desert Botanical Gardens, zoo, art galleries, Rawhide (the western town), the Frank Lloyd Wright Foundation (offers architectural tours); Mount Lemon ski area
Major Schools, Universities Near the B&B Homes: Scottsdale Artists School, U. of Arizona at Tempe, New Mayo Clinic and Research Center

Best B&Bs

■ Spanish contemporary in Paradise Valley, Scottsdale, Arizona. This B&B is right next to Camelback Country Club, and has a beautiful lawn and landscaping. There are three guest rooms, each with private bath, TV, and telephone. Wrote one executive guest from Minnesota about this home, "I haven't been able to think of a superlative appropriate for how outstanding this B&B is. How can one improve on perfection?"

■ Spanish contemporary in Fountain Hills, Scottsdale, Arizona. This three-story, 6,500-square-foot home built in 1986 offers real luxury: two suites (one with a fireplace), a swimming pool, *and* a championship tennis court. For less active guests, a library in the loft, a grand piano, and an electric organ.

■ Historic adobe-style house in Scottsdale, Arizona. Clark Gable and Robert Taylor stayed here. So did many other famous stars and political figures. All rooms have a private entrance, bathroom, TV, and cooking facilities. (Did Clark have to cook his own breakfast?) A separate guesthouse is available.

OLD PUEBLO HOMESTAYS (formerly Barbara Bed and Breakfast)
P.O. BOX 13603, TUCSON, AZ 85732

Offers B&B Homes In: The Tucson area
Reservations Phone: 602/790-2399
Phone Hours: 24-hour answering machine
Price Range of Homes: $25 to $60 single, $35 to $85 double
Breakfast Included in Price: Continental or full American
Brochure Available: Free if you send a stamped, self-addressed no. 10 envelope
Reservations Should Be Made: 2 weeks in advance (last-minute reservations accepted when possible)

Scenic Attractions Near the B&B Homes: Arizona Sonora Desert Museum, Saguaro National Monument, Sabino Canyon, San Xavier Mission, Nogales, Mexico, Old Tucson (movie location and amusement park)
Major Schools, Universities Near the B&B Homes: U. of Arizona

Best B&Bs

■ Famous B&B in Tucson, Arizona. This home is in the historic district, and was featured in the book *Desert Southwest* and in many magazine articles. You can stay in a carriage house suite with a queen-size bed, private bath, and a kitchenette stocked with complimentary wine and snacks. The living room of this suite is furnished with period antiques. Or you could choose a gatehouse suite with sitting/bedroom and a queen-size bed. The kitchenette also has a stocked refrigerator. Or a Victorian room with a queen-size bed and antiques.

CALIFORNIA

─────── B&B Reservation Services ───────

EYE OPENERS BED & BREAKFAST RESERVATIONS
P.O. BOX 694, ALTADENA, CA 91001

Offers B&B Homes In: California, from San Diego to San Francisco
Reservations Phone: 213/684-4428 or 818/797-2055
Phone Hours: 24 hours daily
Price Range of Homes: $30 to $80 single, $35 to $85 double
Breakfast Included in Price: Continental or full American (juice, eggs, bacon, toast, coffee) and regional specialties
Brochure Available: Free if you send a stamped, self-addressed no. 10 envelope; $1 for home descriptions
Reservations Should Be Made: 2 weeks in advance (last-minute reservations accepted if possible)

Scenic Attractions Near the B&B Homes: Angeles National Forest, Huntington Library and Gardens, San Diego and Los Angeles Zoos, Universal Studios, Rose Bowl, Norton Simon Museum, Asia Pacific Museum, Dodger Stadium, Santa Anita Race Track, NBC-TV Studios, Yosemite, Balboa, Golden Gate Park
Major Schools, Universities Near the B&B Homes: California Institute of Technology, Art Center College of Design, Fuller Theological Seminary, UCLA, USC, the Claremont Colleges, San Francisco State, UC San Diego

Best B&Bs ────────────────────────────
■ See their "50 Best B&Bs" winner in Part III.

■ Private home in Newport, California. This beach home has a crow's nest with a 360° view. Stained glass is featured throughout.

CAROLYN'S BED & BREAKFAST HOMES IN SAN DIEGO

416 THIRD AVE., #25, CHULA VISTA, CA 92010

Offers B&B Homes In: San Diego city and county
Reservations Phone: 619/422-7009
Phone Hours: 9 a.m. to 6 p.m. Monday through Saturday
Price Range of Homes: $30 to $75 single, $45 to $85 double, $65 to $90 for cottages
Breakfast Included in Price: Continental or full American, depending on the individual home (fresh-baked muffins often served)
Brochure Available: Free if you send a stamped, self-addressed no. 10 envelope
Reservations Should Be Made: 2 weeks in advance (last-minute reservations accepted if possible)

Scenic Attractions Near the B&B Homes: Pacific Ocean, Torrey Pines Golf Course, Sea World, San Diego Zoo, Scripps Aquarium, Scripps Institute of Oceanography, Del Coronado Hotel, Disneyland, Tijuana (Mexico), Wild Animal Park, Cabrillo National Monument
Major Schools, Universities Near the B&B Homes: USC, Cal State San Diego, UC San Diego, U. of San Diego, San Diego State U.

HOSPITALITY PLUS

P.O. BOX 336, DANA POINT, CA 92629

Offers B&B Homes In: 80 cities throughout California
Reservations Phone: 714/496-7050
Phone Hours: 9 a.m. to 5 p.m. Monday through Friday, plus Saturday and Sunday evenings
Price Range of Homes: $15 to $40 single, $20 to $55 double
Breakfast Included in Price: About 20% of homes serve continental; others serve full breakfasts with specialties such as Swedish round pancakes, Ortega omelets, and cinnamon rolls
Brochure Available: For 50¢
Reservations Should Be Made: 2 weeks in advance (last-minute reservations accepted if possible); phone reservations preferred

Scenic Attractions Near the B&B Homes: Disneyland, Sequoia National Park, Yosemite, San Diego Zoo, Wild Animal Park,

Lion Country Safari, Amtrak to Missions of California, Pageant of the Masters, Pacific Ocean, Lake Tahoe, redwoods

Major Schools, Universities Near the B&B Homes: Stanford, UCLA, UC Berkeley, plus other U. of California campuses, USC

Best B&Bs

■ Pelican Rock at Laguna Beach, California. The only oceanfront B&B in town.

■ Monarch Pacific at Laguna, California. Beautiful four-acre setting with great sunsets and ocean views. Private bath.

■ Hideaway cottage in San Francisco, California. Your whole family can stay in this secluded cottage behind a Victorian house. It has a bedroom, kitchen, and living room. And you are within walking distance of the trolley.

BED & BREAKFAST RENT-A-ROOM
11531 VARNA ST., GARDEN GROVE, CA 92640

Offers B&B Homes In: Los Angeles, Disneyland, San Diego, Huntington Beach, Laguna Beach, Lake Arrowhead, and along the coast

Reservations Phone: 714/638-1406

Phone Hours: 8 a.m. to 10 p.m. daily

Price Range of Homes: $25 to $35 single, $30 to $60 double

Breakfast Included in Price: Continental (some hosts serve a different continental breakfast every day, with crêpes, French toast, etc.), and some full American

Brochure Available: Free if you send a stamped, self-addressed no. 10 envelope

Reservations Should Be Made: 2 weeks in advance (last-minute reservations accepted if possible)

Scenic Attractions Near the B&B Homes: Hollywood, Universal City, Marineland, Ports O' Call, *Queen Mary,* Disneyland, Knott's Berry Farm, Lion Country Safari, San Diego Zoo, Wild Animal Park, Sea World, Tijuana (Mexico), missions in San Diego, San Juan Capistrano

Major Schools, Universities Near the B&B Homes: UCLA, USC, Long Beach State, Fullerton State, UC Irvine, U. of San Diego, San Diego State

Best B&Bs

■ Ranch-style home at Portuguese Bend, California. This B&B has its own private beach. It also has a double fireplace and a great front porch overlooking the ocean. The full breakfast includes quiche, waffles, ham and eggs, and a platter of fresh fruit. *Insider's Tip:* Discount tickets are available from your host to many major southern California attractions. Childcare is available.

WINE COUNTRY RESERVATIONS
P.O. BOX 5059, NAPA, CA 94581

Offers B&B Homes In: The Napa Valley
Reservations Phone: 707/257-7757, 707/944-1222, or 707/944-1109
Price Range of Homes: $66 to $400, single or double
Breakfast Included in Price: Continental (juice, roll or toast, coffee), which may include muffins, home-baked breads, fruit, cheese, coffee, teas, and juices; some have full breakfast.
Brochure Available: For $2
Reservations Should Be Made: 3 to 4 weeks in advance (last-minute reservations accepted if possible); two nights required on weekends

Scenic Attractions Near the B&B Homes: 150 premium wineries, ballooning, hiking, bike trails, Calistoga mud and mineral baths, walking tours of old homes
Major Schools, Universities Near the B&B Homes: Napa Jr. College, Pacific Union College

Best B&Bs

■ See their "50 Best B&Bs" winner in Part III.

■ An 1898 Queen Anne home in Napa Valley, California. This B&B is called Gallery Osgood. It sits amid a showplace flower garden, and offers three guest rooms with shared bath. The home has period furnishings, stained-glass windows, crystal, and fine arts. *Insider's Tip:* Complimentary wine is served in the evening.

■ Country home in Napa Valley, California. The Stahlecker B&B is surrounded by 1½ acres of country charm. Three guest rooms are available: Amy's Blue Rose Room, Royal Oak Room, and the Emerald Tool Room (they don't have names like those in your typical motel!). Each room has a queen-size bath and is beautifully decorated. Guests are invited to share the front room with its fireplace and the television room with a large corner brick fireplace. Afterward, take a stroll through the rose garden or sit by a creek under old oaks and laurel trees. *Insider's Tip:* This B&B follows an Irish tradition of serving complimentary tea at 4 p.m.

EL CAMINO REAL BED & BREAKFAST
P.O. BOX 7155, NORTHRIDGE, CA 91327

Offers B&B Homes In: Southern California
Reservations Phone: 818/363-6753
Phone Hours: Evenings (answering machine 24 hours)
Price Range of Homes: $35 to $45 single, $40 to $115 double
Breakfast Included in Price: Continental to full American, except in dormitory accommodations and apartments
Brochure Available: Free
Reservations Should Be Made: As far in advance as possible

Scenic Attractions Near the B&B Homes: Pacific Ocean, Southern California
Major Schools, Universities Near the B&B Homes: UCLA, USC

Best B&Bs _____

■ Home in Malibu, California. Located high on a hill, this B&B provides a panoramic view of the Pacific Ocean. The home is filled with artwork. *Insider's Tip:* This is a particularly good place to stay if you want to spend some time at the famous Getty Museum, which is nearby. The host is very knowledgeable about fine local restaurants.

■ House at Seal Beach, California. The B&B offers attractive accommodations with a garden, right on the beach. One guest room has a king-size bed; the other, twins. Walk out the backdoor through the garden and you're at the ocean. Hot tub available.

AMERICAN FAMILY INN/BED & BREAKFAST SAN FRANCISCO
P.O. BOX 349, SAN FRANCISCO, CA 94101

Offers B&B Homes In: San Francisco, Marin County, Monterey/ Carmel, and the California Wine Country

Reservations Phone: 415/931-3083

Phone Hours: 9:30 a.m. to 5 p.m. Monday through Friday (answering machine all other hours)

Price Range of Homes: $45 to $125 single, $55 to $125 double, $70 to $100 for family accommodations, $100 and up for boats

Breakfast Included in Price: Full hearty American

Brochure Available: Free

Reservations Should Be Made: By phone, when you know the exact dates (last-minute reservations accepted if space allows)

Scenic Attractions Near the B&B Homes: San Francisco cable cars, Fisherman's Wharf, Chinatown, Moscone Convention Center, Golden Gate Park

Major Schools, Universities Near the B&B Homes: UC Medical Center, San Francisco State

Best B&Bs

▪ Contemporary home in San Francisco, California. The reservation service says, "The best view of San Francisco!" This home combines modern architecture and classic antiques. The large bedroom has a panoramic view of the city. For extra creature comforts: a king-size bed, Jacuzzi, and fireplace in the room. The small bedroom has a view of the bay and a queen-size bed. Close to public transportation. The host is an architect.

▪ Private cottage in San Francisco, California. This B&B is located on the famous crooked Lombard Street on Russian Hill (you've probably seen this street in dozens of photographs and movies). The tastefully decorated living room has a view of the bay and bay bridge, a fireplace, and a TV.

▪ Modern home in San Francisco, California. This three-level home is high on a San Francisco hill with great views of the city and nearby Glen Canyon. It's near all the sights. *Insider's Tip:* Don't skip breakfast. The hostess serves Swedish pancakes with homemade orange syrup, fancy omelets, and other breakfast specialties. A number of her recipes have been published.

▪ This reservation service can also book you on a most unusual B&B: a yacht or a houseboat on San Francisco Bay.

WINE COUNTRY BED & BREAKFAST
P.O. BOX 3211, SANTA ROSA, CA 95403

Offers B&B Homes In: Santa Rosa and approximately 35-mile radius, including Healdsburg, Sebastopol, Sonoma, St. Helena, and Calistoga
Reservations Phone: 707/578-1661
Phone Hours: 10 a.m. to 8 p.m. daily
Price Range of Homes: $45 to $60 single, $60 to $95 double
Breakfast Included in Price: Full American (juice, eggs, bacon, toast, coffee)
Brochure Available: Free if you send a stamped, self-addressed no. 10 envelope
Reservations Should Be Made: 2 weeks in advance (no last-minute reservations, but will accept 1 week ahead if deposit is sent)

Scenic Attractions Near the B&B Homes: Over 24 world-famous wineries and vineyards, Redwood Forest in Armstrong State Park, Bodega Bay, Sonoma Old Spanish Mission, Jack London House and Museum, Russian River resorts, historic Russian settlement at Fort Ross, Luther Burbank Gardens
Major Schools, Universities Near the B&B Homes: Sonoma State, Santa Rosa Jr. College

Best B&Bs

▪ Redwood country home in Sonoma, California. You're surrounded by trees and garden, yet only minutes from the center of town. After a day of exploring the Napa Valley and the town of Sonoma, the Valley of the Moon, and Jack London Park, you'll come home at night to a large bedroom with a king-size bed and private bathroom. The hostess serves big country-style breakfasts.

▪ Modern houseboat on San Francisco Bay, California. An unusual accommodation that floats near the picturesque town of Sausalito, close to the Golden Gate Bridge. The bedroom has a double bed, a private bathroom, and a great view of the water. Weather permitting, you can breakfast on the deck.

▪ Historic home in Healdsburg, California. Located close to the Napa Valley and Alexander Valley and the coast, this B&B offers a bedroom with a double bed, private sitting room, TV, and private bath. The hostess serves a full breakfast. *Insider's Tip:* Take a picture of yourself in front of the home and its whimsical Queen Anne tower.

CALIFORNIA HOUSEGUESTS INTERNATIONAL, INC.

18653 VENTURA BLVD., #190B, TARZANA, CA 91356

Offers B&B Homes In: California (statewide), including the Los Angeles area, Carmel, Monterey, Santa Barbara, San Francisco, San Diego, Wine Country (also throughout the U.S., France, Britain, Canada, Mexico)
Reservations Phone: 818/344-7878
Phone Hours: 7 a.m. to 5 p.m. daily (answering machine for off-hours with callback)
Price Range of Homes: $40 to $80 single, $45 to $160 and up double
Breakfast Included in Price: Special continental (croissants, cheese, hot beverage, preserves, fresh fruit, with a flower), or full in selected locations
Brochure Available: Free if you send a stamped self-addressed no. 10 envelope
Reservations Should Be Made: 1 week in advance (last-minute reservations accepted if possible)

Best B&Bs

■ Modern beachside home in Hermosa Beach, California. Exceptional décor and art throughout, including a white leather sectional in a sunken living room, a black lacquer grand piano, and a magnificent stained-glass door to the beachfront patio. The private room has a queen-size bed and a private bath.

■ Modern home in Los Angeles, California. Has a pool and well-tended garden. This B&B is near Universal Studios (be sure to take the studio tour). The private guest suite is decorated with Laura Ashley wallpapers and has a queen-size bed, private bath, and a sitting room with a queen-size sofa bed, TV, microwave, and refrigerator. *Insider's Tip:* A babysitter is available.

BED AND BREAKFAST OF LOS ANGELES

32074 WATERSIDE LANE, WESTLAKE VILLAGE, CA 91361

Offers B&B Homes In: Los Angeles, Ventura, and Orange Counties; also along the California coast (San Diego to San Francisco)
Reservations Phone: 818/889-8870 or 818/494-9622
Phone Hours: 9 a.m. to 9 p.m. Monday through Friday

Price Range of Homes: $30 to $50 and up single, $35 to $85 and up double

Breakfast Included in Price: Continental or full American (juice, eggs, bacon, toast, coffee), with some homes serving regional specialties

Brochure Available: For $2 with a legal-sized stamped, self-addressed envelope

Reservations Should Be Made: 1 month in advance (last-minute reservations accepted if possible)

Scenic Attractions Near the B&B Homes: All Southern California tourist attractions

Major Schools, Universities Near the B&B Homes: USC, UC Occidental, Pepperdine, Marymount, Loyola, Whittier, Cal College Long Beach, Northridge, Saddleback, Domingas Hills, Los Angeles, Fullerton, Polytech at Pomona, and UC Riverside

Best B&Bs

■ Condominium guest room in Beverly Hills, California. You'll be right in the heart of this celebrity community when you stay here. Your room has twin beds, TV, a private bath, and a view of the garden. Good public transportation. Inexpensive: about $45 for two. You can save some money for fancy shopping on Rodeo Drive.

■ English country home in Playa Del Rey, California. This house has been described by the reservation service as a *"very* special place, with a European atmosphere!" It's filled with antiques, has garden views, and is only one mile to the ocean. The two first-floor guest rooms each have a private bath and sitting area. The upstairs guest room has a private bathroom in the hall (bring a robe).

■ Guesthouse in Malibu, California. You'll have a view out through the canyon to the ocean. The living room has a hide-a-bed couch, TV, and a large balcony. *Note:* A car is essential if you stay in this pretty, private place.

_____ **B&B Inns** _____

SANDPIPER INN AT THE BEACH
2408 BAY VIEW AVE., CARMEL-BY-THE-SEA, CA 93923

Reservations Phone: 408/624-6433
Description: This European-style country inn opened in 1929 in a
    quiet residential area just 50 yards from the beach. The 15
    rooms and cottages all have private baths.
Amenities: Continental breakfast

Nearby Attractions: Point Lobos State Reserve, Old Carmel Mis-
    sion Basilica, Big Sur, 17-Mile Drive, Monterey Bay Aquarium
Special Services: Tennis, golf, swimming
Rates: $85 to $140 double

VAGABOND'S HOUSE INN
FOURTH AND DOLORES (P.O. BOX 2747),
CARMEL-BY-THE-SEA, CA 93921

Reservations Phone: 408/624-7738
Description: This brick half-timbered Tudor country inn is in the
    heart of the village. Each of the rooms faces a flagstone
    courtyard of ferns and flowers.
Amenities: Continental breakfast served each morning to the
    rooms from 8:30 to 10:30 a.m.

Nearby Attractions: The Carmel Mission, Sunset Center, 17-Mile
    Drive, Point Lobos Reserve, the Tor House, Monterey Bay
    Aquarium
Special Services: Each room is supplied with a coffee pot,
    fresh-ground coffee, fresh flowers, and a fruit basket
Rates: $75 to $115 double

CARTER HOUSE
1033 3RD ST., EUREKA, CA 95501

Reservations Phone: 707/445-1390
Description: This Victorian mansion has seven rooms for guests,
    three with private bath. The house has been stylishly restored

with antiques and Oriental rugs, yet with modern paintings and ceramics by local artists.

Amenities: Breakfast specialties might include a tart with almond filling, eggs Florentine or Benedict, or kiwi with raspberries

Special Services: Airport pickup with a 1958 Bentley, wine and brie in the afternoon, tea, cookies, and cordials at bedtime, can be arranged.

Rates: $55 to $350 double

THE OLD TOWN BED & BREAKFAST INN
1521 3RD ST., EUREKA, CA 95501

Reservations Phone: 707/445-3951

Description: This 1871 house was moved to its present location in 1915. The five rooms for guests are all individually decorated in soft colors with period furniture; two of the rooms have a shared bath.

Amenities: Full breakfast

Nearby Attractions: Redwoods State Park, Seashore State Park, museums, tubing, tennis, golf, racquetball

Special Services: Complimentary evening social hour

Rates: $55 to $70 single, $60 to $75 double

CLEONE LODGE INN
24600 N. HWY. 1, FORT BRAGG, CA 95437

Reservations Phone: 707/964-2788

Description: In a quiet setting on three acres of wooded grounds, each unit in the lodge varies in design and décor and may include antiques, wicker furniture, colorful prints, fireplaces, garden views, and kitchens.

Nearby Attractions: Mendocino's rugged coast, redwood groves, wineries, MacKerricher State Park, Lake Cleone, canoeing, trout fishing, horseback riding, bicycling, hiking

Special Services: Outdoor decks and trails.

Rates: $52 to $103 double; MasterCard and VISA accepted

HOTEL LEGER
MAIN AND LAFAYETTE, MOKELUMNE HILL, CA 95245

Reservations Phone: 209/286-1401
Description: Over 100 years ago George Leger came from Europe to this gold-rush boomtown and opened a hotel. His spirit of service and hospitality lives on today at the hotel, which combines nostalgia with modern comfort.

Nearby Attractions: Historic and scenic attractions, golf courses and summer and winter sports areas a short drive away
Special Services: The Court House Theater seating 128 presents popular stage productions in summer and is available for meetings, weddings, and banquets.
Rates: $40 to $65 double on weekends, $34 to $59 double weekdays

THE NAPA INN
1137 WARREN ST., NAPA, CA 94559

Reservations Phone: 707/257-1444
Description: This three-story turn-of-the-century home in the quaint preservation area of Napa has four spacious accommodations with bath, and furnished with antiques.
Amenities: Hearty breakfast

Nearby Attractions: Napa Valley wineries, balloon rides, lakes and rivers
Special Services: Afternoon refreshments
Rates: $80 to $90 double occupancy

TALL TIMBERS CHALETS
1012 DARMS LANE, NAPA, CA 94558

Reservations Phone: 707/252-7810
Description: The inn's country cottages are sited on two acres. Each separate cottage is decorated in country style (Laura

Ashley fabrics), and contains a bedroom, a living room (with a queen-size sofa bed), a breakfast area, and a bath.
Amenities: Continental breakfast, with fresh fruit in season

Nearby Attractions: Wineries, a geyser-fed hot spring with mud baths and massage available, Marine World/Africa
Special Services: The inn accepts well-behaved children.
Rates: $65 to $90 double, February to October; prices vary November to January.

PORTOFINO BEACH HOTEL
2306 W. OCEAN FRONT, NEWPORT BEACH, CA 92663

Reservations Phone: 714/673-7030
Description: The remodeled rooms are furnished with antiques and have private baths and an ocean view. An antique bar and gourmet Italian restaurant are available to guests.
Amenities: Continental breakfast

Nearby Attractions: McFaddens Wharf, the beach at Newport, Disneyland, Universal Studio Tour
Special Services: Beach chairs, towels, and umbrellas; local airport pickup
Rates: $100 to $210 double in summer, $90 to $190 double in winter

THE SHERMAN HOUSE
2160 GREEN ST., SAN FRANCISCO, CA 94123

Reservations Phone: 415/563-3600
Description: An 1876 historic landmark converted from a private mansion into a 14-room accommodation, the house has been meticulously restored to its original beauty with French Second Empire interiors featuring a splendid three-story music room with gallery salon, a carriage house, formal gardens, a Victorian greenhouse, and a gazebo. Rooms have canopied feather beds and fireplaces.

Nearby Attractions: Historic landmarks, cable cars, Fisherman's Wharf
Special Services: Airport limousine service, courtesy membership in one of San Francisco's best athletic clubs
Rates: $170 to $650 double

PETITE AUBERGE
863 BUSH ST., SAN FRANCISCO, CA 94108

Reservations Phone: 415/928-6000
Description: This French country inn has antiques, fresh flowers, and fireplaces.
Amenities: Juice, eggs, quiche, or French toast, croissants, muffins, granola, and coffee, tea, or milk

Nearby Attractions: All of San Francisco
Special Services: Afternoon tea and hors d'oeuvres
Rates: $105 to $195 double

THE PARSONAGE
1600 OLIVE ST., SANTA BARBARA, CA 93101

Reservations Phone: 805/962-9336
Description: This two-story, restored Queen Anne is filled with Oriental rugs and antiques.
Amenities: Fresh-squeezed orange juice, homemade breads and muffins, apple pancakes, chili cheese soufflé featured on the breakfast menu

Nearby Attractions: Santa Barbara Mission, Botanical Gardens, the Pacific Ocean
Special Services: Complimentary wine offered each evening
Rates: $65 to $125 single, $70 to $130 double

UTAH

——————— **B&B Inns** ———————

PETERSON'S BED & BREAKFAST
95 N. 300 WEST (P.O. BOX 142), MONROE, UT 84754

Reservations Phone: 801/527-4830
Description: Parts of the building are 100 years old, but fit in well with the later additions. The rooms are fitted with king-size beds, sitting areas, kitchens, private baths, and private entrances.

Amenities: Full breakfast with such specialties as country ham, Dutch apple pancakes, and homemade coffee cake

Nearby Attractions: Five national parks, museum of Indian artifacts, tennis, golf, Monroe Hot Springs
Special Services: Complimentary beverages
Rates: $35, single or double; $45 for a suite

Alaska & Hawaii

ALASKA

─────────── B&B Reservation Services ───────────

ALASKA PRIVATE LODGINGS
P.O. BOX 200047F, ANCHORAGE, AK 99520

Offers B&B Homes In: Anchorage, Seward, Homer, Palmer, Willow, Talkeetna, Fairbanks, Kenai, Wasilla, Denali Park area
Reservations Phone: 907/258-1717
Phone Hours: 9 a.m. to 5 p.m. Monday through Friday
Price Range of Homes: $35 to $55 single, $40 to $75 double
Breakfast Included in Price: Breakfasts vary with each home
Brochure Available: Call or write for free brochure and directory.
Reservations Should Be Made: Advance reservations preferred; one-night deposit required; VISA and MasterCard accepted

Scenic Attractions Near the B&B Homes: Alaska Oil Pipeline; Alaska Railroad; glaciers, gold mines, salmon-spawning waters, mountain ranges, native wildlife; city, state, and national parks
Major Schools, Universities Near the B&B Homes: U. of Alaska at Anchorage, Alaska Pacific U.

Best B&Bs ─────────────────────────────

■ Private home in Anchorage, Alaska. This B&B is close to the airport, and offers three guest rooms, each with private bath. The hostess serves a full breakfast. Easy access to public transportation.

■ Carriage house in Anchorage, Alaska. In a downtown but quiet area. This B&B is close to restaurants and sightseeing tour stops. You will stay in a private apartment with breakfast provisions available.

■ Log home in Rock Creek, Alaska. Located only 20 miles north of the entrance to Denali National Park (this park with its grazing grizzlies, elk and moose, and spectacular Mount McKinley is one of the wonders of the world). Two guest rooms are available with twin beds and a shared bath. Full breakfast is served to the guests. *Insider's Tip:* Use the free bus inside Denali to travel to the various points of interest. In the spring you'll see grizzlies and their cubs playing on the plains below.

ACCOMMODATIONS ALASKA STYLE—STAY WITH A FRIEND
3605 ARCTIC BLVD., SUITE 173, ANCHORAGE, AK 99503

Offers B&B Homes In: Anchorage, Fairbanks, Juneau, Sitka, Homer, Soldotna, Anchor Point, Valdex, Seward, Palmer, Wasilla, Willow, Trapper Creek, Glennallen, Denali Park, Gustavus

Reservations Phone: 907/344-4006

Phone Hours: 8 a.m. to 8 p.m. May to September; shorter hours off-season

Price Range of Homes: $35 to $75 single, $40 to $85 double

Breakfast Included in Price: Continental to full American

Brochure Available: $1 for descriptive listing

Reservations Should Be Made: In advance for best selection

Scenic Attractions Near the B&B Homes: Denali National Park, Kanai Fjord National Park, Glacier Bay National Park, glaciers, Home Spit, volcanic mountains, salmon and halibut fishing, kayaking, floating, and canoeing

Major Schools, Universities Near the B&B Homes: U. of Alaska, Alaska Pacific U., Sheldon Jackson College

Best B&Bs

- New home on a hillside in Sitka, Alaska. This home offers great views—of Cascade Creek below, and in the distance Sitka Sound, Mount Edgecume, and the Pacific Ocean. On crisp mornings you can take a brisk two-mile walk to downtown Sitka. Rooms are furnished with antiques and reproductions. Home no. 111P.

- Home in downtown Anchorage, Alaska. Near a small park and close to the new Anchorage Coastal Trail. The home is large and plainly furnished. Good views of Mount Susitna outside. *Insider's Tip:* Want to know about the early days of Alaska. Talk with your host, a pioneer goldmining engineer. This home was presented with two "Wild about Anchorage" awards in 1987. Home no. 1D.

■ European-style country home in Palmer, Alaska. In Palmer
you're near good fishing, the Matanuska Valley, Knik Glacer, and
jet-boat tours. This B&B is located in a pine forest. The pets may
surprise you; six good-natured llamas graze around the house.
Good walking trails nearby. A full breakfast is served (eggs,
toast, cold cuts, cake). The host speaks English and German and
understands Dutch. Home no. 93N.

FAIRBANKS BED & BREAKFAST
P.O. BOX 74573, FAIRBANKS, AK 99707

Offers B&B Homes In: Fairbanks
Reservations Phone: 907/452-4967
Phone Hours: 8 a.m. to 8 p.m. daily
Price Range of Homes: $36 and up single, $48 and up double
Breakfast Included in Price: Continental (juice, roll or toast,
  coffee), cereals
Brochure Available: Free
Reservations Should Be Made: Reservations accepted anytime if
  guaranteed with $25 deposit

Scenic Attractions Near the B&B Homes: Cruises on sternwheel-
  er *Discovery*, Alaska Salmon Bake, mining valley at Alaskaland
Major Schools, Universities Near the B&B Homes: U. of Alaska at Fairbanks

Best B&Bs _____
■ See their "50 Best B&Bs" winner in Part III.

_____ **B&B Inns** _____

GUSTAVUS INN
P.O. BOX 60, GUSTAVUS, AK 99826

Reservations Phone: 907/697-2254
Description: The inn combines a traditional homestead atmosphere and magnificent Alaskan setting with modern accommodations and convenient transportation. Bedrooms have queen-
  size or twin beds and private baths.
Amenities: Full breakfast

Nearby Attractions: Glacier Bay National Park, fishing for salmon or halibut, kayaking, biking, nature walks
Special Services: Boat tours of Glacier Bay, three meals a day served
Rates: $69.50 single, $139 double

ALASKAN HOTEL
167 S. FRANKLIN ST., JUNEAU, AK 99801

Reservations Phone: 907/586-1000, or toll free 800/327-9347
Description: Alaska's oldest hotel opened in 1913. It has 10 rooms with private bath and 30 rooms with shared bath. Over 50 pieces of stained glass adorn the hotel. The hotel is on the National Register of Historic Places.

Nearby Attractions: The capital city of Juneau
Special Services: Hot tubs and sauna, oak antique phones, kitchenettes, TVs
Rates: $36 to $50 single, $41 to $55 double, in spring and summer; $25 to $36 single, $30 to $41 double, in fall and winter

HAWAII

---------- B&B Reservation Services ----------

BED & BREAKFAST HONOLULU (STATEWIDE)
3242 KAOHINANI DR., HONOLULU, HI 96817

Offers B&B Homes In: Islands of Oaho, Kauai, Maui, Hawaii, Molokai, Lanai
Reservations Phone: 808/595-7533, or toll free 800/288-4666
Phone Hours: 8 a.m. to 8 p.m. Monday through Saturday
Price Range of Homes: $25 to $250
Breakfast Included in Price: For 90% of homes
Brochure Available: Free
Reservations Should Be Made: As far in advance as possible, but last-minute reservations possible

Scenic Attractions Near the B&B Homes: All Hawaiian attractions
Major Schools, Universities Near the B&B Homes: U. of Hawaii (all campuses), Chaminade U.

PACIFIC-HAWAII BED & BREAKFAST
19 KAI NANI PL., KAILUA, OAHU, HI 96734

Offers B&B Homes In: Oahu and almost all the other Hawaiian islands
Reservations Phone: 808/262-6026 or 808/263-4848; telefax 808/261-6573
Phone Hours: 8 a.m. to 10 p.m. Monday through Friday (also on weekends and holidays)
Price Range of Homes: $20 single, $25 to $100 double
Breakfast Included in Price: Continental with Hawaiian fruits
Brochure Available: For $2
Reservations Should Be Made: Anytime; can accept short-notice reservations

Scenic Attractions Near the B&B Homes: Miles of beaches, Pali Lookout, Queen Emma Summer Palace
Major Schools, Universities Near the B&B Homes: U. of Hawaii

Best B&Bs

■ Hillside home in Anahola, Kauai, Hawaii. A California artist has created a unique personal "statement" with this unusual home. It is surrounded by terraced gardens and overlooks the beautiful Anahola Bay. The home is decorated with the artist's own paintings and objets d'art gathered from around the world. You can stay in a separate guest wing that features an individual lanai in the center of a redwood-beamed living room and library. A continental breakfast is served in the garden courtyard amid tropical plants. This B&B is located halfway between the Ne Pali Coast and the popular South Shore. *Insider's Tip:* The artist/host is available for private art instruction in his studio. Several different types of accommodations are available in this B&B. You may want to walk around and choose what's best for you (depending on availability). Home MATL-13.

■ Executive home, Oahu, Hawaii. A Kailua home with everything: a swimming pool, a stream, all right next to a golf course, and within walking distance of Kailua Beach Park. The master bedroom offers a double bed and a private entrance. A continental breakfast is served on the patio. Home TSU-8.

▪ Spanish-style home on Oahu, Hawaii. You can stay in a Spanish hacienda—style home and go to sleep to the sound of waves. Two rooms and one bath have a separate entrance, with a patio leading to a sandy beach. One room is furnished with a king-size bed, color TV, desk, and table. The other features a double bed, a single bed, a large refrigerator, and some outside cooking facilities (if you're in the mood to grill a steak). You can walk to some good restaurants. Home EP-5.

BED & BREAKFAST HAWAII
P.O. BOX 449, KAPAA, HI 96746

Offers B&B Homes In: All Hawaiian islands except Lanai
Reservations Phone: 808/822-7771
Phone Hours: 8:30 a.m. to 4:30 p.m. Monday through Saturday
Price Range of Homes: $15 to $45 single, $20 to $75 double
Breakfast Included in Price: Continental (juice, roll or toast, coffee), plus such regional specialties at some homes as banana cakes, papaya and mango breads, Hawaiian French toast with coconut syrup, fresh fruit
Brochure Available: Free
Reservations Should Be Made: 3 weeks in advance (last-minute reservations accepted if possible)

Scenic Attractions Near the B&B Homes: All national and state parks, famous zoos, historic homes, all the beauty and romance of the tropics
Major Schools, Universities Near the B&B Homes: U. of Hawaii and branches on other islands

Best B&Bs
▪ See their "50 Best B&Bs" winner in Part III.

▪ Two-story home in Honolulu, Oahu, Hawaii. Two guest rooms are available, each with a private bath. Each room has its own lanai (Hawaiian for patio) with either a garden view or a view of Diamond Head. Your hostess is a practicing artist, and very active as an officer in the State Foundation on Culture and the Arts.

▪ Home on Sprecklesville Beach, Maui, Hawaii. Shrubbery blocks the view of the beach from the home, but walk around the greenery and you're on a beautiful white sand beach. The accommodation offered is a large guest room with a private bath and a queen-size bed. An additional bedroom is available with a double bed. Guests can enjoy a large enclosed porch surrounded by the garden. Sprecklesville is just a few miles from the airport and very convenient for touring Maui. Home M-12.

■ Llama farm in Kailua-Kona, Big Island of Hawaii, Hawaii. That is no misprint. This B&B is located on a farm filled with lovable llamas. They are unusually gentle and make good pets (a llama craze is continuing to grow in the U.S.). Your unit is spacious and private, with a pullman kitchen where you can prepare light meals. You can breakfast on your own or join your hosts downstairs. Your view is terrific from this five-acre farm—the blue Pacific with green flashes at sunset. Home H-34.

GO NATIVE . . . HAWAII
P.O. BOX 13115, LANSING, MI 48901

Offers B&B Homes In: Almost all of the Hawaiian islands
Reservations Phone: 517/349-9598
Phone Hours: 24 hours
Price Range of Homes: $30 and up
Breakfast Included in Price: Varies at each location
Brochure Available: Free; $2 for a directory of homes
Reservations Should Be Made: Confirmed in writing upon receipt of required deposit

Scenic Attractions Near the B&B Homes: All Hawaiian attractions
Major Schools, Universities Near the B&B Homes: U. of Hawaii and branches on other islands

Best B&Bs
■ Former missionary home on the Big Island of Hawaii. This historic home will drive history buffs mad. The windows are hand-poured glass panes. The Franklin fireplace was manufacturered in New York City in 1867. Those stairway rails were made of natural untreated koa wood branches. *Insider's Tip:* Long-term guests may want to stay in the pleasant garden studio apartment with a full kitchen and bath. Home 1-23.

■ A B&B in Pacific Heights, Honolulu, Hawaii. The view from this home is tremendous, and includes the city and the ocean. You can relax in the huge common living room. *Insider's Tip:* Head for the balcony for some great views of the sunsets. Hawaii seems to have the most beautiful sunsets in the world. Home 2-20.

▪ Home and cottage in Kailua, Kona, Hawaii. Tropical fruit grows right outside your door. You can stay in a bedroom in the main house which has a private bath and color TV. Or you can choose the cottage, which has a complete kitchen and TV. *Note:* Breakfast is not served in the cottage. Home 2-19.

Canada

BRITISH COLUMBIA

―――――――― B&B Reservation Services ――――――――

AB&C BED & BREAKFAST OF VANCOUVER
P.O. BOX 66109, STN F, VANCOUVER, BC V5N 5L4,
CANADA

Offers B&B Homes In: Vancouver and Victoria
Reservations Phone: 604/263-5595
Phone Hours: 9 a.m. to 5 p.m. daily; answering service after
   hours
Price Range of Homes: $35 ($30 U.S.) to $45 ($38 U.S.)
   single, $50 ($42 U.S.) to $60 ($51 U.S.) double
Breakfast Included in Price: Continental to full American
Brochure Available: Free
Reservations Should Be Made: As soon as possible, but last-
   minute reservations accepted

Scenic Attractions Near the B&B Homes: Stanley Park,
   Capilano Suspension Bridge, Queen Elizabeth Park
Major Schools, Universities near the B&B Homes: U. of British
   Columbia

OLD ENGLISH BED & BREAKFAST REGISTRY
P.O. BOX 86818, NORTH VANCOUVER, BC V7L 4L3,
CANADA

Offers B&B Homes In: Vancouver, North Vancouver, West Vancouver
Reservations Phone: 604/986-5069
Phone Hours: 9 a.m. to 5 p.m. daily; answering machine other
   hours
Price Range of Homes: $30 ($26 U.S.) to $40 ($34 U.S.)
   single, $45 ($38 U.S.) to $70 ($59 U.S.) double

Breakfast Included in Price: Full breakfast
Brochure Available: Free
Reservations Should Be Made: Best to reserve ahead, although same-day calls are accepted when possible.

Scenic Attractions Near the B&B Homes: Stanley Park; Grouse Mountain, offering tramway to top; Nitobe Memorial Gardens
Major Schools, Universities Near the B&B Homes: U. of British Columbia, Simon Fraser U.

Best B&Bs

■ **Home in West Vancouver, B.C.** This contemporary B&B offers rooms with queen-size beds, private baths, and color TV. There is a swimming pool available to guests. The home is located right across from the Cypress Park ski/hiking area. You can take some great pictures of Vancouver from a nearby viewpoint. You will be close to Grouse Mountain, Capilano Canyon, and the fish hatchery, and about a ten-minute drive from cafés, bistros, shops, and a beach walk in Ambleside park. *Insider's Tip:* The hosts, the Pages, can book you on a city tour or a day trip to Victoria.

■ **Home in North Vancouver, B.C.** The Krouzelka family will be your hosts in this B&B with a self-contained suite: bedroom with a queen-size bed, a bathroom with an oversize tub, and a living room which has its own fireplace, TV, and sofa bed. Guests can make their own breakfast from the fixings in the refrigerator or join the hosts. They are also welcome to relax on the patio and in the backyard. Bus service to downtown Vancouver is nearby.

■ **New town house in Vancouver, B.C.** This B&B offers guest accommodations with a private bath. When you stay here, you are only a block away from the beach at English Bay, and just a few blocks from Derman Street (with cafés, shops, and entertainment). Breakfast fixings are left in the refrigerator for breakfast at your leisure. *Insider's Tip:* On weekends the host likes to cook for guests. You are welcome to use the washing machine and the telephone (when you charge calls to your credit card).

VANCOUVER BED & BREAKFAST LTD.

1685 INGLETON AVE., VANCOUVER, BC V5C 4I8, CANADA

Offers B&B Homes In: The Greater Vancouver area
Reservations Phone: 604/291-6147
Phone Hours: 8:30 a.m. to 4:30 p.m. Monday through Friday
Price Range of Homes: $40 ($34 U.S.) to $65 ($55 U.S.) per room

Breakfast Included in Price: Continental to full American
Brochure Available: Free
Reservations Should Be Made: 48 hours in advance; minimum two-night stay

Scenic Attractions Near the B&B Homes: Vancouver city sights, Stanley Park, mountains, ocean, public markets
Major Schools, Universities Near the B&B Homes: U. of British Columbia, Simon Fraser U.

Best B&Bs

■ The Bavarian, in Vancouver, B.C. This large family home offers guests a bedroom with queen-size brass canopy bed, sitting area, and private full bathroom. You can view the deep woods from the deck, while immersed in a deluxe Jacuzzi tub.

■ Writer's retreat in West Vancouver, B.C. The home is lighted by many leaded windows. For inspiration—a living room with a stone fireplace, oak beams, with a gentle creek by the side of the house. A full Canadian breakfast is served.

V.I.P. BED & BREAKFAST LTD.

1786 TEAKWOOD RD., VICTORIA, BC V8N 1E2, CANADA

Offers B&B Homes In: Victoria, Sidney
Reservations Phone: 604/477-5604
Phone Hours: 7 a.m. to 10 p.m. daily
Price Range of Homes: $30 ($26 U.S.) to $35 ($30 U.S.) single, $45 ($38 U.S.) to $50 ($42 U.S.) double
Breakfast Included in Price: Full American (juice, eggs, bacon, toast, coffee)
Brochures Available: Free
Reservations Should Be Made: 2 weeks in advance (last-minute reservations accepted if possible)

Scenic Attractions Near the B&B Homes: Butchart Gardens, Provincial Museum, Craigdarroch Castle, Beacon Hill Park, Parliament Buildings
Major Schools, Universities Near the B&B Homes: U. of Victoria, Camosun College

NOVA SCOTIA

_____ **B&B Reservation Services** _____

NOVA SCOTIA FARM & COUNTRY VACATION ASSOCIATION
NEWPORT STATION, HANTS CO., NS B0N 2B0, CANADA

Offers B&B Homes In: Rural Nova Scotia
Information Phone: 902/798-5864
Phone Hours: 9 a.m. to 7 p.m. daily
Price Range of Homes: $15 ($13 U.S.) to $25 ($21 U.S.)
  single, $25 ($21 U.S.) to $40 ($34 U.S.) double
Breakfast Included in Price: Continental or full American; in
  some homes, all meals can be provided if the guest so wishes.
Brochure Available: Free
Reservations Should Be Made: Anytime (last-minute reservations
  accepted)

Best B&Bs _____

■ Sea-view fisherman's home in Musquodoboit, N.S. From this
1860 home you have a picture view of the ocean, islands, and
fishing boats. There are three guest rooms on the second floor,
with a full breakfast served. *Insider's Tip:* There's a historic lighthouse right on the property, a great spot to set up an artist's
easel or to take some sunset photographs. Your hosts are fifth-
generation owners and enjoy sharing some of the "mystery" stories
about this lighthouse.

■ Turn-of-the-century home in Newport Station, N.S. Known as
Wavertree Inn, this B&B is filled with antiques and collectibles. It's
located about 45 minutes from Halifax, at the gateway to the
Annapolis Valley, and only 5 minutes away from the Windsor and
Matrock ski hill. Breakfast includes homemade bread, muffins,
jams and jellies, and "eggs—if the chickens cooperate!"

■ Doiremaple farm in Mabou, N.S. About 35 miles north of Port
Hastings on the Ceilidh Trail is a B&B that is also a working dairy
farm. You and your family can watch many of the daily activities
or take a walk in the woods. Scottish music and culture abounds
in this area. Two double rooms are available with a shared bath.
A country-style breakfast is included in the very modest rate: $35
($29 U.S.) per couple.

---------- B&B Reservation Services ----------

BED & BREAKFAST PRINCE EDWARD COUNTY
P.O. BOX 160, BLOOMFIELD, ON K0K 1G0, CANADA

Offers B&B Homes In: Prince Edward County, on the north shore of Lake Ontario
Reservations Phone: 613/393-3046
Phone Hours: 9 a.m. to 8 p.m. daily
Price Range of Homes: $21 ($18 U.S.) to $26 ($22 U.S.) single, $30 ($26 U.S.) to $44 ($37 U.S.) double
Breakfast Included in Price: Full American, including homemade muffins, bread, tea biscuits, jams, jellies, etc.
Brochure Available: Free if you send 48¢ (40¢ U.S.) postage and a self-addressed envelope
Reservations Should Be Made: 1 month in advance in July and August (last-minute reservations accepted if possible)

Scenic Attractions Near the B&B Homes: Famous sand dunes, beaches, sailing, windsurfing, birdwatching, museums, "Bird City," bicycling, the White Chapel Meeting House, Macaulay House

Best B&Bs
■ A century-old home in Rednersville, Ontario. In a quiet location near Trenton and Belleville, this home is furnished with antiques and caters to adults. The hostess enjoys cooking and shares her interests in travel with guests over fresh muffins. The home is one mile from the water and near several art galleries.

OTTAWA AREA BED & BREAKFAST
P.O. BOX 4848, STATION E, OTTAWA, ON K1S 5J1,
CANADA

Offers B&B Homes In: Ottawa and area
Reservations Phone: 613/563-0161
Phone Hours: 10 a.m. to 9 p.m. preferred, but available 24
  hours daily
Price Range of Homes: $34 ($29 U.S.) single, $44 ($37 U.S.)
  double
Breakfast Included in Price: Full American (juice, eggs, bacon,
  toast, coffee)
Brochure Available: Free
Reservations Should Be Made: 2 weeks in advance (last-minute
  reservations accepted if possible)

Scenic Attractions Near the B&B Homes: Parliament Buildings
  of Canada, Rideau Canal, museums, art galleries
Major Schools, Universities Near the B&B Homes: U. of Ottawa, Carleton U., Algonquin College, St. Paul's U.

Best B&Bs

■ Renovated home in Center Town, Ottawa. Located within walking distance of the Parliament Buildings. You have a choice of a
room with a double or single bed—with a balcony. Breakfast is
included. *Insider's Tip:* Take a peek at the kitchen. It was created
by one of Ottawa's top designers.

■ Suburban home in Ottawa. The house is furnished with country
and Victorian furniture. You can walk to the Nepean Sailing Club
overlooking the Ottawa River. Guests are welcome to use the
in-ground swimming pool and the TV room.

■ Grain farm outside Ottawa. This B&B is located about 45
minutes from downtown Ottawa. It was built in 1867 and offers
guests a variety of activities, including swimming in the in-ground
pool, taking country walks, and viewing various farm animals. The
breakfast "will last you all day."

COUNTRY HOST
R.R. #1, PALGRAVE, ON L0N 1P0, CANADA

Offers B&B Homes In: Ontario, from Toronto, northwest almost
  300 miles to Tobermory; also at Point Pelee National Park area

on Lake Erie (where thousands of birds migrate in spring and fall) and on Lake Nipissing at North Bay
Reservations Phone: 519/941-7633
Phone Hours: 8 a.m. to midnight daily (no collect calls)
Price Range of Homes: $35 ($30 U.S.) single, $40 ($34 U.S.) to $50 ($42 U.S.) double
Breakfast Included in Price: Full American (juice or fruit in season, bacon or sausage, eggs, toast, coffee); real maple syrup, Canadian bacon and hot muffins, often served (lunches and dinners available in some homes if requested in advance)
Brochure Available: Free—send for personal answer, including stamped, self-addressed envelope
Reservations Should Be Made: At least 1 week in advance (last-minute reservations accepted if possible)

Scenic Attractions Near the B&B Homes: Bruce Trail, conservation areas, swimming, fishing, golfing, skiing, ice-fishing, snowmobiling, antiques and craft shops, wildflowers and hundreds of bird species

Best B&Bs
■ See their "50 Best B&Bs" winner in Part III.

QUÉBEC

———— B&B Reservation Services ————

MONTRÉAL BED AND BREAKFAST
4912 VICTORIA, MONTRÉAL, PQ H3W 2N1, CANADA

Offers B&B Homes In: Montréal and nearby communities (Dorval, where Dorval Airport is located; the Eastern Townships; Laurentian Mountains area)
Reservations Phone: 514/738-9410 or 514/738-3859
Phone Hours: 9 a.m. to 9 p.m. daily
Price Range of Homes: $30 ($26 U.S.) to $40 ($34 U.S.) single, $50 ($42 U.S.) to $100 ($84 U.S.) double
Breakfast Included in Price: Full American (juice, eggs, bacon, toast, coffee), plus regional specialties
Brochure Available: For $1

Reservations Should Be Made: 3 weeks in advance, if by mail; telephone reservations accepted; deposit by VISA, MasterCard, or American Express

Scenic Attractions Near the B&B Homes: Mount Royal Park, Olympic Stadium, St. Joseph Oratory, Botanical Gardens, Place des Arts, Old Montréal, Museum of Fine Arts, Underground City
Major Schools, Universities Near the B&B Homes: McGill, U. de Montréal

Best B&Bs ─────────────────────────────────
■ See their "50 Best B&Bs" winner in Part III.

═══

GÎTE QUÉBEC BED & BREAKFAST
3729 AVE. LE CORBUSIER, STE-FOY, PQ G1W 4R8, CANADA

Offers B&B Homes In: Québec City and area
Reservations Phone: 418/651-1860
Phone Hours: 8 a.m. to 9 p.m. daily
Price Range of Homes: $40 ($34 U.S.) single, $60 ($51 U.S.) double
Breakfast Included in Price: Full American (juice, eggs, bacon, toast, coffee)
Brochure Available: Free
Reservations Should Be Made: 2 weeks in advance (last-minute reservations accepted if possible)

Scenic Attractions Near the B&B Homes: Château Frontenac, the Citadel and Governors' Promenade, Dufferin Terrace, the Plains of Abraham, Ste. Anne de Beaupré, Winter Carnival, Montmorency Falls, Île d'Orléans, Fort Museum Artillery Park, Chevalier House, Place d'Armes, Ursuline Convent and Museum

PART

The 50 Best B&B Homes in North America

A Note on My Selections

In the Depression era bed-and-breakfast may have only been a sparsely furnished room and a thin cup of coffee in a modest frame house somewhere along the highway. But today the B&B movement has become the Cinderella of the U.S. travel industry, and the accommodations, services, and thoughtfulness of hosts have created a delightful new way to travel. To help honor these new standards, *Frommer's Bed & Breakfast North America* guidebook has created a new category "The 50 Best B&B Homes in North America."

In making these selections I have relied heavily on the recommendations of the bed-and-breakfast reservation services. Each was invited to nominate just one home, the best home on its list. The men and women who operate these services may see and judge hundreds of homes and are in a unique position to point with pride at a home that rises above the rest in their areas. I have also selected certain individual homes that are not connected with any reservation service, based on recommendations of travel writer colleagues, published reviews in the media, photographs, and written comments of guests who have stayed in the homes.

Of course, I couldn't resist selecting a home where the host is a professional magician who entertains his guests with magic tricks after breakfast. Or the B&B home that takes guests on a stagecoach tour of California's wine country. Or the granddaughter of a famous American artist who welcomes guests to the artist's studio home and serves them "ethereal eggs" with sour cream and cheese.

Some homes are truly spectacular southern mansions that rival *Gone with the Wind*'s Tara. Others are beautiful apartments with skyline views. Still others are more modest rural dwellings with a spectacular mountain or ocean view, unbelievable gourmet breakfasts, or a hostess who babysits and leaves a glass of sherry and cheeses on a bedstand at night.

Is each a perfect "10"? No, but I think each offers something really special to guests.

There is one confusing element. Some of the B&B homes I have selected call themselves "inns." But I have arbitrarily decided that any B&B operation in a private home is a "B&B home," to distinguish it from the larger commercial inns which are basically small hotels that serve breakfast and also call themselves "B&B inns."

Homes change owners and standards can change. If you stay at any of these homes and are disappointed—or find what you believe is a superior B&B in the same area—you're invited to become one of our "B&B Critics" and write to me with your evaluations and discoveries. The collective judgment of our readers will play a major part in future selections of the "50 Best."

But meanwhile you can use this list to help plan a wonderful B&B vacation for yourself and your family all across North America.

Note: In the case of homes nominated by reservations services, I have given only partial addresses. Please contact the service at the phone number listed. Some hosts prefer not to be contacted directly. For homes not listed by reservation services I have provided complete addresses and each host's phone number.

NEUBAUER HOUSE

FAIRBANKS, ALASKA

(Nominated by Fairbanks Bed & Breakfast)

This is a new two-story frame house with a large yard and deck. It's located in a quiet residential neighborhood, close to local historic houses and eight blocks from the downtown area. For breakfast the host serves juice, rolls, and cereal. In the summertime there will be fresh fruit, honeydew melons, and pancakes. There is a TV in the room. Guests (for a donation) can use the laundry facilities.

Rates: $48 to $68 double, May to September; $30 double, October to April
Reservations: 907/452-4967

FRENCH COUNTRY HOME

SEDONA, ARIZONA

(Nominated by Bed & Breakfast in Arizona)

This is a home with elegant décor, nestled among the red rocks and pines of Sedona. It uses passive solar energy. The lower-level rooms have private entries that lead to an outdoor patio. One bedroom has a queen-size bed, TV, and radio. One bedroom has a double bed. (*Note:* You will have complete privacy. The hosts will take only one guest party, one to four people, at a time.) You will be greeted with afternoon refreshments: coffee, tea, homemade cookies. Wine and snacks are served at 5 p.m. The host couple is very helpful. They will tell you about local points of interest and make dinner reservations for you at some of the area's best restaurants.

Rates: $75 to $85 double
Reservations: 602/995-2831

THE HOPE-MERRILL HOUSE

P.O. BOX 42, GEYERVILLE, CA 95441

Bob and Rosalite Hope purchased this house in 1980 and brought it back to its early Victorian life. All of the wallpapers and trim bring back the full sense of the period. The house was once an early stagecoach stop. The hosts go out of their way to welcome guests, with a glass of wine at the end of the day and a home-cooked breakfast at the beginning. They have also created a unique diversion for guests, "Stage a Picnic," an idea which was featured on national TV. Guests are taken by horse-drawn stage to wineries in Sonoma County, followed by a picnic: smoked meats, poultry, fresh garden vegetables, local cheeses, and—of course—some good California wine.

Rates: $60 to $150
Reservations: 707/857-3356

SANTA NELLA HOUSE

12130 HWY. 16, GUERNEVILLE, CA 95446

This 1870 Italian-Victorian-style farmhouse with a white circular veranda and artistic latticework is the perfect hideaway in the redwood Russian River wine country. It's located on the site of the first olive and lumber mills in the area, and was the main dwelling of the Santa Nella winery, established in 1880. The house is heated with wood-burning stoves. Two of the guest rooms have fireplaces. Turn-of-the-century furnishings, high ceilings, and deep red carpets are featured. Each bedroom has special character. The genial innkeepers serve what one guest praised as "almost sinful" breakfasts, including freshly ground coffee, eggs (Benedict on Sunday), omelets, homemade date-nut bread and jams, large fresh-fruit plates of mango, papaya, kiwi, melon, pineapple, etc., in season. Santa Nella House is within 2½ miles of Redwood Grove State Park, and there are 25 wineries to visit within 25 miles.

Rates: $70 to $80 double on weekends and holidays; $65 to $75 on weekdays
Reservations: 707/869-9488

TERRACE MANOR

1353 ALVARADO TERRACE, LOS ANGELES, CA 90006

A pleasant way to stay right in the midst of downtown L.A., this 1902 home is a registered National Historic Landmark and has original stained-glass windows and oak paneling. Period furnishings, unusual collectibles, and a gallery of artwork complete the early-century mood. This home and five other landmark homes surround a small park, yet the Los Angeles Convention Center is only eight blocks away. You're approximately one mile from downtown businesses and shopping areas. For breakfast, strawberries and cream, eggs Florentine, peach flan pie, fried bananas, lemon mousse with berries, and melon with piña colada yogurt dressing are just some of the surprises. The host is a professional magician who performs for guests after breakfast or during the afternoon social hour, when wine and refreshments are served. Arrangements can be made for guests to attend the exclusive "Magic Castle," a private club for magicians and their guests.

Rates: $60 to $90 double
Reservations: 213/381-1478

THE MILCAN HOME

PASADENA, CALIFORNIA

*(Nominated by Eye Openers Bed & Breakfast
Reservations)*

Imagine living in a Spanish-style stucco home with a walled garden, patio, and swimming pool. Then think about being on a lovely boulevard in Pasadena, a small charming city known for its gracious homes and cultural offerings—just 15 miles northeast of Los Angeles. The home is only a mile from the Huntington Library and two miles from museums and numerous good restaurants. The hostess serves a full breakfast of cheese, meat, eggs, coffee, tea, and breads.

Rates: $40 to $50 double
Reservations: 213/684-4428 or 818/797-2055

THE WILSON HOME

3995 SPRING MOUNTAIN RD., ST. HELENA, CA 94574

This "lodge" nestled in a forest, a rustic gem on four acres, has two guest units in the main residence. Each has a private entrance and bath, and one has a fireplace. Rooms are decorated with antiques, and fully carpeted. All possible amenities for total comfort are stressed. Breakfast consists of half a cantaloupe filled with fresh-grown strawberries/raspberries; fresh-ground coffee; homemade nut and fruit breads; orange juice; jams, jellies, and hand-pressed butter; muffins; and croissants. The Wilson Home is just minutes from major wineries, restaurants, spas, balloon rides. Private wineries accept Wilson Home guests, including the "Falcon Crest" location for the TV series. You can swim in the pool on the property, walk mountain paths, or picnic on the grounds.

Rates: $77 to $80 double
Reservations: 707/963-3794

DAVIS HOME

WHITTIER, CALIFORNIA

(Nominated by CoHost, America's Bed & Breakfast)

Want to take your children or grandchildren to Disneyland, Knott's Berry Farm, and Universal Studios—and then return to a luxurious home surrounded by exotic plants? All bedrooms here are decorator-designed with elegant private baths. From the deck you can see Los Angeles, Long Beach, and Catalina Island. Cooking is southern style, with bacon, sausage or ham, eggs, potatoes or grits, fresh fruit, and juice. Regional California dishes such as huevos rancheros, frijoles refritos, and fresh fruit, or pancakes, waffles, and popovers, are also served. The host may pick you up at the airport (for about what you'd pay a local bus service). The host will also plan and escort tours of the area, provide babysitting, and even host patio brunches or dinners for guests. Golf or tennis can also be arranged.

Rates: $55 to $60 double, May to September; $50 to $55 double,
October to April
Reservations: 213/699-8427

WEBBER PLACE

YOUNTVILLE, CALIFORNIA

(Nominated by Wine Country Reservations)

This is a romantic hideaway for lovers and wine lovers. This B&B was built in the 1850s as a farmhouse and you will see many traces of its ancestry in such touches as clawfoot bathtubs. Every room has its own distinctive antiques. When you arrive you'll be served complimentary wine. Each morning at breakfast you'll have home-baked muffins and fresh fruit. After a day of wine-country touring, you can sit out on that big front porch and enjoy the gardens.

Rates: To $99 double
Reservations: 707/257-7757 or 707/944-1109

MANOR HOUSE

NORFOLK, CONNECTICUT

(Nominated by Covered Bridge Bed & Breakfast)

An 1898 Victorian English Tudor estate on five park-like acres. Guests who have stayed here are very enthusiastic. Wrote one, "I felt the need to tell you again what a lovely time we had while staying with you. You have created such a comfortable, friendly atmosphere in your home, making one feel part of a family." Another waxed poetic: "A peaceful wind blows gently around the Victorian palace." Still another said, "Simply breathtaking and charming." Many of the guest rooms have working fireplaces. Norfolk is a lovely little town surrounded by pine trees and a center of music during the summer.

Rates: $65 to $135 double
Reservations: 203/542-5690

1900 VICTORIAN MANSION

WASHINGTON, D.C.

(Nominated by the Bed & Breakfast League/Sweet Dreams & Toast)

This B&B is located in the Dupont Circle section of Washington. One guest described it as "that fabulous old house." It is old—built right at the start of the century. And it's fabulous. The place is filled with fireplaces, original woodwork, high ceilings—the kind of place where politicians would party in smoke-filled rooms prior to the surgeon-general's warnings about smoking. (It's not allowed in the house.) Guests can play visiting celebrities (which they are) and read in the library or join other guests for a glass of sherry at the end of the day. With advance notice, the host will provide breakfast in your room. You have a choice of six guest bedrooms. Five of them have a full bath complete with old-fashioned tub and modern shower. Guests are welcome to store snacks in the refrigerator and use the small bar.

Rates: $60 to $65 double
Reservations: 202/363-7767

THE BERNARD HOME

ST. PETERSBURG BEACH, FLORIDA

(Nominated by B&B Suncoast Accommodations)

This one-story, five-bedroom Spanish home on a waterway with dock, hot tub, and rooftop deck is located on the Paradise Island of St. Petersburg Beach, overlooking milky-white sand beaches in the Gulf of Mexico. Each room has a refrigerator, television, air conditioning, heating unit, and separate entrance. Additional rooms are available for children. Guests are invited to use the kitchen, laundry, horseshoe pit, and gas grill. Breakfast consists of fruit in season, coffee, danish, muffins, juice, and jams. You're invited to "help yourself" to bacon and eggs as well. The home is less than an hour from Busch Gardens, Dale Museum, and Sunken Gardens, and two hours from Disneyland. As one guest recently summed it up: "We always felt at home and that makes a vacation something special and unforgettable." The hosts will take you on local tours as well.

Rates: $60 double, December 1 to April 30; $45 double, May 1 to November 30 (weekly rate available)
Reservations: 813/360-1753

DOWNTOWN MANSION

ATLANTA, GEORGIA

(Nominated by Bed & Breakfast Atlanta)

It's hard to believe, but some vacationers in Atlanta are actually waiting to cram themselves into tiny hotel cubbyholes and pay a small fortune for the privilege. Other knowledgeable B&B travelers have discovered the space and luxury of this Atlanta mansion. It was built in 1916 as the honeymoon cottage. The home has been completely restored without losing such marvelous touches as those high ceilings, heart-pine floors, and an antique tile fireplace hearth. You have a choice of two guest rooms, each with private bath. The first has a double bed, lace curtains, and an adjoining full bath. The other has an old sleigh bed (double) and antique furniture. After touring Atlanta, you can join the friendly cat on the front porch. The host is a real estate marketing consultant, a good person to ask where the current real estate market is headed.

Rates: $60, single or double
Reservations: 404/875-0525

REMSHART-BROOKS HOUSE

106 W. JONES ST., SAVANNAH, GA 31401

The Remshart-Brooks House was built in 1853–1854, the second house of a four-house row. Authentically restored, this row is now the focal point of many historic tours. Take a closer look at the bricks on the front, for you may never see their like again; the source of the clay and the formula for these lovely handmade Savannah gray bricks have been lost. You can stay in a suite furnished with country antiques. There's a fireplace in the living room, the original cooking fireplace of the home. Breakfast is provided in the suite, and guests can dine at their leisure on such items as sour cream coffee cake, molasses and rum muffins and sausage-cheese biscuits, all home-baked by your hostess, Anne Barnett.

Rates: $60 double
Reservations: 912/234-6928

HOME ON THE BAY

HANALEI, KAUAI, HAWAII

(Nominated by Bed & Breakfast Hawaii)

When you awake in the morning on the "Garden Isle," you are just a 100-yard dash from Hanalei Bay. You can view the bay from a second-story deck, and the rest of the scenery is right out of a Hollywood tropical isle film: lush green mountains and waterfalls. The upstairs bedroom has a queen-size bed, antique furniture, and an ocean view. The second accommodation is a one-bedroom apartment on the ground floor. You can sleep on the queen-size bed or go native on the futon. The continental breakfast includes fresh island fruit. The town of Hanalei is only a short distance away. *Insider's Tip:* While staying on Kauai, check out those helicopter tours that take you soaring over some incredible mountains, beaches, and falls. It is one of life's most memorable experiences.

Rates: $55, single or double, for one bedroom; $70 double for the private apartment; $75 triple

Reservations: 808/822-7771

HOLMES RETREAT

178 N. MINK CREEK RD., POCATELLO, ID 83204

How can you resist a B&B that makes this offer: "Breakfast in bed, beside big windows, or on a deck where hummingbirds play." The hostess, Shirley Holmes, mother of seven grown children, extends the art of mothering to her guests. She serves her homemade muffins on blue china, with butter and chokecherry jelly. Each morning she tries to plan a different breakfast experience, even playing background music on the stereo (Frank Mills's "Sunday Morning Suite" is the odds-on favorite). Breakfast may also include "shirred eggs baked in their own ramekin . . . sprinkled with herbs and onion. Julienne slices of ham and slices of mushroom top the white of the eggs, then cheddar cheese is grated over all." You can work off the calories by going horseback riding nearby, canoeing on the Snake River, birdwatching, or just enjoying the over-six acres of Holmes Retreat. On summer eves you can even arrange to have your hostess plan a romantic dinner by a small bonfire on the grounds. The fireside table is set with linen, crystal goblets, china, and flowers—with love songs playing from a nearby speaker. Who said romance was dead?

Rates: $45 double
Reservations: 203/232-5518

HAAGEN HOUSE

617 STATE ST., ALTON, IL 62002

This Victorian-style home with Italian influence was built by Bavarian immigrant and dry-goods store owner, Louis Haagen, in 1868. The one-room studio suite with private bath, kitchenette, fireplace, four-poster queen-size bed, and period antiques has a private entrance. Haagen House is located in the heart of the Christian Hill historic district, just 25 minutes from downtown St. Louis, 20 minutes from Père Marquette State Park, and 10 minutes from the village of Elsah, first to be listed in the National Register of Historic Places. It is within walking distance of bicycle and walking paths. Continental breakfast is left in the guest refrigerator to be prepared at leisure. A full breakfast (for $7.50 per guest) consists of bacon, sausage, eggs, English muffin, fresh fruit. Free transportation is offered from the train station, and transportation from the airport for an extra charge.

Rates: From $75 double
Reservations: 618/462-2419

WELCOME HALL

VERSAILLES, KENTUCKY

(Nominated by Bluegrass Bed & Breakfast)

This handsome 1792 stone house and grounds are a perfect example of that period's self-sufficient country estate. It's set in the gently rolling pastures of Kentucky's famous bluegrass region, an area devoted to thoroughbred horses, with some 400 farms producing most of the world's supply of race horses. Four-poster beds, fireplaces, and delicious breakfasts are the specialties. You awake to a breakfast of fresh strawberries in season, biscuits with country ham, and eggs just plucked from beneath the hen. It's all served in an atmosphere of charm and grace nearly two centuries old. A brick-floored summer house in the middle of an extensive walled garden provides a pleasant retreat to read or converse.

Rates: $60 double
Reservations: 606/873-3208

ACADIAN HOME

LAFAYETTE, LOUISIANA

(Nominated by Southern Comfort Bed & Breakfast Reservation Service)

This antebellum Acadian raised mansion is in the heart of Louisiana's Cajun Country and listed on the National Register of Historic Homes. It has two fully restored Victorian carriage houses on the grounds where guests can stay in three bedrooms and a suite, all with private baths. The rooms are decorated with a wonderful collection of furniture of native woods. Breakfast is a Cajun treat featuring pain perdu and other delicacies. It is served on the glassed-in porch overlooking the New Orleans—style courtyard. Or in winter, in the dining room with its original fireplace. The host is a petroleum geologist who collects guns and Samurai swords. The hostess spins, weaves, and deals in antiques. Fortunately for all the guests, she's also a gourmet cook. They both delight in helping visitors see the many points of interest in the area. The host can arrange fishing or duck-hunting trips.

Rates: $75 to $85 double
Reservations: 504/346-1928 or 504/928-9815

THE GOTT HOUSE

KENNEBUNKPORT, MAINE

(Nominated by Bed & Breakfast of Maine)

This is a historic home of Dutch colonial architecture, with antiques, sundecks, a swimming dock, a storage area for guests' bicycles, in a quiet country setting in a pine grove by a river. A full gourmet breakfast with a view includes homemade breads and fresh fruit. Private baths are available. A studio apartment is available at weekly rates. The house is located near museums, amusement parks, day cruises to offshore islands, and charter sailing or fishing boats. And it's less than two hours from Boston.

Rates: $40 to $85 double (depending on the season)
Reservations: 207/781-4528

OCEANFRONT HOME

SCARBOROUGH, MAINE

(Nominated by Pineapple Hospitality, Inc.)

When you walk the grounds of this lovely 1779 home overlooking the ocean, you'll come across a curious marker. It commemorates a violent episode right on this spot with Indians, an incident that started the Indian Wars. The Indians are friendly now and so is the hostess. She was once a star of the English stage, and her home reflects her career and her worldwide travels. Your suite consists of a large bedroom with a panoramic view. It is furnished with a double bed with a canopy, comfortable chairs, and a large private bath and adjoining dressing room, and a living room with a fireplace. Guests have access to a glassed-in sun room. An upstairs bedroom also has a glorious view. For dinner you can walk to the nearby Black Point Inn (which also offers golf, tennis, and entertainment). A private beach and yacht club is right across the street. The yacht club offers charter sailing to the public.

Rates: $75 double, $85 for a suite
Reservations: 508/990-1696

CELIE'S B&B

BALTIMORE, MARYLAND

(Nominated by the Traveller in Maryland, Inc.)

This town house has an enclosed, landscaped garden and a deck with an unbeatable view of Baltimore. It's located in the Fells Point area, just 1½ blocks from where the tugs come in. You can take a boat shuttle from Fells Point to the Baltimore Inner Harbor (May to October). There's a king-size bed by a woodstove in the bedroom.

Rates: $75 double, plus tax
Reservations: 301/269-6232

VICTORIAN HOME

BOSTON, MASSACHUSETTS

(Nominated by the Bed & Breakfast Registry Ltd.)

You can be the guest in a renovated Victorian town house located in a 19th-century landmark district adjacent to Back Bay. The three guest rooms have lovely furnishings which include an antique bed with a large oak headboard, overstuffed chairs, and sitting area. Symphony Hall is a two-block stroll, and you're only six blocks from the Boston Museum of Fine Arts. For breakfast you may get the host's favorite—"Uncle Willie's Yam Hash with poached eggs." You may often find cut flowers or a complimentary sherry in your room when you arrive home.

Rates: $60 to $75 double
Reservations: 617/646-4238

HEBERT HOUSE

WILLIAMSBURG, MASSACHUSETTS

(Nominated by Berkshire Bed & Breakfast Homes)

This 200-year-old restored farmhouse is set on 27 acres of fields and woodlands overlooking Unquemonk Mountain. It has a large country kitchen with a fireplace and Dutch oven, a screened porch and dining room for breakfast, and a private sitting room with a TV, games, and wood-burning stove. Guest rooms have antique brass and iron beds. Flowers in the room and mints on the pillow are extra touches. Breakfast goodies include homemade applesauce, rhubarb sauce, bacon and eggs, freshly baked breads, buttermilk pancakes, and homemade jams. Snowshoes and sleds are available.

Rates: $50 for one night ($45 for two or more nights) double
Reservations: 413/268-7244

WOODS INN

ANN ARBOR, MICHIGAN

(Nominated by Bed & Breakfast in Michigan)

This fine country home, decorated with the best antiques, has four rooms for guests—three doubles and one single—and a guest den and extensive screened porch. So superior are the antiques, wicker furniture, paintings, and other ornaments that Woods Inn is open as well for antiques tours. Breakfast is hearty and features Michigan produce served on antique dishes and in the 1800s mode. This historic inn is ideally located to enjoy the sports, art, theater, music, and other attractions of Ann Arbor. It is described as the "All American" city, and one of the ten best in which to retire or start a new business. The Henry Ford Museum is only 30 minutes away.

Rates: $45 to $50 double
Reservations: 313/561-6041

HIDDEN POND FARM

P.O. BOX 461, FENNVILLE, MI 49408

A friend told Edward X. Kennedy, "Have a dream, but don't be a dreamer. Make your dream into a reality." That's exactly what Mr. Kennedy did when he bought and completely restored a Michigan farm near the Lake Michigan beaches, Saugatauk and Fennville. There are two B&B bedrooms upstairs, but guests have access to seven rooms of the 13-room house, including a living room with fireplace, and a den. An outside deck overlooks the hidden pond. Guests can hike over woodland trails or cross-country ski. Mr. Kennedy offers his own special brew of coffee in the morning. He is a practical dreamer. He has been heavily landscaping his grounds and garden this year so that you can enjoy the foliage and flowers.

Rates: $75 to $90 double
Reservations: 615/561-2491

VICTORIAN HOME

MERIDIAN, MISSISSIPPI

(Nominated by Lincoln Ltd. Bed & Breakfast;
Mississippi Reservation Service)

Mississippi hospitality in every sense of the word is extended in this turn-of-the-century Victorian-style home. Gracious hosts offer a welcome beverage and genial conversation if desired. They share a wonderful collection of antiques from around the world that decorate the home. They are noted gourmet cooks and will include guests for dinner as well as breakfast by prior arrangement. For breakfast, southern cheese grits, ham, eggs, homemade muffins, omelets, Mississippi Muscadine Jellies, and "much, much more" are offered. There is plenty of acreage to jog, walk, or just relax in. Dogs are welcome, but children cannot be accommodated. There's plenty to see in this cultural, medical, industrial, and retail center of eastern Mississippi, with antebellum homes to tour. Among other things to do in Meridian are fishing and boating on beautiful lakes, or attending the Jimmie Rodgers Festival every May, the Lively Arts Festival in April, the symphony, art museum, and Little Theater.

Rates: $65 double
Reservations: 601/482-5483

JOHN F. PETO STUDIO

102 CEDAR AVE., ISLAND HEIGHTS, NJ 08732

John F. Peto was a 19th-century artist who really began to receive recognition and fame many years after his death. Today he is considered one of the major painters of his era. You can stay in the home studio he built for himself, now occupied by his granddaughter, Joy Peto Smiley. There are reproductions of his most famous paintings throughout the house. Mrs. Smiley has operated the house as a B&B for almost ten years. "It has been a wonderful human experience," said Mrs. Smiley, "especially meeting so many interesting people." She makes them welcome by serving what she calls "ethereal eggs"—two eggs with bacon, cheese, and sour cream. Many guests come to go sailing or walk around the three beaches of Island Heights.

Rates: $75 double
Reservations: 201/270-6058

ADOBE HOME

SANTA FE, NEW MEXICO

(Nominated by Bed & Breakfast Rocky Mountains)

This is a modest home (in rates) but one that offers some great, luxurious amenities. It has the natural charm of the Southwest with wooden beams, Kiva fireplaces, and hardwood floors adorned with Indian rugs. One special guest room offers a double brass bed, fireplace, writing desk, and private phone. The adjacent private bath has a heated towel rack and scented soaps. (Eat your heart out, Hyatt.) You are less than five minutes by foot from the art galleries of Canyon Road. Your host is a real estate agent who likes to talk about photography and interior design.

Rates: $65 double
Reservations: 719/630-3433

THE ALEXANDER HAMILTON HOUSE

CROTON-ON-HUDSON, NEW YORK

(Nominated by Bed & Breakfast U.S.A. Ltd.)

This 1889 Victorian home has a 20th-century swimming pool, which guests are invited to use. The house is located near the village, and it's possible to get there from New York City without using a car. (You take a 50-minute train ride, which affords scenic views of the Hudson). Historic Van Cortlandt Manor is a short ride away. Racquet sports enthusiasts will be happy to know that tennis courts are only a short walk away. Breakfast is served on the patio by the in-ground pool (weather permitting). The hostess is the author of a B&B guidebook.

Rates: $55 double
Reservations: 914/271-6228

NEW YORK CITY APARTMENT

NEW YORK, NEW YORK

(Nominated by Bed & Breakfast in the Big Apple—Urban Ventures, Inc.)

In the sedate Gramercy Park section of Manhattan (16th Street and Third Avenue), this apartment has two terraces and excellent views of the city. The hostess is a native Mississippian, who has re-created the lushness of her native state in the décor. She has been described as "an incredibly caring person, who does everything to make guests feel at home."

Rates: $65 double
Reservations: 212/594-5650

SUMMERWOOD HOUSE

RICHFIELD SPRINGS, NEW YORK

(Nominated by Bed & Breakfast Leatherstocking Reservations)

Picture yourself on a weekend in a pretty little village in New York State, just 15 miles from Cooperstown. You are a house guest in a Queen Anne home that has stained-glass windows and period furnishings, and sits on three acres covered with maple, oak, and pine trees. You come down to breakfast that could include homemade coffee cakes and breakfast rolls, sausage-and-grits casserole, and fruits of the season. The hostess shares with guests the refrigerator, laundry facilities, a games table, and a TV. With advance notice she will even prepare a box lunch for your picnic. When you take your trip to Cooperstown, you can visit the Baseball Hall of Fame, the Farmer's Museum, and a bevy of antique shops.

Rates: $50 double with private bath, $45 double with shared bath
Reservations: 315/733-0040

WATERFRONT CONTEMPORARY

SAYVILLE, LONG ISLAND, NEW YORK

(Nominated by Bed & Breakfast of Long Island)

The exterior of this unique home (right across from Fire Island) says "contemporary" and "modern." But the inside harks back to another era, with Tiffany lamps, brass beds, and beautiful oak pieces—the kind of good taste you'd expect from a host couple who are an interior designer and an artist. You reach your room via a private entrance. Guests with their own boats can pull right into the bulkhead. The hosts will also arrange to ferry guests on their own boat to the beaches of Fire Island. You can walk to nearby excellent restaurants. Breakfast includes fruit, cold cereal, croissants, and sometimes cheese or eggs, toast, coffee, tea. The house specialties are sautéed mushrooms, quiche, and carrot cake.

Rates: $80 double (suite)
Reservations: 516/334-6231

THE JENKINS HOUSE

CINCINNATI, OHIO

(Nominated by Ohio Valley Bed & Breakfast)

This stone Victorian home in one of the oldest, most exclusive of Cincinnati's neighborhoods is convenient to downtown and to shopping. It's the last house on a private street. An iron gate leads to a double-door entry and into a large hall. Stained glass and natural woodwork, plus a grand stairway and fireplaces, reflect another era. The bedroom has inlaid Wedgwood near the ceiling, and the décor is all art deco. Other perks include an outside deck, a gourmet kitchen, and a fountain in the yard large enough to wade in. The hostess asks what guests desire for breakfast and tries "to meet their needs." She will also pick up guests at the airport.

Rates: $55 to $60 double for one night
Reservations: 606/356-7865

THE CIDER MILL

2ND STREET (P.O. BOX 441), ZOAR VILLAGE, OH 44697

Built in 1863 and refurbished in 1972, the Cider Mill, located in the famed religious communal village of Zoar, offers comfort and serenity. Private guest rooms have exposed ceiling beams and select antiques. Shared baths provide complete, modern comfort. A spiral staircase links each level of the house. The living room brick wall has survived more than a century. A complimentary breakfast features broiled grapefruit, sausage-and-egg soufflé, and apple-taffy coffee cake. Complimentary wine or hot-spiced cider is served on arrival. There's plenty to do in Zoar all day long: tour antique, craft, and gift shops; play golf; canoe on the river; cycle or hike on scenic paths along the old Ohio-Erie Canal. Airport pickup is offered.

Rates: $50 double
Reservations: 216/874-3133

THE JOHNSON HOUSE

216 MAPLE ST., FLORENCE, OR 97439

Just ask for the Johnson House when you drive into town—it's the oldest house in Florence. Of Victorian Italianate design, it was built in 1892 by Dr. O. J. Kennedy, the town's first resident physician. The building and grounds have been perfectly restored by the Fraeses, the current owners. Furnishings and décor are original—there are no reproductions in the house. The town is located on Oregon's spectacular central coast, part of the Oregon Dunes National Monument. For breakfast you can expect fresh juice and fruit in season (home-grown strawberries, blackberries, blueberries, cherries). And there are home-baked muffins (banana muffins are a house specialty). The main course might be frittata, soufflé, or eggs Benedict, served with freshly ground coffee. Local wild berry conserves and salmon and crabmeat crêpes aux herbes are specialties of the house. The owners will pick up guests at the nearby airport. Bicycles are available at no charge.

Rates: $45 to $75 double
Reservations: 503/997-8000

SPRING HOUSE

MUDDY CREEK FORKS, AIRVILLE, PA 17302

This 1798 stone house is tucked away in a quiet country village not far from York, Lancaster, and Gettysburg. The house is furnished throughout with antiques: one bedroom has an early Pennsylvania quilt; another, original stenciling. It all makes you feel as if you've taken a step back into the past. The library and the porch provide cozy areas where you can meet other guests or retire into a private corner to read. The house has a piano. The innkeeper serves two- or three-course breakfasts, which might include such specialties as coriander sausage, zucchini frittatas, and blackberry cobbler. She grows most of the fruit, vegetables, and herbs, and makes her own preserves. The Spring House is an excellent place to escape to. You can poke around antique shops, wineries, and galleries, and wander along country roads. More traveled areas, such as Lancaster County, are nearby. Horseback riding through the orchards is available near this B&B.

Rates: $60 to $85 double ($10 extra for one-night stay)
Reservations: 717/927-6906

BUCKS COUNTY BARN

BUCKS COUNTY, PENNSYLVANIA

(Nominated by Bed & Breakfast of Philadelphia)

If you've ever been to New Hope, you know what a great place this is to shop for antiques and try trendy new restaurants before they move to New York City. Well, after a day in New Hope, have we got a deal for you! Just 20 minutes away is a 1760 B&B barn, on a quiet backcountry road in a historic area. Like all good historic barns, this one has fieldstone walls and original beams and rafters. The advantage of remodeling a large barn is how much living space you can enjoy. This one has five separate levels of such space. Each guest bedroom has its own fieldstone fireplace and sitting area with TV. (Who's going to watch TV in such a pretty setting?)

Rates: $95 double
Reservations: 215/827-9650

THE VARS HOME

NEWPORT, RHODE ISLAND

(Nominated by Bed & Breakfast of Rhode Island, Inc.)

This 1850 home is located in Newport's historic Point Section, a neighborhood of 18th- and 19th-century houses, two blocks away from the harbor and a five-minute walk from the center of town. A brick walk banked with ivy and a colorful flower bed welcome you into this cheerful home, where great effort has gone into even the table settings. Breakfast comes complete with china, stemware, and fresh flowers. The hostess serves fresh fruits (peaches, strawberries, blueberries, melon, kiwi), homemade banana breads, German pancakes with fresh apples, blueberry pancakes (always on Sunday), and a variety of other delights. Guests are invited to use the piano and to relax in the glider in the yard. You'll find the fixings for tea, coffee, and bouillon, as well as an electric coffee pot, in your room.

Rates: $65 to $70 double
Reservations: 401/849-1298

CAPERS MOTTE HOUSE

69 CHURCH ST., CHARLESTON, SC 29401

This is considered one of Charleston's greatest early Georgian mansions, and is associated with prominent families in local and state history. Four rooms are provided for guests, and two more in the quaint kitchen building, all with private baths. Guests are usually invited to use the swimming pool in the yard. They meet other guests at tea time or cocktail hour in the drawing room on the second floor. This historic home is filled with antiques, original Georgian paneling, wing chairs, drop-leaf table, and wig stand. Breakfast is served in the dining room downstairs—banana bread, and blueberry pancakes, and a "hominy surprise." Located on historic Church Street, it's just a block from the Battery, close to the Market area and outstanding restaurants and shops.

Rates: $70 to $90 double, depending on season
Reservations: 803/722-2263

THE THOMAS HOME

CHARLESTON, SOUTH CAROLINA

(Nominated by Historic Charleston Bed and Breakfast)

Right in the center of Charleston's historic district in this unique home, a national historic landmark and Category I building. There are two bedrooms, study and bath, living room, dining room, and kitchen. The home is decorated with antiques and reproductions. A large patio is encircled by a flourishing garden. Stables and kitchen lead to the main house. Daily maid service is provided and fresh flowers decorate the guest rooms. Breakfast consists of fresh fruit, juice, croissants or pastries, and coffee and tea. Many historic homes, quaint shops, museums, parks, and restaurants are nearby; beaches are ten miles away, and Fort Sumter where the Civil War began.

Rates: $110 double, March to June; $100 double, July to February; and $175 for four people

Reservations: 803/722-6606

THE 1790 HOUSE

630 HIGHMARKET, GEORGETOWN, SC 29440

Right in the middle of Georgetown's Historic District is this 200-year-old historic home. Eight guests in four rooms with private bath can be accommodated at one time. Decanted sherry and fresh fruit and flowers are provided in the rooms. Four public rooms are available for chatting, reading, or relaxing. This classic colonial home with mansard roof is three stories tall. It has a handmade English brick foundation and coral stone porch. A full breakfast is served with juice, fruit, bacon, ham, sausage, fresh muffins, biscuits, eggs or custard French toast (a house specialty), grits, and pancakes. Guests are treated as part of the family, not as customers. It's just two blocks to the revitalized downtown Front Street on the Sampit River, 15 minutes to Brookgreen Gardens and Huntington State Beach, one hour to Charleston, 35 minutes to Myrtle Beach, and walking distance to restaurants. One visitor wrote to the hostess, "You have a great talent for making your guests feel welcome."

Rates: $45 to $50 single, $55 to $60 double
Reservations: 803/546-4821

THORNROSE HOUSE

531 THORNROSE AVE., STAUNTON, VIRGINIA, 24401

Southern hospitality prevails in this modified Georgian Revival brick residence, circa 1912. It's located in a historic Victorian town adjacent to a 300-acre park with tennis, golf, lakes with ducks and swans, and swimming. Three guest rooms are tastefully decorated, furnished with antiques. All rooms have air conditioners and bathrooms. You can watch television or play the grand piano by a working fireplace in the guest sitting room. Or you can read books and play games. You can linger on a wrap-around veranda among vine-covered colonnades or sit on park benches on spacious, shaded grounds. Breakfast is varied with the specialty "Birchermuesli," a popular concoction of oats, raisins, fruits, nuts, and whipped cream. Afternoon tea is provided and a decanter of sherry. Literature on many local historic sites is provided. The hosts cater to nonsmokers. [*Author's Note:* I received many letters in 1988 praising this B&B.]

Rates: $35 to $45 single (plus 6¼% total tax); $45 to $55 double
(plus 6¼% total tax)
Reservations: 703/885-7026

CREGER HOUSE

835 E. CHRISTENSON RD., WIDBEY ISLAND, GREENBANK,
WA 98253

This guesthouse complex on Whidbey Island, amid historic towns, near the nation's first historic land preserve and five state parks, is close to Seattle yet light-years away in peace, quiet, and beauty. Included are a luxurious log home just for two, three cottages, plus the Wildflower Suite in a 1920s farmhouse. All are equipped with kitchenettes, fireplaces, stained-glass windows, country antiques, microwave ovens, video players, color television, and small libraries. The hosts describe it as the "fun and romance" spot. As many as five honeymoons have gone on at one time here. Breakfasts include omelets, quiches, eggs Benedict, shirred eggs, biscuits, blueberry muffins, strawberry waffles, ham, bacon, sausage, juices, and fresh fruits among the choices. Special amenities include a spa and swimming pool, an exercise room, rowboating on a wildlife pond, badminton, horseshoes, hammocks, barbecues, and picnics—all on 25 acres of woods and pasture.

Rates: $85 to $125 double in cottages, $75 double in the Wildflower
Suite, and $150 double in the lodge
Reservations: 206/678-3115

CEDARYM COLONIAL HOME

1011 240TH AVE., NE, REDMOND, WA 98053

This authentic colonial Cape Cod reproduction with its pine floors, large cooking fireplace, wrought-iron lift latches, and bull's-eye glass above the front door, offers true tranquility. Grounds are extensive with rolling lawns, natural-wood walks, a formal rose garden, and two cottage gardens. A gazebo comes complete with hot tub. In the barn is a Model T car used for sightseeing jaunts. Located within minutes of Seattle, guests can enjoy major Northwest sights. In each room are fresh flowers and a fruitbasket. In case of chilly weather, fires are lit in fireplaces. The inn hosts respect the privacy of guests, but conduct tours for those interested in colonial lifestyle or antiques.

Rates: $45, single or double (plus tax)
Reservations: 206/868-4159

THE BRETL HOME
MAPLEWOOD, WISCONSIN

(Nominated by Bed & Breakfast Guest Homes)

This Colonial-style family home is situated in a tiny town at the south end of Door County. It is farm country and a favorite vacation destination in the Middle West. The home is beautifully maintained, with two guest rooms plus a hide-a-bed for a child or children and a shared bath. A full farmer-type breakfast of eggs, sausage, home-made baked goods, and fresh fruit is provided. You'll find plenty to do in the five nearby state parks, at summer theater, music festivals with artists in residence, and both winter and summer sporting events. The hosts go out of their way to serve guests. They have been known to wash guests' cars.

Rates: $45 double
Reservations: 414/743-9742

PENTHOUSE APARTMENT
MILWAUKEE, WISCONSIN

(Nominated by Bed & Breakfast of Milwaukee, Inc.)

This recently constructed ninth-floor apartment atop a warehouse is located in the historic Third Ward district of downtown Milwaukee. The area is undergoing dynamic change with condominium conversion within warehouses. The professional talents of the hostess, an interior designer, is reflected in the furnishings of the living area, kitchen, full bath, and bedroom. A king-size bed converts to twin beds and a queen-size hide-a-bed is in the living area. The skyline view is spectacular. A solarium, spa, and deck are at the disposal of guests. It is described as the perfect setting for a honeymoon or true getaway. You have a choice of a hearty continental breakfast or a full breakfast. Downtown, the fruit and vegetable district, several excellent restaurants, and the lakefront are within walking distance.

Rates: $125 per night
Reservations: 414/271-2337

TETON TREE HOUSE

WILSON, WYOMING

(Nominated by Bed & Breakfast Western Adventure)

   This unique house perched on the side of a mountain is only about eight miles from Jackson. It's an ideal base for skiing or touring the area, including the Grand Tetons. The house is being built in stages by a very friendly couple, Chris and Denny Becker. The rooms are spacious and most have great mountain views. In warm weather you can even sit out on the deck and have oatmeal with granola, fresh fruit, and delicious muffins made with oats and sunflower seeds. The hosts know the area thoroughly and can help plan your hiking, skiing, or white-water rafting expeditions. The area is so remote that in the winter peeping-tom mooses have been known to appear at the windows. The Beckers have two young children who will soon make you part of the family.

Rates: $55 double
Reservations: 406/259-7993

POWELL HOUSE

ONTARIO, CANADA

(Nominated by Country Host)

   The ducks quack, the sheep and cows bleat, and the little goats are birthed and bottle-raised on this 109-acre farm complete with an 80-year-old refurbished farmhouse. Inside are antiques galore, plus original pine floors and wainscotting. Located in a rolling countryside farm community, Powell House is accessible to hiking trails, fishing, fairs, and festivals, with guest transportation provided. All summer sports are featured on Georgian Bay; it has the best downhill skiing in winter in Ontario, and 20 miles of cross-country skiing on groomed trails. Breakfasts are plentiful, with fruits in season, fresh juice, eggs according to choice with ham, bacon, or sausage, topped off with hot muffins or toast, homemade jams and jellies, or pancakes and maple syrup.

Rates: $45 ($37.50 U.S.) to $50 ($42 U.S.) double; lunch for hikers is $3.50 ($3 U.S.) each; dinner, $9 ($7.50 U.S.) each.
Reservations: 519/941-7633

JOHANNE HARRELLE HOUSE

MONTRÉAL, QUÉBEC, CANADA

(Nominated by Montréal Bed & Breakfast)

In this most unusual renovated rowhouse in Montréal's Latin Quarter, guests have the first level of the house for themselves—double bedroom with private bath, living area, courtyard patio, and quaint dining area. This two-story B&B has an interior courtyard, skylight, and wrought-iron spiral staircase. It's located one street parallel to St. Denis Street, the heart of the Latin Quarter district with cafés, restaurants, shops, Métro. It's an easy walk to St. Louis Square, a park haven, and to Old Montréal and everything downtown. This is considered an ideal setup for honeymoon couples, but "appreciated by all guests." Breakfasts include choice of juices, yogurts, pancakes, eggs, crêpes, and superior coffee.

Rates: $100 ($83 U.S.) double
Reservations: 514/738-9410

Would You Like to Become One of Our B&B Critics-at-Large?

Have you discovered a great bed-and-breakfast home that belongs in our list of "50 Best"? Have you stayed in an elegant B&B inn that should be featured in this book?

Or have you been dissatisfied in any way with any of the homes and inns mentioned in this book?

You're invited to become one of our secret B&B critics. Just complete and send in the attached B&B *home* or B&B *inn* rating forms. There's no need to tear up the book—just photocopy as many forms as you need right from the book.

If you have been dissatisfied in any way with a B&B home, inn, or reservation service currently featured in this book, please let me know with a short note explaining the problem.

If you have really been pleased with your B&B experience, one of the nicest things you could do is send a copy of your evaluation to your host. They would be delighted to know that you thought enough of them and their home or inn to nominate them as "one of the best in North America."

Mail the completed form to:

B&B Critics
c/o Bed & Breakfast North America
Frommer Books
Prentice Hall Trade Division
One Gulf + Western Plaza
New York, NY 10023

Reader Nomination For
"One of the Best B&B <u>Homes</u> in North America"

Name of B&B Hosts _____
Address _____
City _____ State _____ ZIP _____
Phone _____

Criteria

(Please check one box for each category)

	Excellent	Good	Fair	Poor
1. Quality of room and furnishings	☐	☐	☐	☐
2. Quality of breakfast	☐	☐	☐	☐
3. Housekeeping	☐	☐	☐	☐
4. Friendliness/helpfulness of host and hostess	☐	☐	☐	☐

Why do you believe this home qualifies as one of the 50
best in North America? _____
_____
_____
_____

Your name _____
Address _____
City _____ State _____ ZIP _____

May we quote you by name in the next edition of this book
if your nominee is selected as one of the 50 best?

☐ Yes   ☐ No

Reader Nomination For
"One of the Better B&B <u>Inns</u> in North America"

(*Note:* Many B&B homes also call themselves "inns." But this category is primarily for the large commercial establishments of eight rooms or more and closer in feeling to a hotel than to a private home.)

Name of B&B Inn _____
Address _____
City _____ State _____ ZIP _____
Phone _____

Criteria

(Please check one box for each category)

	Excellent	Good	Fair	Poor
1. Quality of room and furnishings	☐	☐	☐	☐
2. Quality of breakfast	☐	☐	☐	☐
3. Housekeeping	☐	☐	☐	☐
4. Friendliness/helpfulness of the innkeeper and the personnel of the inn	☐	☐	☐	☐
5. Quality of the public rooms	☐	☐	☐	☐

Why do you believe this home qualifies as one of the better B&B inns in North America? _____
_____
_____
_____

Your name _____

Address _____

City _____ State _____ ZIP _____

May we quote you by name in the next edition of this book if your nominee is selected as one of the 50 best?

☐ Yes   ☐ No

Index

GENERAL

Acapulco (Mexico), 202
Alabama:
  B&B inn, 175
  reservation services, 173–4
  state tourist office, 12
Alaska:
  B&B inns, 239–40
  best B&B home in, 258–9
  reservation services, 237–9
  state tourist office, 12
American Automobile Association
  (AAA), 11–12
American Samoa, 16
Annapolis (MD), 111–12
Arcadia National Park (ME), 50–1
Arizona:
  best B&B home in, 259
  reservation services, 217–20
  state tourist office, 12
Arkansas:
  B&B inn, 195
  reservation services, 193–4, 207
  state tourist office, 12
Aspen (CO), 197–8
Atlanta (GA):
  best B&B home in, 264–5
  reservation services, 180–2

Baltimore (MD), 111–12
Barbados, 180
B&B home(s):
  cost of, 3–4, 6
  definition of, 7
  50 best in North America,
    finding, 10–12
  guests, 17–19
  history of, 6–7
  hosts, 4–5, 20–31, 258–83
  operating a, 20–31
Berkshires (MA), 46–7, 67–8
Boston:
  best B&B home in, 269
  reservation services, 57–64
British Columbia (Canada):

reservation services, 167, 169,
  247–9
see also Vancouver; Victoria
Buffalo (NY), 83
Business travel, 8

California, 4
  B&B inns, 229–33
  best B&B homes in, 259–62
  reservation services, 35–7, 41–2,
    220–8
  state tourist office, 13
  see also Wine Country (CA); *and spe-*
    cific cities
Cambridge (MA), 59–63
Canada:
  reservation services, 39–40
  see also British Columbia; Nova Sco-
    tia; Ontario; Québec
Cape Cod (MA), 58–9, 64–7
Cape May (NJ), 115–6
Caribbean, 39, 176
Charleston (SC):
  B&B inns, 137–8
  best B&B homes in, 278–9
  reservation services, 117, 134–6
Charlotte (NC), 117
Chicago (IL), 39, 147–8
Colorado:
  B&B inns, 198–200
  reservation services, 195–8
  state tourist office, 13
Columbus (OH), 151
Connecticut:
  B&B inns, 47–8
  best B&B homes in, 263
  reservation services, 45–7, 63–4
  state tourist office, 13
Corpus Christi (TX), 209–10
Cost of B&Bs, 3–4, 6

Delaware:
  reservation service, 109, 117, 123,
    131

RESERVATION SERVICES

Aaah! Bed & Breakfast #1 Ltd. (NY), 79–80
A & A Bed & Breakfast of Florida, Inc. (FL), 178
AB&C Bed & Breakfast of Vancouver (BC, Canada), 247
Accommodations Alaska Style—Stay With A Friend (AK), 238–9
Adobe Bed & Breakfast Ltd. (NY), 80–1
Alaska Private Lodgings (AK), 237–8
Amanda's Bed & Breakfast Reservation Service (MD), 112
American Country Collection of Bed & Breakfast Homes and Country Inns (NY), 85–6
American Family Inn/Bed & Breakfast San Francisco (CA), 224–5
American Historic Homes Bed & Breakfast (CA), 35
Anna's Victorian Connection (RI), 90–1
A Reasonable Alternative, Inc.—Bed & Breakfast in Long Island (NY), 85
Arkansas & Ozarks Bed & Breakfast (AR), 194
Atlanta Hospitality—A B&B Reservation Service (GA), 180

Barbara Bed & Breakfast (AZ), 219–20
Bed & Biscuits (NC), 117
Bed & Breakfast, Brookline/Boston (MA), 58–9
Bed & Breakfast, Inc., Reservation Service (LA), 203–4
Bed & Breakfast Agency (MA), 57
Bed & Breakfast in the Albemarle (NC), 116–17

Bed & Breakfast in Arizona (AZ), 217–18
Bed & Breakfast Atlanta (GA), 180–2
Bed & Breakfast in the Big Apple (Urban Ventures, Inc.) (NY), 82–3
Bed & Breakfast Birmingham (AL), 173–4
Bed & Breakfast—Cambridge and Greater Boston (MA), 61
Bed & Breakfast Cape Cod (MA), 66–7
Bed & Breakfast of Chester County (PA), 126–7
Bed & Breakfast/Chicago, Inc. (IL), 147–8
Bed & Breakfast Co. Tropical Florida (FL), 176–7
Bed & Breakfast Colorado, Ltd. (CO), 195–6
Bed & Breakfast Connections (PA), 124–5
Bed & Breakfast of Delaware (DE), 109
Bed & Breakfast Down East, Ltd. (ME), 50–1
Bed & Breakfast of the Florida Keys, Inc. (FL), 175–6
Bed & Breakfast Folks (MA), 67
Bed & Breakfast of Fredericksburg (TX), 212
Bed & Breakfast of Grand Rapids (MI), 149–50
Bed & Breakfast Guest Homes (WI), 153
Bed & Breakfast Hawaii (HI), 242–3
Bed & Breakfast Honolulu (Statewide) (HI), 240–1
Bed & Breakfast Hospitality (CA), 36
Bed & Breakfast Host Homes of Tennessee (TN), 189–90

B&B INNS

Acadian Home (LA), 267–8
Adobe House (NM), 272
Alaskan Hotel (AK), 240
Alexander Hamilton House (NY), 273
Aspen Lodge, The (CO), 200
Auburn Street Cottage, The (OR), 166

Bay Breeze Guest House (MA), 69
Bernard Home (FL), 264
Big Moose Inn (NY), 89
Black Bear Inn (VT), 96
Black Lantern Inn (VT), 99
Blue Boar Lodge (NC), 120–1
Bluehill Farm Country Inn (ME), 52
Bradford Inn, The (NH), 74
Bretl Home (WI), 281
Brigadoon (CT), 45
Bucks County Barn (PA), 277
Bullis House Inn (TX), 213
Butternut Inn at Stowe (VT), 102

Cabbage Key, Inc. (FL), 179
Campton Inn, The (NH), 76
Candlelight Inn (MA), 71
Capers Motte House (SC), 278
Carter House (CA), 229–30
Cassena Inn (SC), 138–9
Castle Inn (VT), 100
Cecce Bed & Breakfast Inn (NY), 88–9
Cedar Run Inn (PA), 132
Cedars, The (SC), 143
Cedarym Colonial Home (WA), 280–1
Celie's B&B (MD), 269
Center Bridge Inn (PA), 132
Chauga River House (SC), 139
Cider Mill (OH), 275
Cleone Lodge Inn (CA), 230
Clifford Lake House (MI), 150–1
Colonial Inn, The (NC), 119
Coppers Beach Inn (CT), 48
Crab Apple Acres Inn (ME), 53

Craignair Inn (ME), 55
Creger House (WA), 280

Davis Home (CA), 262
Deefield Inn (MA), 70
Dockside Guest Quarters (ME), 56
Downtown Mansion (GA), 264–5

East Wind Inn and Meeting House (ME), 55
Echo Ledge Farm Inn (VT), 97
Evergreen, The (VT), 95
Evergreen Inn (SC), 136

Fiddlers Green Inn (VT), 103
Fireside Inn (CO), 199
Foxwood Inn (MT), 164
Franconia Inn (NH), 75
French Country Home (AZ), 259

Gott House (ME), 268
Great Southern Hotel, The (AR), 195
Green Heron Inn, The (ME), 54
Greenhurst Inn (VT), 96
Green Mountain Tea Room and Guest House (VT), 101
Greystone Inn, The (NC), 119
Gunflint Lodge (MN), 162
Gustavus Inn (AK), 239–40

Haagen House (IL), 266–7
Harvey Mountain View Farm and Inn (VT), 101
Haus Rohrbach Pension (WA), 169–70
Hebert House (MA), 270
Hedges, The (NY), 87–8
Hidden Pond Farm (MI), 271
Highland Lodge, The (VT), 97–8
Holly House (NJ), 115–16
Holmes Retreat (ID), 266
Home on the Bay (HI), 265–6

50 BEST HOMES

SIGHTS AND ATTRACTIONS

SCHOOLS, COLLEGES, AND UNIVERSITIES

Adelphi University (NY), 80, 84, 85
Agnes Scott College (GA), 181
Alabama, University of, at Birming-
ham (AL), 173
Alabama State University (AL), 174
Alaska, University of, at Anchorage
(AK), 237, 238
Alaska, University of, at Fairbanks
(AK), 239
Alaska Pacific University (AK), 237,
238
Albemarle, College of the (NC), 116
Albertus Magnus College (CT), 46
Albright College (PA), 122
Algonquin College (ON, Canada), 252
Allentown College of St. Francis de
Sales (PA), 122
Alvernia College (PA), 122
American College of Physicians (PA),
123
American Graduate School of Busi-
ness (AZ), 217
American University (DC), 38, 110
Amherst College (MA), 68, 69
Anna Maria College (MA), 58
Antioch College (OH), 152
Arizona, University of, at Tempe (AZ),
217, 218
Arizona, University of, at Tucson
(AZ), 217
Arizona, University of (AZ), 219
Arkansas, University of (AR), 193, 194
Arkansas College (AR), 194
Armstrong State College (GA), 182
Art Center College of Design (CA),
220
Art & Design, College of (GA), 182
Atlanta University (GA), 180, 181
Atlantic Union College (MA), 58
Auburn University (AL), 173, 174
Avila College (KS), 201

Babson College (MA), 60, 62
Baptist College (SC), 134
Baruch College (NY), 80

Bates College (ME), 49, 50
Baylor University (TX), 211
Bay Pines VA Hospital (FL), 178
Beaver College (PA), 123
Belhaven College (MS), 187
Bennington College (VT), 47, 86
Bentley College (MA), 63
Berkeley School of Music (MA), 63
Berkshire Christian College (CT),
47
Boston University (MA), 57, 59–63
Bowdoin College (ME), 49, 50
Brandeis University (MA), 60, 62,
63
Brewster Academy (NH), 73
Bridgewater State College (MA), 65
British Columbia, University of (BC,
Canada), 168, 247, 249
Brockport (NY), 78
Brown University (RI), 91
Bryant College (RI), 91
Bryn Mawr (PA), 123, 124, 130, 131
Bucknell University (PA), 128
Buffalo State University (NY), 83

Cabrini College (PA), 123
Cal College Long Beach (CA), 228
California, University of, Irvine (CA),
222
California, University of, at Los Ange-
les (UCLA) (CA), 220, 222, 224
California, University of, Medical
Center (CA), 225
California, University of, Riverside
(CA), 228
California, University of, San Diego
(CA), 220–2
California Institute of Technology
(CA), 220
Cal State San Diego (CA), 221
Calvin College (MI), 149
Camosun College (BC, Canada), 249
Canisius College (NY), 83
Cape Cod Community College (MA),
66

308

NOW, SAVE MONEY ON ALL YOUR TRAVELS!
Join Frommer's™ Dollarwise® Travel Club

Saving money while traveling is never a simple matter, which is why, over 27 years ago, the **Dollarwise Travel Club** was formed. Actually, the idea came from readers of the Frommer publications who felt that such an organization could bring financial benefits, continuing travel information, and a sense of community to economy-minded travelers all over the world.

In keeping with the money-saving concept, the annual membership fee is low—$18 (U.S. residents) or $20 U.S. (Canadian, Mexican, and foreign residents)—and is immediately exceeded by the value of your benefits which include:

1. The latest edition of any TWO of the books listed on the following pages.

2. A copy of any Frommer City Guide.

3. An annual subscription to an 8-page quarterly newspaper *The Dollarwise Traveler* which keeps you up-to-date on fastbreaking developments in good-value travel in all parts of the world—bringing you the kind of information you'd have to pay over $35 a year to obtain elsewhere. This consumer-conscious publication also includes the following columns:

Hospitality Exchange—members all over the world who are willing to provide hospitality to other members as they pass through their home cities.

Share-a-Trip—requests from members for travel companions who can share costs and help avoid the burdensome single supplement.

Readers Ask . . . Readers Reply—travel questions from members to which other members reply with authentic firsthand information.

4. Your personal membership card which entitles you to purchase through the club all Frommer publications for a third to a half off their regular retail prices during the term of your membership.

So why not join this hardy band of international Dollarwise travelers now and participate in its exchange of information and hospitality? Simply send $18 (U.S. residents) or $20 U.S. (Canadian, Mexican, and other foreign residents) along with your name and address to: Frommer's Dollarwise Travel Club, Inc., Gulf + Western Building, One Gulf + Western Plaza, New York, NY 10023. Remember to specify which *two* of the books in section (1) and which *one* in section (2) above you wish to receive in your initial package of member's benefits. Or tear out the next page, check off your choices, and send the page to us with your membership fee.

FROMMER BOOKS
PRENTICE HALL PRESS
ONE GULF + WESTERN PLAZA
NEW YORK, NY 10023

Date_____

Friends:
Please send me the books checked below:

FROMMER™ GUIDES

(Guides to sightseeing and tourist accommodations and facilities from budget to deluxe, with emphasis on the medium-priced.)

☐ Alaska $13.95	☐ Cruises (incl. Alask, Carib, Mex, Hawaii,	
☐ Australia. $14.95	Panama, Canada, & US). $14.95	
☐ Austria & Hungary $14.95	☐ California & Las Vegas. $14.95	
☐ Belgium, Holland, Luxembourg. $13.95	☐ Florida $13.95	
☐ Brazil $14.95	☐ Mid-Atlantic States. $13.95	
☐ Egypt $13.95	☐ New England. $13.95	
☐ France $14.95	☐ New York State $13.95	
☐ England & Scotland. $14.95	☐ Northwest $14.95	
☐ Germany. $13.95	☐ Skiing in Europe. $14.95	
☐ Italy $14.95	☐ Skiing USA—East. $13.95	
☐ Japan & Hong Kong $13.95	☐ Skiing USA—West. $13.95	
☐ Portugal, Madeira, & the Azores. $13.95	☐ Southeast & New Orleans $13.95	
☐ South Pacific $13.95	☐ Southeast Asia. $14.95	
☐ Switzerland & Liechtenstein $13.95	☐ Southwest. $14.95	
☐ Bermuda & The Bahamas. $13.95	☐ Texas $13.95	
☐ Canada. $13.95	☐ USA $15.95	
☐ Caribbean. $13.95		

FROMMER'S™ $-A-DAY® GUIDES

(In-depth guides to sightseeing and low-cost tourist accommodations and facilities.)

☐ Europe on $30 a Day. $14.95	☐ New Zealand on $40 a Day $12.95
☐ Australia on $30 a Day $12.95	☐ New York on $50 a Day. $12.95
☐ Eastern Europe on $25 a Day $13.95	☐ Scandinavia on $60 a Day $13.95
☐ England on $40 a Day. $12.95	☐ Scotland and Wales on $40 a Day $12.95
☐ Greece on $30 a Day. $12.95	☐ South America on $30 a Day $13.95
☐ Hawaii on $50 a Day. $13.95	☐ Spain and Morocco (plus the Canary Is.)
☐ India on $25 a Day $12.95	on $40 a Day. $13.95
☐ Ireland on $35 a Day $13.95	☐ Turkey on $25 a Day $12.95
☐ Israel on $30 & $35 a Day $12.95	☐ Washington, D.C., & Historic Va. on
☐ Mexico (plus Belize & Guatemala)	$40 a Day $12.95
on $25 a Day. $13.95	

FROMMER'S™ TOURING GUIDES

(Color illustrated guides that include walking tours, cultural & historic sites, and other vital travel information.)

☐ Australia. $9.95	☐ Paris. $8.95
☐ Egypt $8.95	☐ Scotland. $9.95
☐ Florence $8.95	☐ Thailand $9.95
☐ London. $8.95	☐ Venice $8.95

TURN PAGE FOR ADDITONAL BOOKS AND ORDER FORM.

FROMMER'S™ CITY GUIDES

(Pocket-size guides to sightseeing and tourist accommodations and facilities in all price ranges.)

☐ Amsterdam/Holland $5.95
☐ Athens $5.95
☐ Atlantic City/Cape May $5.95
☐ Belgium $5.95
☐ Boston $5.95
☐ Cancún/Cozumel/Yucatán $5.95
☐ Chicago $5.95
☐ Dublin/Ireland $5.95
☐ Hawaii $5.95
☐ Las Vegas $5.95
☐ Lisbon/Madrid/Costa del Sol $5.95
☐ London $5.95
☐ Los Angeles $5.95
☐ Mexico City/Acapulco $5.95

☐ Minneapolis/St. Paul $5.95
☐ Montreal/Quebec City $5.95
☐ New Orleans $5.95
☐ New York $5.95
☐ Orlando/Disney World/EPCOT $5.95
☐ Paris $5.95
☐ Philadelphia $5.95
☐ Rio $5.95
☐ Rome $5.95
☐ San Francisco $5.95
☐ Santa Fe/Taos $5.95
☐ Sydney $5.95
☐ Washington, D.C. $5.95

SPECIAL EDITIONS

☐ A Shopper's Guide to the Caribbean $12.95
☐ Beat the High Cost of Travel $6.95
☐ Bed & Breakfast—N. America $11.95
☐ California with Kids $14.95
☐ Guide to Honeymoon Destinations
  (US, Canada, Mexico, & Carib) $12.95
☐ Manhattan's Outdoor Sculpture $15.95

☐ Motorist's Phrase Book (Fr/Ger/Sp) $4.95
☐ Paris Rendez-Vous $10.95
☐ Swap and Go (Home Exchanging) $10.95
☐ The Candy Apple (NY for Kids) $11.95
☐ Travel Diary and Record Book $5.95
☐ Where to Stay USA (Lodging from $3
  to $30 a night) $10.95

☐ Marilyn Wood's Wonderful Weekends (NY, Conn, Mass, RI, Vt, NH, NJ, Del,Pa) $11.95
☐ The New World of Travel (Annual sourcebook by Arthur Frommer previewing: new travel trends, new modes of travel, and the latest cost-cutting strategies for savvy travelers) (2nd ed.) $14.95

SERIOUS SHOPPER'S GUIDES

(Illustrated guides listing hundreds of stores, conveniently organized alphabetically by category)

☐ Italy $15.95
☐ London $15.95

☐ Los Angeles $14.95
☐ Paris $15.95

GAULT MILLAU

(The only guides that distinguish the truly superlative from the merely overrated.)

☐ The Best of Chicago (avail. June 1989) $15.95
☐ The Best of France (avail. July 1989) $15.95
☐ The Best of Italy (avail. July 1989) $15.95
☐ The Best of Los Angeles $15.95

☐ The Best of New England (avail. July 1989) . . .$15.95
☐ The Best of New York $15.95
☐ The Best of San Francisco $15.95
☐ The Best of Washington, D.C. $15.95

ORDER NOW!

In U.S. include $1.50 shipping UPS for 1st book; 50¢ ea. add'l book. Outside U.S. $2 and 50¢, respectively.

Allow four to six weeks for delivery in U.S., longer outside U.S.

Enclosed is my check or money order for $_____

NAME _____

ADDRESS _____

CITY _____ STATE _____ ZIP _____